KNOWING JESUS

To the memory of
Jim Punton

Knowing Jesus Through the Old Testament

Christopher
J.H.Wright

INTERVARSITY PRESS
DOWNERS GROVE, ILLINOIS 60515

Published in the United States of America by InterVarsity Press, Downers Grove, Illinois, with permission from HarperCollins Publishers Ltd., London.

InterVarsity Press® is the book-publishing division of InterVarsity Christian Fellowship®, a student movement active on campus at hundreds of universities, colleges and schools of nursing in the United States of America, and a member movement of the International Fellowship of Evangelical Students. For information about local and regional activities, write Public Relations Dept., InterVarsity Christian Fellowship, 6400 Schroeder Rd., P.O. Box 7895, Madison, WI 53707-7895.

ISBN 0-8308-1693-3

Printed in the United States of America ♾

Library of Congress Cataloging-in-Publication Data

Wright, Christopher J. H., 1947-
    Knowing Jesus through the Old Testament/Christopher J. Wright.
      p.   cm.
    Originally published: England: Marshall Pickering, 1992.
    Includes bibliographical references (p.).
    ISBN 0-8308-1693-3
      1. Jesus Christ—Messiahship.   2. Jesus Christ—Genealogy.
   3. Jesus Christ—Historicity.   4. Bible. O.T.—Criticism,
interpretation, etc.   I. Title.
BT230.W84   1995
232'.1—dc20
                                         94-42149
                                           CIP

---

16   15   14   13   12   11   10   9   8   7   6   5
08   07   06   05   04   03   02   01   00   99

Preface

My love for the Hebrew scriptures of the Old Testament came somewhat later in life than my love for Jesus Christ. But each has reinforced the other ever since I entered the world of biblical studies. In the midst of the many intrinsically fascinating reasons why Old Testament study is so rewarding, the most exciting to me is the way it never fails to add new depths to my understanding of Jesus. I find myself aware that in reading the Hebrew scriptures I am handling something that gives me a closer common link with Jesus than any archaeological artefact could do.

For these are the words *he* read. These were the stories he knew. These were the songs he sang. These were the depths of wisdom and revelation and prophecy that shaped his whole view of 'life, the universe and everything'. This is where he found his insights into the mind of his Father God. Above all, this is where he found the shape of his own identity and the goal of his own mission. In short, the deeper you go into understanding the *Old Testament*, the closer you come to the heart of Jesus. (After all, Jesus never actually *read* the New Testament!) That has been my conviction for a long time, and it is the conviction that underlies this book.

For it saddens me that so many Christians in these days love Jesus, but know so little about who he thought he was and what he had come to do. Jesus becomes a kind of photo-montage composed of a random mixture of Gospel stories, topped up with whatever fashionable image of him is current, including, recently, the New Age caricatures of him. He is cut off from the historical Jewish context of his own day, and from his deep roots in the Hebrew scriptures.

It is ironic that this widespread lack of biblically informed knowledge about Jesus is growing at the very time when there is a new impetus and enthusiasm in scholarly circles, both Christian and Jewish, for historical research on Jesus. The so-called Third Quest, for the historical Jesus has already generated numbers of exciting and fascinating works of scholarship, which at times almost persuaded me I would rather be a student of the New Testament than of the Old!

That feeling usually evaporated fairly quickly as I felt my own amateur status in that field, which needs to be made clear at this point. I have been acutely aware that to write anything at all on the New Testament in general or Jesus in particular is like crawling through a minefield under cross-fire. However, with the help of several friends of undoubted New Testament scholarship, I have been bold enough to crawl on, trying to take into account as much of current scholarship as was feasible. My constant comfort has been to remind myself that I am not writing for fellow scholars, but for people who want to deepen their knowledge of Jesus and of the scriptures that meant so much to him. In that sense, I found it hard to decide whether this is a book about Jesus in the light of the Old Testament, or a book about the Old Testament in the light of Jesus. Perhaps it is both.

I have also managed to fulfil one other minor life's ambition with this book, which was to write at least one book entirely without footnotes. This again was dictated by the sort of reader I had in mind. Biblical experts will detect in every paragraph the sources of so many of my ideas, but it is tedious to hang them out at the bottom of every page. My acknowledgement to all those from whose books I have learnt so much is paid by the bibliographical list at the end of the book.

More personal gratitude is due to many who have helped me through the minefield in various ways. First to my students at the Union Biblical Seminary, in Pune, India, who bore my first gropings in this area, under the title, 'Old Testament

Preface

Hermeneutics'. It was while teaching that course, that I came across John Goldingay's articles on 'The Old Testament and Christian faith: Jesus and the Old Testament in Matthew 1–5' in *Themelios* 8.1–2, (1982–83). They provided an excellent framework, first for that course, and then, with his kind permission, for the broad structure of this book, which is rather loosely linked to the themes of the early chapters of Matthew's Gospel. Secondly, to Dick France, who helped to prime the pump for my amateur New Testament researches with some very helpful bibliographical suggestions which generated a flood of other discoveries. Needless to say, neither of these two friends bear any responsibility for the final content of this book.

My thanks are due also to Kiruba Easteraj and the Selvarajah family for their hospitality and kindness in Montauban Guest House, Ootacamund, India, where the first chapters were written during summer vacations.

My wife, Elizabeth, and our four children know only too well how much I depend on their love and support, and over the years they have learned to share or bear my enthusiasm for the Old Testament. They need no words to know my appreciation, but this at least puts my deep gratitude on paper.

Finally a word of explanation for the dedication. It was Jim Punton, a man who always made me think simultaneously of Amos in his prophetic passion for justice and of Jesus in his warmth and friendship, who first sowed the seed of this book. 'Chris', he said to me once, putting his arm around me like an uncle, 'you must write a book on how the Old Testament influenced Jesus.' That was nearly ten years ago. Sadly, Jim's untimely death means that he cannot judge whether I have achieved what he had in mind.

Chris Wright
All Nations Christian College,
Ware, England.

CHAPTER ONE

Jesus and the Old Testament Story

Jesus: A man with a story

Judging from the selection of readings in an average Christmas carol service, the New Testament begins, in the consciousness of the average Christian, at Matthew 1:18, 'This is how the birth of Jesus Christ came about . . .'. A natural enough assumption, we might agree, since Christianity began with the birth of Jesus and this verse proposes to tell us how it happened. What more do you need at Christmas?

If the average Christian pauses between carols to wonder what the previous seventeen verses are all about, his or her curiosity is probably offset by relief that at least they weren't included in the readings! And yet they are there, presumably because that is how Matthew wanted to begin his Gospel, and also how the minds that shaped the order of the canonical books wanted to begin what we call the New Testament. So we need to respect those intentions and ask why it is that Matthew will not allow us to join in the adoration of the Magi until we have ploughed through his tedious list of begettings. Why can't we just get on with the story?

Because, says Matthew, you won't understand that story – the one I am about to tell you – unless you see it in the light of a much longer story which goes back for many centuries but leads up to the Jesus you want to know about. And that longer story is the history of the Hebrew Bible, or what Christians came to call the Old Testament. It is the story which Matthew 'tells' in the form of a schematized genealogy – the ancestry of the Messiah.

His opening verse sums up the whole story: Jesus, who is the Messiah was the son of David and the son of Abraham. These two names then become the key markers for the three main section of his story:

from Abraham to David;
from David to the Babylonian exile;
from the exile to Jesus himself.

For any Jew who knew his scriptures (and Matthew is usually reckoned to have been writing primarily for Jewish Christians), every name recalled stories, events, periods of history, memories of their national past. It was a long story, but Matthew compresses it into 17 verses just as Jesus could later on compress it into a single parable, about a vineyard and its tenant farmers.

What Matthew is saying to us by beginning in this way is that we will only understand Jesus properly if we see him in the light of this story which he completes and brings to its climax. So when we turn the page from the Old to the New Testament, we find a link between the two which is more important than the attention we usually give it. It is a central historical interface binding together the two great acts of God's drama of salvation. *The Old Testament tells the story which Jesus completes.*

This means not only that we need to look at Jesus in the light of the history of the Old Testament, but also that he sheds light backwards on it. You understand and appreciate a journey in the light of its destination. And certainly as you journey through the history of the Old Testament it makes a difference to know that it leads to Jesus and that he gives meaning to it. We shall look at that in more depth after we have reviewed that journey in the next section. First let us note several things as regards Jesus himself which Matthew

wishes us to understand from his chosen means of opening
his story.

JESUS WAS A REAL JEW

In Jewish society genealogies were an important way of establishing your right to belong within the community of God's
people. 1 Chronicles 1–9 and Ezra 2 and 8 are examples of
this. Your ancestry was your identity and your status. Jesus,
then, was not just 'a man'. He was a particular person born
within a living culture. His background, ancestry and roots,
were shaped and influenced, as all his contemporaries were,
by the history and fortunes of his people. We need to keep
this in mind, because it often happens that we can talk and
think (and sing) about Jesus in such general and universal
terms that he becomes virtually abstract – a kind of identikit
human being. The Gospels bind us to the particularity of
Jesus and Matthew anchors him in the history of the Jewish
nation.

There are (and always have been) those who do not like
this Jewishness of Jesus, for a wide variety of reasons. Yet it
is the very first fact about Jesus that the New Testament
presents to us, and Matthew goes on to underline it in countless ways in the rest of his Gospel. And as we shall see
throughout this book, it is this very Jewishness of Jesus and
his deep roots in his Hebrew scriptures which provide us
with the most essential key to understanding who he was,
why he came and what he taught.

JESUS WAS A REAL MAN

He was 'the son of Abraham'. Now when Abram first makes
his appearance in the Old Testament story, in Genesis 12, the
stage is already well set and populated. Genesis 10 portrays a
world of nations – a slice of geographical and political reality.

It is a world of real human beings, which we would have recognized if we'd been there – not some mythological Utopia full of heroes and monsters. This is the human world whose sinful arrogance is described in the story of the tower of Babel in Genesis 11. And this is the world within which, and for which, God called Abram as the starting point of his vast project of redemption for humanity.

Now the main point of God's promise to Abram was not merely that he would have a son, and thereby descendants who would be especially blessed by God, but that through that people of Abram God would bring blessing to *all nations* of the earth. So although Abraham (as his name was changed to, in the light of this promise regarding the nations) stands at the head of the particular nation of Israel and their unique history, there is a universal scope and perspective to him and them: one nation for the sake of all nations.

When Matthew announces Jesus as the Messiah, the son of Abraham, then, it means not only that he belongs to that particular people (a real Jew, as we have just seen), but that he belongs to a people whose very reason for existence was to bring blessing to the rest of humanity. He shared that mission, and indeed, as the Messiah, he had come to make it a possibility and a reality at last. A particular man, but with a universal significance.

At several points in his most Jewish of all four Gospels Matthew shows his interest in the universal significance of Jesus for those beyond the boundaries of Israel. It emerges for the first time here in the opening genealogy in an unexpected and easily overlooked feature of it. In his long list of fathers, Matthew includes just four mothers, all in the space of vv. 3–6: Tamar, Rahab, Ruth and Bathsheba. It may be that one reason for Matthew including them is that there were question marks and irregularities in their marriages, which may be Matthew's way of showing that there was scriptural precedent even for the 'irregularity' of Jesus's birth from an unmarried mother. But probably more significant is the other thing they all have in common. They were all, from a Jewish point of view, foreigners. Tamar and Rahab were Canaanites (Gen. 38, Josh. 2); Ruth was a Moabitess (Ruth 1); Bathesheba was the wife of Uriah, a Hittite, so probably a Hittite herself (2 Sam. 1). The implication of Jesus being the heir of Abraham and his universal promise is underlined: Jesus the Jew, and the Jewish Messiah, had Gentile blood!

JESUS WAS THE SON OF DAVID

Matthew here states at the outset what he will develop and demonstrate through his Gospel, that Jesus was the expected Messiah, of the royal line of David, with the rightful claim to the title 'King of the Jews'. He establishes this further by tracing Jesus's descent through the royal line of kings descended from David that ruled over Judah (vv. 6–11). Probably this represents an 'official' genealogy, whereas Luke (3:23–38) has recorded Jesus's actual biological parentage (or rather, that of Joseph his legal, but not biological father). The two lists are not contradictory, but rather trace two lines through the same 'family tree' from David to Jesus.

Much more was involved in asserting that Jesus was the Davidic Messiah than mere physical ancestry. We shall look at the implications in chapters three and four. It included the expectation that the arrival of the true son of David would coincide with the intervention of God himself to establish his reign. It would mean the rule of God's justice, liberation for the oppressed, the restoration of peace among mankind and in nature itself. Furthermore, the mission of the Messiah was also connected to the ingathering of the nations. The universal scope of being the son of Abraham was not cancelled out by the particular identity of being the son of David. In fact, in Old Testament expectation there was a link between the two. It would be through the son of David, the heir to God's promise to David, that the promise to Abraham himself would be fulfilled.

Psalm 72 is a good illustration of this. It is a prayer on behalf of the Davidic king, headed 'Of Solomon'. As well as looking forward to prosperity and justice, it includes this hope and expectation:

> May his name endure for ever;
> > may it continue as long as the sun.
> All nations will be blessed through him,
> > and they will call him blessed.
>
> (v. 7)

This is a very clear echo of the personal and universal promise of God to Abraham in Genesis 12:2–3. (Cf. also Ps. 2:7–8; Isa. 55:3–5).

JESUS IS THE END OF THE TIME OF PREPARATION

At the end of his genealogy, in v.17, Matthew makes an observation about it before he moves on to the birth of Jesus:

> Thus there were fourteen generations in all from
> Abraham to David, fourteen from David to the exile
> to Babylon, and fourteen from the exile to the Christ.

Matthew is very fond of threes and sevens in his presentation of material in his Gospel. Both were symbolic numbers for completeness or perfection. Three double-sevens is pretty complete! His purpose is not merely statistical, or just a matter of a historical curiosity. From that point of view his observation is not strictly accurate, since at several places in the genealogy biological generations are skipped over (as was quite common in Old Testament genealogy). Rather he is being deliberately schematic, with a theological intention. He is pointing out that Old Testament history falls into three approximately equal spans of time between the critical events:

from the foundational covenant with Abraham to the establishing of the monarchy under David;

from David to the destruction and loss of the monarchy in the Babylonian exile;

and from the exile to the coming of the Messiah himself who alone could occupy the throne of David.

Jesus is thus 'the end of the line', as far as the Old Testament story goes. It has run its completed course in preparation for him, and now its goal an climax has been reached.

The Old Testament is full of future hope. It looks beyond itself to an expected end. This forward movement, or eschatological thrust (from Greek 'eschaton', 'ultimate event' or 'final conclusion') is a fundamental part of the faith of Israel. It was grounded in their experience and concept of God himself as a God who was constantly active within history for a definite purpose, working towards his desired goal for the earth and humanity. Just as Matthew has summarized that history in the form of his genealogy, so his concluding observation in v. 17 points out that it is a history whose purpose is now achieved. The preparation is complete. The Messiah has come. In that sense, Jesus is the end. The same note is echoed throughout the Gospel in the urgency of Jesus's preaching about the Kingdom of God. 'The time is fulfilled; the Kingdom of God is at hand.'

JESUS IS ALSO A NEW BEGINNING

Matthew's Gospel (and the New Testament itself) opens with the words, literally, 'An account of the genesis of Jesus, the Messiah . . .' A Jewish reader would immediately be reminded of Genesis 2:4 and 5:1, where exactly the same expression is used in the Greek translation of the Hebrew scriptures. The same word in the plural (*geneseis*, 'origins', 'generations') is used several more times in the book of Genesis to introduce genealogies and narratives, or to conclude them and mark off important divisions in the book.

So the use of the word 'genesis' here, by a careful author like Matthew, is fairly certainly deliberate. With the echo of the book of Genesis we are meant to realize that the arrival of Jesus the Messiah marks a new beginning, indeed a new creation. God is doing his 'new thing'. Good news indeed. Jesus, then, is not only (looking back) the end of the beginning; he is also (looking forward) the beginning of the end.

So much of significance, then, is contained within Matthew's opening seventeen verses. In its own way, though more indirectly, it is rather like the prologue of John's Gospel, pointing out dimensions of the significance of Jesus before introducing him in the flesh. We see Jesus in the particularity of his context in Jewish history, and yet with the universal significance which was attached to that history since the promise to Abraham. We see him as the messianic heir of the line of David. We see him as the end and also the beginning. Only with such understanding of the meaning of the story so far, can we proceed to a full appreciation of the Gospel story itself.

Returning, however, to our average carol-singing Christian, it is doubtful if the succession of names in Matthew's genealogy will be as effective in recalling the outline of Old Testament history for her as it would have been for Matthew's original readers. So at this point it may be helpful to step back and very briefly review the Old Testament story, following the three broad divisions that Matthew observes.

The story so far

FROM ABRAHAM TO DAVID

i) The problem

Matthew begins with Abraham, at the point of God's promise from which Israel took their existence. Luke begins further back with Adam. And indeed we can only understand Abraham himself in the light of what goes before. For it is Genesis 1–11 which poses the question to which the rest of the Bible, from Genesis 12 on, is the answer.

Having created the earth and human beings to dwell with him upon it, God witnessed the rebellion of the human race against his love and authority. The earlier stories portray this at the level of individual and family life. The later ones go on to show how the whole of human society is enmeshed in a growing web of corruption and violence, which even the judgement of the flood did not eradicate from human life. The climax of this 'prehistory' is reached with the story of the tower of Babel in Genesis 11. At the end of that story we find the effects of sin have reached a 'global' scale, with humanity scattered in division and confusion across the face of the earth, an earth still under the curse of God. Is there any hope for the human race in such a condition? Can the nations of the earth ever be restored to the blessing and favour of God?

ii) Election

God's answer was a seventy-five-year-old man. To that man and his as yet childless and elderly wife, God promised a son. And through that son, he promised a nation which, in contrast to the nations since Babel, would be blessed by God. And through that nation, he promised blessing to all the nations.

No wonder Abraham and Sarah both laughed on different occasions, especially as they neared their century and God kept renewing the promise in spite of it becoming ever more remote. But the promise was kept. The laughter turned into Isaac ('he laughs'), and the family that was to become a great nation began to take shape and increase. So important was this choice that it formed part of the identity of the God of the Bible thereafter. He is known, and indeed chooses to be known, as 'The God of Abraham, Isaac and Jacob'. That description was enough to characterize him as the God of promise and fulfilment, and the God whose purpose ultimately embraced all nations.

It also defined the identity of the people of Israel. Who were Israel? The chosen people, yes, but chosen, as Moses reminded them deflatingly and often, not because of their numerical greatness or moral superiority, but only because God had loved and chosen Abraham, for his own redemptive purpose (Deut. 7:7–8, 9:4–6).

iii) Redemption

Having migrated to Egypt as guests in time of famine, the descendants of Abraham ended up as slaves, an oppressed ethnic minority in a hostile land. The book of Exodus vividly describes their exploitation and then goes on to an even more vivid description of their liberation by God. In the process of this great story of deliverance, God acquires a new name alongside this fresh dimension of his character: 'Yahweh', the God who acts out of faithfulness to his promise, in liberating justice for the oppressed. The exodus thus becomes the primary model of what redemption means in the Bible, and gives substance to what an Israelite would have meant by calling God 'Redeemer'.

iv) Covenant

Three months after the exodus, God at last has Israel to himself, at the foot of Mount Sinai. There, through Moses, he gave them his law, including the ten commandments, and entered into a covenant with them as a nation. He would be their God and they would be his people, in a relationship of sovereignty and blessing on the one hand, and loyalty and obedience on the other.

It is important to see that this covenant was based on what God had already done for them (as they had just recently seen, Ex. 19:4–6). His grace and redemptive action came first. Their obedience to the law and covenant was to be as a grateful response, and in order to enable them to be what God wanted them to be as his people in the midst of the nations. We shall explore the meaning of this in chapter five.

v) Inheritance

The generation of the exodus, through their own failure, unbelief and rebellion, perished in the wilderness. It was given to the succeeding generation to take possession of what had been the purpose of the exodus liberation – the promised land itself. Under the leadership of Joshua, the Israelites gained strategic control of the land. But there followed a lengthy process of settlement in which the tribes struggled – sometimes in co-operation, and sometimes in competition – to possess fully the land allotted to them.

During the centuries of the period of the judges there was much disunity, caused by internal strife and external pressures. Alongside this went chronic disloyalty to the faith of Yahweh, though it was never lost altogether, and was sustained, like the people themselves, by the varied ministries and victories of the figures called 'judges', culminating in the great Samuel.

The pressures eventually led to the demand for monarchy (1 Sam. 8–12). This was interpreted by Samuel as a rejection of God's own rule over his people, especially since it was motivated by a desire to be like the other nations, when it was precisely the vocation of Israel to be different. God, however, elevated the sinful desires of the people into a vehicle for his own purpose, and after the failure of Saul,

David established the monarchy firmly and became its glorious model.

Possibly the most important achievement of David was that he at last gave to Israel complete and unified control over the whole of the land that had been promised to Abraham. Up to then it had been fragmentarily occupied by loosely federated tribes, under constant attack and invasion from their enemies. David defeated those enemies systematically, giving Israel 'rest from their enemies round about', and established secure borders for the nation.

There is, therefore, a kind of natural historical arch from Abraham to David, in the sense that with David the covenant with Abraham had come to a measure of fulfilment: Abraham's offspring had become a great nation; they had taken possession of the land promised to Abraham; they were living in a special relationship of blessing and protection under Yahweh.

But then, as often in the Old Testament, no sooner has a promise 'come to rest', so to speak, than it takes off again in a renewed form as history moves forward (we shall look at this characteristic of the Old Testament in the next chapter). And so, in a personal covenant with David, God tied his purpose for Israel to his promise to the house of David himself. As in the covenant with Abraham, the promise to David included a son and heir, a great name, and a special relationship (2 Sam. 7). So then, with this new royal dimension, the story of God's people moves forward to its next phase.

FROM DAVID TO THE EXILE

i) Division

Solomon glorified and consolidated the empire that David had built, and built the temple his father had desired and planned. That temple then became the focal point of God's presence with his people for the next half millenium, until it was destroyed, along with Jerusalem, at the time of the exile.

Solomon also introduced Israel to foreign trade, foreign culture, foreign wealth and foreign influences. The golden age of Solomon's wealth and wisdom, however, had its dark side in the increasing burden of the cost of empire that fell on the ordinary population. With the onset of forced labour, taxation, conscription and confiscation, the accuracy of Samuel's warnings in 1 Samuel 8:10–18 was painfully proved. All of this was totally contrary to the authentic Israelite tradition of covenant equality and freedom and it produced increasing discontent among the people, especially in the northern tribes who seemed to suffer more than the royal tribe of Judah.

When Rehoboam, Solomon's son, refused the people's request and his elders' advice to lighten the load, and instead deliberately chose the way of oppression and exploitation as state policy, the discontent boiled over into rebellion. Led by Jeroboam, the ten northern tribes seceded from the house of David and formed a rival kingdom, taking for themselves the name of Israel, leaving Rehoboam and his Davidic successors with the remnant – the kingdom of Judah. The date was about 931 BC. From then on the story of Israel is one of the divided kingdoms, of which the northern state was the first to be destroyed.

ii) The ninth century BC

The northern kingdom of Israel, as with many states founded by revolution, however just the cause, went through a period of instability, with successive *coups d'état* after the death of Jeroboam, and four kings in twenty-five years.

Eventually in the ninth century BC, Omri established a dynasty and built up the political and military strength of the country. This was sustained by his son Ahab, whose wife Jezebel had been chosen for him as a marriage alliance with powerful Phoenicia, the maritime trading nation to the north of Israel. Jezebel's influence, however, was more than political and economic. She set about converting her adoptive kingdom to the religion of her native Tyre. She imposed the cult of Baal, and systematically tried to extinguish the faith of Yahweh.

The crisis that this produced led to the call and challenge of Elijah in the mid-ninth century. He not only courageously brought about a (temporary) revival and reconversion of the people to their ancestral faith, through the judgement of drought followed by the fiery climax of Mount Carmel (1 Kgs 18), but also addressed the anger of God against the economic and social evil that was threatening the material structure of Israel's faith, as typified in Ahab and Jezebel's treatment of Naboth (1 Kgs 21). Elijah was followed by Elisha, whose long ministry lasted throughout the rest of the ninth century and influenced both national and international politics.

In Judah, the ninth century was a quieter affair. With its established capital, court, bureaucracy and dynasty, Judah proved much more stable than the northern state. The first fifty years saw the reigns of only two kings: Asa and Jehoshaphat. Both were strong and comparatively godly and preserved the faith of Yahweh. Jehoshaphat also introduced a major judicial reform.

The second half of the ninth century saw an attempt by Athaliah, of the house of Omri, who had been married to Jehoshaphat's son Jehoram (as another of Omri's marriage alliances), to capture the throne of David for the house of Israel after her husband's death. Her reign only lasted five years, however, before she was removed in a counter-revolution and the Davidic succession restored in the person of seven year old Joash.

iii) *The eighth century* BC

Meanwhile, in northern Israel, the dynasty of Omri had been overthrown in a bloody revolution led by Jehu, a fanatical Yahwist who considered it his mission to remove all traces of Baal, his prophets and his worshippers, by fair means or foul – mostly foul. His blood purge weakened the kingdom and lost him his allies. But by the second quarter of the eighth century his great-grandson, Jeroboam II, restored Israel to a degree of political, military and material prosperity which it had not seen since the days of Solomon.

But, as in the days of Solomon, the prosperity was not enjoyed by all. Underneath the upper and external extravagance, and in spite of the thriving and popular religious cult, lay an increasing poverty gap and a world of exploitation and oppression. Economic problems of debt and bondage, corruption of the markets and the courts, divided the nation and led to another upsurge of the prophetic voice of Yahweh's anger.

Amos and Hosea both prophesied in the northern kingdom of Israel in the mid to late eighth century. Amos fiercely denounced the social injustices that he observed on all sides, defending the poor and exploited as 'the righteous' (i.e. those with right on their side in the situation), and attacking the wealthy, luxury-loving class, especially in Samaria, as 'the wicked' – a total and revolutionary reversal of popular religious understanding of the day. At the same time he claimed that the thriving religious practices at Bethel and Gilgal, though not necessarily idolatrous in the sense of worshipping other gods than Yahweh, were not only not pleasing in the sight of God as the people believed, but actually stank in his nostrils. The rampant injustice and oppression in the nation was not only a complete betrayal of all their history as God's covenant people (a history Amos recounts accusingly), but also turned their pretended worship into a mockery and an abomination.

Hosea, through the bitter experience of his own marriage to an unfaithful and adulterous wife, saw more of the internal spiritual reality of the people's condition. He saw the syncretistic Baal worship with its attendant sexual perversions including ritual prostitution and by analogy accused the people of being infected with a 'spirit of prostitution'. Amos had predicted that the kingdom would be destroyed and king and people exiled. It must have seemed laughable in the prosperous days of Jeroboam II, but within 25 years of his death, it happened and Hosea probably witnessed it.

By the middl· of the eighth century BC, Assyria had become the dominant world power and was rapidly expanding westward to the Palestinian states. After several rebellions, Israel was attacked by Assyria in 725. Samaria was besieged and eventually fell in 721. The bulk of the Israelite population (the ten northern tribes) was deported and scattered throughout other parts of Assyria's empire, while populations of foreigners from other parts were brought into Israel's territories. In this act of Assyria – an example of its policy of imperial subjugation – lies the origins of the mixed race of 'Samaritans'. So the northern kingdom of Israel ceased to exist, its territory now nothing more than a province under the paw of the Assyrian lion – a paw now poised ominously close to Judah.

In Judah, the eighth century began, as in Israel, with half a century of prosperity and stability, mainly under the strong king Uzziah. His successor Jotham was also a good king, but all was not well among the people who, according to the chronicler 'continued their corrupt practices' (2 Chron. 27:2). Apparently the same social and economic evils had penetrated Judah as were blatant in Israel. This provides the background for the ministries of two great eighth-century prophets in Judah – Isaiah and Micah, who began during the reign of Jotham.

The Assyrian threat loomed over Judah also in the last third of the eighth century. King Ahaz, in 735, in an attempt to protect himself from threatened invasions from Israel and Syria, however, appealed to Assyria for assistance against these more local enemies. They readily obliged, smashing Syria, Israel and Philistia, and then turned to demand of Judah a heavy tribute for the favour. Ahaz's action, which had been directly opposed by Isaiah, proved politically and religiously disastrous, since Judah became virtually a vassal state of Assyria and was forced to absorb much of her religious practices as well.

Ahaz's successor, Hezekiah, reversed that policy. He linked major religious reforms to a renewed bid for freedom from Assyrian domination. His rebellion brought Assyrian invasions of devastating force, and indeed he surrendered and paid up. But Jerusalem itself was remarkably delivered, in fulfilment of a prophetic encouragement from Isaiah. But instead of producing national repentance and return to Yahweh and the demands of the covenant, as preached by Isaiah, this miraculous deliverance served only to make the people complacent in the belief that Jerusalem and her temple were indestructible forever.

iv) The seventh century BC

The seventh century in Judah was like a see-saw. The reforming, anti-Assyrian policies of Hezekiah were completely reversed by Manasseh. His long, half-century reign became a time of unprecedented apostasy, of religious decay, corruption and a return even to ancient Canaanite practices long abominated and forbidden in Israel, such as child sacrifice. His reign was violent, oppressive and pagan (cf. 2 Kgs 21 and 2 Chron. 33), and as far as can be seen, no voice of prophecy penetrated the darkness.

His grandson Josiah, however (Amon the son only reigned two years), brought in yet another reversal of state policy: both resistant to Assyria, and religiously reforming. In fact the reformation of Josiah, lasting about a decade from 629, and including the discovery of a book of the law (probably Deuteronomy) during repairs to the temple, was the most thorough and severe in its effects of any in Judah's history. And yet, as it was observed by Jeremiah, only slightly younger than Josiah himself and called to be prophet in the early flush of the reformation, its effects were largely external and did not purge the idolatry from the hearts of the people, or the corruption from their hands.

In the passion of his youth, Jeremiah denounced the religious, moral and social evils of Jerusalem society, from top to bottom, but appealed movingly for repentance, believing that God's threatened judgement could thereby be averted. As his ministry wore on into his middle age, Jeremiah, forbidden by God even to pray for the people, so advanced was their hardness of heart, foretold nothing but calamity for his own generation at the hands of their enemies. Their disbelief turned to outrage when he predicted even the destruction of the very temple itself, against the popular mythology which, since Isaiah's day, believed it to be safe forever under Yahweh's protection, like Jerusalem itself. He suffered arrest, beating and imprisonment for so unpopular a message. Unpopular but accurate.

In the later seventh century the weakening Assyrian empire quite rapidly collapsed and was replaced by the resurgent power of Babylon under an energetic commander, Nebuchadnezzar. Irritated by repeated rebellions in Judah, which after the death of Josiah in 609 was ruled by a succession of weak and vacillating kings, Nebuchadnezzar finally besieged Jerusalem in 588, capturing it in 587. The destruction was total: the city, the temple, and everything in them went up in smoke. The bulk of the population, except for the poorest in the land, were carried off in captivity to Babylon. The unthinkable had happened. God's people were evicted from God's land. The exile had begun and engulfed a whole generation. The monarchy was ended. The exile of Jehoiachin ('Jeconiah') and his brother Zedekiah, the last two kings of Judah, brings to an end the second section of Matthew's genealogy.

v) Some lessons of history

We saw some of the important features of the first period of Israel's history (Abraham to David): the nature of Yahweh as a God of faithfulness to covenant promise, and of liberating justice for the oppressed; and the nature of his people, called into existence for the sake of God's redemptive purpose for all the nations, standing in the grace of God's redemption and under the demand of his covenant, living within the inheritance of the land he had given to them. This central section (from David to the exile) also had its vital lessons, which the historical books and the books of the prophets made clear.

One affirmation was that Yahweh, the God of Israel, was in sovereign control of world history – not merely the affairs of Israel. The prophets had asserted this with incredible boldness – arrogance, one might say, had it not been true. They looked out on the vast empires that impinged upon the life of Israel and at times appeared to threaten its existence, and regarded them as mere sticks and tools in the hands of Yahweh, the God of little divided Israel. Those who edited the historical books of Israel, from Joshua to Kings, did so most probably during the exile itself, when Israel was in captivity to one of those empires. Yet they continued to make the same affirmation of faith: Yahweh has done this. God is still in control, as he always has been.

A second vital truth that permeates this period is the moral character and demand of Yahweh. The God who acted for justice at the exodus remained committed to maintaining it among his own people. The law had expressed this commitment institutionally. The prophets gave it voice directly, each to his contemporary generation and context. God's moral concern is not only individual (though the masses of individual stories show that it certainly does claim every individual), but social. He evaluates the moral health of society as a whole, from international treaties to market economies, from military strategy to local court procedures, from national politics to the local harvest. This dimension of the message of the Old Testament would vibrate from Matthew's list of kings, since so many of them were associated with (not to say, the victims of) the unforgettable rhetoric of the great prophets of the monarchy period.

A third unmistakeable dimension of this era was the realization that Yahweh cared little, if at all, for the external rituals of the faith of his people in the absence of practical social obedience to his moral demands. This was all the more surprising in the light of the strong Pentateuchal tradition that ascribed the religion of Israel – its festivals, sacrifices, and priesthood – to the gift and commandment of Yahweh himself. Of course, even in the law itself the essential covenant requirements of loyalty and obedience had come before the detailed sacrificial regulations. And since the days of Samuel there had been the awareness that 'obedience is better than sacrifice' (1 Sam. 15:22). Nevertheless there was still something radically shocking when Amos and Isaiah told the people that Yahweh hated and despised their worship, and was fed up and sickened by the very sacrifices they thought he wanted, while Jeremiah told them that they could mix up all their rituals the wrong way round for all that God cared (Amos 5:21ff., Is. 1:11ff., Jer. 7:21ff). God will not be worshipped and cannot be known apart from commitment to that righteousness and justice, faithfulness and love, which are his own character and delight (Jer. 9:23f., 22:15f.).

All three of these prominent features of the message of the Old Testament in the period of the monarchy are to be found in the teaching of Jesus, son of David: the sovereignty (kingship) of God, perceived and affirmed only by faith, even against appearances; the essentially moral quality of God's rule and the demand made upon those who submit to it; and the priority of moral and practical obedience over any and all religious observance. In these, as in so many ways as we shall see, especially in chapter five, Jesus recaptured and amplified the authentic voice of his Hebrew Bible.

FROM THE EXILE TO THE MESSIAH

i) The exile

The exile lasted fifty years (that is, from 587 BC to the first return of some Jews to Jerusalem in 538 BC). The period from the destruction of the temple to the completion of its rebuilding was approximately seventy years.

It is remarkable that Israel and her faith survived at all. That they did survive was largely due to the message of the prophets – particularly of Jeremiah up to, and of Ezekiel after, the fall of Jerusalem. They consistently interpreted the terrifying events as the judgement of Yahweh, punishment for the persistently evil ways of his people. From that perspective, the exile could be seen as a punishment that was *logical* (it showed God's consistency in terms of his covenant threats as well as his promises), but also *limited* (so there could be hope for the future). Both Jeremiah and Ezekiel foretold a return to the land and a restoration of the relationship between God and his people. Jeremiah portrayed it in terms of a new covenant (Jer. 31:31ff.). Ezekiel had visions of nothing short of national resurrection (Ezek. 37), with reunified tribes of Israel living once again in God's land, surrounding God's temple, and enjoying God's presence (Ezek. 40–48).

Nevertheless, by the later years of the exile it seemed that many had abandoned hope. The Israelites accused Yahweh of having forgotten and forsaken them (e.g. Is. 40:27, 49:14) – a rich irony in view of the fact that it was they who for centuries had treated him that way! Into this lethargic despair came the message of Isaiah 40–55, either the preserved words of

Isaiah himself from the eighth century now at last relevant, or, as many scholars believe, the words of an anonymous prophet of the calibre of Isaiah (and greatly influenced by him) who lived at the time of the exile itself and addressed his stirring message to the exiles. At a time when all they could see was the threatening rise of yet another empire (the Persians), this prophet calls on them to lift up their eyes and hearts once more to see their God on the move bringing liberation at last.

The ringing affirmation of Isaiah 40–55 is that Yahweh is not only still the sovereign Lord of all creation and all history (and is utterly uniquely so), but that he is about to act again on behalf of his oppressed people with a deliverance which will recall the original exodus, but dwarf it in significance. The clouds they so much dread – the meteoric rise of Cyrus, ruler of the new, expanding Persian empire – would burst in blessings on their head. Babylon would be destroyed and they would be released, free to return to Jerusalem, which, sings the prophet, was already exulting in joy at the sight of God leading his captives home.

In the midst of all this directly historical prediction, the prophet also perceives the true ministry and mission of Israel as the servant of God, destined to bring his blessing to all nations – a destiny in which they are manifestly failing. The task will be accomplished however, through a true Servant of Yahweh, whose mission of justice, teaching, suffering, death and vindication will ultimately bring God's salvation to the ends of the earth. The particular story of tiny Israel and the universal purposes of God are again linked together tantalizingly.

ii) The restoration

The historical predictions were fulfilled. Cyrus defeated Babylon in 539 and granted freedom to the captive peoples of the Babylonian empire to take up their gods and go home – under his 'supervision', of course. In 538 the first return of some (by no means all) of the exiled Jews began. They were a tiny community facing enormous problems. Jerusalem and Judah were in ruins after half a century of neglect. They experienced intense opposition and a campaign of political and physical obstruction from the Samaritans. Their early harvests were disappointing, creating further problems. Not surprisingly, after a start was made and the foundations laid, work on the rebuilding of the temple was soon neglected. However, as a result of the encouragement of two of the post-exilic prophets, Haggai and Zechariah, it was eventually completed in 515.

Throughout this period Judah had no independence, of course. They formed just a small sub-province of the vast Persian empire, which stretched from the shore of the Aegean sea to the borders of India, and lasted for two centuries. In the fifth century it appears that disillusionment and depression set in again, partly as a result of the apparent failure of the hopes raised by Haggai and Zechariah. And this led to a growing laxity in religious and moral life. This was challenged by the last of the Old Testament prophets, Malachi, probably about the middle of the fifth century. He was concerned about the slovenliness of the sacrifices, the spread of divorce and the widespread failure of the people to honour God in practical life.

The same kind of situation was addressed a little later by Ezra and Nehemiah, whose terms of office overlapped somewhat in Jerusalem. Ezra's achievement was the teaching of the law and the re-ordering of the community around it, consolidated by a ceremony of covenant renewal. Nehemiah's achievements included the rebuilding of the walls of Jerusalem, giving its inhabitants not only physical safety, but also a sense of unity and dignity. As the officially appointed Persian governor, he was able to give the needed political patronage and authority to the reforms of Ezra, as well as engaging in some social and economic reforms of his own.

iii) The inter-testamental period
The canonical history of the Old Testament comes to an end
in the mid-fifth century, with Malachi, Ezra and Nehemiah.
But of course, the Jewish community went on, as does
Matthew's genealogy. The Jews lived through two more
changes of imperial power before Christ.

Twice during the early fifth century Persia tried, and failed,
to conquer the Greek mainland and spread their power to
Europe. They were heroically beaten back by the Spartans
and Athenians – who then fell to fighting with each other.
Not until the mid-fourth century were the Greek states forced
into a unity by the power of Macedon, which then turned its
attention east to the wealth of the Persian empire just across
the Aegean Sea. Under Alexander the Great, Greek armies
sliced through the Persian empire like a knife through butter,
with amazing speed. The whole vast area once ruled by Persia,
including Judah, then came under Greek rule. This was the
beginning of the 'Hellenistic' (Greek) era, when the Greek
language and culture spread throughout the whole Near and
Middle Eastern world.

After the death of Alexander, prematurely in 323, his
empire was split up among his generals. Ptolemy established
a dynasty in Egypt, and for more or less the whole of the
third century, Palestine and the Jews were under the political
control of the Ptolemies. From about 200 onwards, however,
control of Palestine passed into the hands of the Seleucid
kings of Syria, who ruled over the northern part of the old
Alexandrian empire, from Antioch. Their rule was much more
aggressively Greek, and Jews faced increasing pressure to
conform religiously and culturally to Hellenism. Those who
refused faced persecution. The supreme insult was when Anti-
ochus Epiphanes IV in 167 set up a statue of Zeus, the
supreme god of Greek mythology, in the temple itself.

This sacrilege sparked off a major revolt when Jews under
the leadership of Judas Maccabeus took up arms. It ended

with a successful struggle for independence, climaxing in the cleansing of the temple in 164. For the next century, the Jews more or less governed themselves, under the leadership of the Hasmonean priestly dynasty. This lasted until the power of Greece was replaced by that of Rome, which had been gradually expanding its sphere of influence throughout the whole Mediterranean basin during the second and first centuries BC. In 63 Roman legions under Pompey (also, but less deservedly than Alexander, known as 'the Great'), entered Palestine. Thus began the long period of Roman supremacy over the Jews, within which, because of the imperial need for colonial statistics, a virgin from Nazareth gave birth to her first-born son in Bethlehem of Judea, the city of David, and brought Matthew's genealogy to an end.

Two features of this inter-testamental period are worth noting in view of their influence on the world into which Jesus arrived. The first was an increasing devotion to the law, the *torah*. This became the supreme mark of the faithful Jew. It eventually developed into a somewhat fanatical cause, supported by a systematic building of a whole structure of theology and exposition and application around the law itself. There were professional experts, scribes, involved in this, and there also emerged lay movements devoted to wholehearted obedience to the law – such as the Pharisees. We may be tempted to dismiss all this as legalism. Doubtless it tended in that direction, and we shall hear Jesus with his unique insight and authority exposing some of the failure and mis-guidedness of his contemporary devotees of the law and tradition. But we should also be aware of the positive and worthy motives that lay behind it. Had not the exile, the greatest catastrophe in their history, been the direct judgement of God on the failure of his people precisely to keep his law? Was that not the message of the great prophets? Surely then they should learn the lesson of history and make every effort to live as God required, thus not only avoiding a repetition of such judgement, but also hastening the day of his final deliverance from their present enemies. The pursuit of holiness was serious and purposeful. It was a total social programme – not just a fringe of hyper-religious piety.

The second feature was the upsurge of apocalyptic, messianic hope. As persecution continued and as the nation experienced martyrdoms and great suffering, there developed hopes of a final climactic intervention by God himself, as the prophets had foretold. He would establish his kingdom for ever by destroying his (and Israel's) enemies, vindicating and uplifting the righteous oppressed, and putting an end to their suffering. In varied ways these hopes included the expectation of a coming figure who would realize this intervention of God and lead the people. These expectations were not all linked together, or attached to one single figure. They included terms like messiah (anointed one), son of man, a new David, Elijah, or the Prophet, the branch, etc. We shall look at some of these in chapters three and four. The coming of such a figure would herald the end of the present age, the arrival of the Kingdom of God, the restoration of Israel and the judgement of the wicked.

One can imagine the stirring of hearts and quickening of pulses in Jewish homes and communities when, into this mixture of aspirations and hopes dropped the message of John the Baptist, and then of Jesus himself –

> The time is fulfilled! (what you have been waiting for as something future is now here and present); the kingdom of God is at hand! (God is now acting to establish his reign in the midst of you); so repent and believe the good news (urgent action is required of you now).

Light on the story

This, then, is the story which Matthew condenses into 17 verses of genealogy, the story which leads up to Jesus the Messiah, the story which he completes. It is the story *from which* he acquired his identity and mission. It is also the story *to which* he gave significance and authority. The very form of the genealogy shows the direct continuity between the Old Testament and Jesus himself. This continuity is based on the action of God. The God who is manifestly involved in the events described in the second half of Matthew 1 was also active in the events implied in the first half. In Jesus he brought to completion what he himself had prepared for. This means that it is Jesus who gives meaning and validity to the events of Israel's Old Testament history. So the person who accepts, therefore, the claims of this chapter about *Jesus* (that he is indeed the promised Messiah, that he was conceived by the Holy Spirit of God and therefore uniquely God's Son, that in him the saving presence of God [Jesus, Immanuel] is truly among mankind), also accepts its implied claim about the *history* which leads up to him.

It is important to remember that we are still talking about history here, and not about promises being fulfilled (which is the subject of the next chapter). We are more familiar with the idea that, as Paul put it, 'all the promises of God are "Yes" in Christ' (2 Cor. 1:20). But in a sense all the acts of God are 'Yes' in Christ also. For the Old Testament is much more than a promise box full of blessed predictions about Jesus. It is primarily a story – *the* story of the acts of God in human history out of which those promises arose and in relation to which only they make sense.

If we think of the Old Testament only in terms of promises that are fulfilled we may fall into the trap of regarding the content of the Old Testament as of little value in itself. If it is all 'fulfilled', is it worth anything now? By a perversion of the meaning of the book of Hebrews, it may be asked whether, having the 'reality' of Christ, we need to pay any attention to the 'shadows'. But the events of the Old Testament story were themselves reality – sometimes life and death reality – for those who lived through them. And through them there was a real relationship between God and his people, and a real revelation of God to his people, and through them to us, for it is the same God. That God, to pick up Hebrews in its true sense, who in these last days has spoken to us by his Son, also and truly spoke through the prophets. And those prophets were nothing if not rooted in the earthy specifics of their own historical contexts – 'at many times and in various ways' (Heb. 1:1).

LIGHT ON THE OLD

When we look at events in the history of the Old Testament, then, with these points in mind, it has several effects. It means first that whatever significance a particular event had, in terms of Israel's own experience of God and in the articulation of their faith, is affirmed and validated. 'What it meant for Israel' does not just evaporate in a haze of spiritualization when we reach the New Testament. At the same time, secondly, we may legitimately see in the event, or in the record of it, additional levels of significance in the light of the end of the story – i.e. in the light of Christ. And thirdly, conversely, the Old Testament event may provide levels of significance to our full understanding of all that Christ was and said and did.

Take for example that foundational event in Israel's history – the exodus. The event itself, and the way it is prepared for and described in the Hebrew record, leaves no doubt that God is characterized by care for the oppressed and is motivated to action for justice on their behalf. So prominent is this aspect of the significance of the story in the Hebrew

Bible, that it became permanently definitive of the nature of Yahweh, Israel's God, and of what they meant by the terms redemption and salvation. Now that dimension of the exodus event remains true, as a permanently valid part of God's revelation, after the coming of Christ. His coming in no way alters or removes the truth of the Old Testament story in itself and in its meaning for Israel – namely that God is concerned for the poor and suffering and desires justice for the exploited. On the contrary, it underlines and endorses it.

Looking back on the event, however, in the light of the fulness of God's redemptive achievement in Jesus Christ, we can see that even the original exodus was not merely concerned with the political, economic and social aspects of Israel's predicament. There was also a level of spiritual oppression in Israel's subjection to the gods of Egypt. 'Let my people go *that they may worship/serve me*', was God's demand on Pharoah. And the explicit purpose of the deliverance was that they would *know* Yahweh in the grace of redemption and covenant relationship. So the exodus, for all the comprehensiveness of what it achieved for Israel, points beyond itself to a greater need for deliverance from the totality of evil and restoration to relationship with God than it achieved by itself. Such a deliverance was accomplished by Jesus Christ in his death and resurrection. It was the reality of that accomplishment that Moses and Elijah discussed with him on the Mount of Transfiguration, as, in Luke's words, they talked about 'the exodus he would accomplish in Jerusalem' (Luke 9:31). And indeed when the Hebrew prophets themselves looked hopefully into the future, they pictured God's final and complete salvation in terms of a new and greater exodus, as a result of which salvation would reach to the ends of the earth. So, when we look back on the original historical exodus in the light of the end of the story in Christ, it is filled with rich significance in view of what it points to.

LIGHT ON THE NEW

But it is equally important look at the other end of the story, the achievement of Christ, in the light of all that the exodus was as an act of God's redemption, as it is understood in the Old Testament. The New Testament affirms that the Gospel of the cross and resurrection of Christ is God's complete answer to the totality of evil and all its effects within his creation. But it is the Old Testament which shows us the nature and extent of sin and evil – primarily in the narratives of Genesis 4–11, but thereafter also in the history of Israel and the nations, such as the oppression of the first chapters of Exodus. It shows us that while evil has its origins outside the human race, human beings are morally accountable to God for our own sin. It shows us that sin and evil have a corporate as well as an individual dimension, that is, they affect and shape the patterns of social life within which we live, as well as the personal lives we lead. It shows us that sin and evil affect history itself through inescapable cause and effect and a kind of cumulative process through the generations of humanity. It shows us that there is no area of life on earth in which we are free from the influence of our own sin and the sin of others. In short, the Old Testament portrays to us a very big problem to which there needs to be a very big answer, if there is one at all.

Now, in the New Testament, of course, as Christians we believe we see God's big and final answer to the problem. But in the Old Testament God had already begun to sketch in the dimensions of his answer through successive acts of redemption in history, with the exodus as the prime model. Here we come back to the importance of treating the Old Testament as real history. There is a tendency among Christians to say something like, 'the Old Testament is a foreshadowing of Jesus Christ'. Carefully explained, this is true. But it can lead to the prejudice that dispenses with the Old Testament itself as little more than shadows, or a kind of children's picture book, of no significance in itself but only for what it foreshadowed. That can then allow one so to spiritualize and individualize one's interpretation of the work of Christ that it loses all touch with the dimensions of God's primary and preparatory works of redemption in the history of Israel.

But the exodus was *real* redemption. It was a real act of the living God, for real people, who were in real slavery and it really liberated them. They were liberated from political oppression as an immigrant community into independent nation status. They were liberated from economic exploitation as a slave labour force into the freedom and sufficiency of a land of their own. They were liberated from social violation of basic human rights as a victimized ethnic minority into an unprecedented opportunity to create a new kind of community based on equality and social justice. They were liberated from spiritual bondage to Pharaoh and the other gods of Egypt into undeniable knowledge of and covenant relationship with the living God.

Such was the meaning and scope of redemption in the Hebrew Bible. The very word 'redemption' took its substantial meaning from this event. Ask any Israelite what he meant by saying that Yahweh was a Redeemer, or that he himself was redeemed, and he (or she, if you had asked the likes of Deborah or Hannah) would have told you this story and put Q.E.D. at the end. That is exactly what some of the Psalms do. They celebrate redemption by telling this story. They knew the scale of the problem, and they had experienced the scale of God's answer. No, it was not yet God's last word or act in redemption. Yes, a greater 'exodus' and a complete redemption still lay in their future. But within the limits of history and revelation up to that point, the exodus was a *real* act of God as Redeemer, and it demonstrated unmistakeably the comprehensive scale and scope of his redemptive purpose. The exodus was *God's* idea of redemption. How big,

then, is our 'New Testament Gospel'? It should not fall short
of, or be narrower than, its Old Testament foundation, for
God is the same God and his ultimate purpose is the same.

This means that it is inadequate also merely to put it like
this, as one often hears: 'In the exodus, God rescued Israel
from bondage to Pharoah, and through the cross he rescues
me from bondage to sin.' The mighty act of the exodus was
more than just a parable to illustrate personal salvation. Furthermore, the nature of the bondage is not quite so parallel
as that. Gloriously it is true that the cross breaks the bondage
of my personal sin and releases me from its effects. But the
exodus was a release from bondage to the *sin of others*. The
Israelites were in Egypt and in slavery, not because of their
own sins or God's judgement (as was certainly true of their
later captivity in Babylon during the exile). Their sufferings
were the direct result of the oppression, cruelty, exploitation
and victimization of the Egyptians. Their liberation therefore
was a release from bondage to the evil of others which
enslaved them.

This is not for a moment to imply that the Israelites were
not themselves sinners, as much in need of God's mercy and
grace as the rest of the human race. The subsequent story of
their behaviour in the wilderness proved that beyond a doubt.
Just as it also proved God's infinite patience and forgiving
grace towards their sinful and rebellious ways. The sacrificial
system, indeed, was designed precisely to cope with the
reality of sin on the part of the people of God and to provide
a means of atoning for it. The point here is that atonement
and forgiveness for one's own sin is not what the exodus
redemption was about. It was rather a deliverance from an
external evil and the suffering and injustice it caused, by
means of a shattering defeat of the evil power and an irrevo-
cable breaking of its hold over Israel, in all the dimensions
mentioned above – political, economic, social and spiritual.

If, then, God's climactic work of redemption through the

cross transcends, but also embodies and includes, the scope of all his redemptive activity as previously laid bare in Old Testament history, our Gospel must include the exodus model of liberation, as well as the sacrificial model of atonement, or the restoration model of God's forgiving grace (as after the exile). The New Testament does, in fact, affirm the death and resurrection of Jesus as a cosmic victory over all authorities and powers 'in heaven and on earth' – in other words, over the totality of evil forces which bind and enslave human beings, corrupt and distort human life, and warp, pollute and frustrate the very creation itself. That victory is an essential part of the biblical Good News. And applying that victory to every dimension of human life on earth is the task of Christian mission.

So then we can see that when we take Old Testament history seriously in relation to its completion in Jesus Christ, a two-way process is at work, yielding a double benefit in our understanding of the whole Bible. On the one hand, we are able to see the full significance of the Old Testament story in the light of where it leads – the climactic achievement of Christ; and on the other hand, we are able to appreciate the full dimensions of what God did through Christ in the light of his historical declarations and demonstrations of intent in the Old Testament. We have concentrated on the exodus so far. But the same principles could be applied to other major dimensions of Israel's story, such as the land itself – the story of its promise, gift and inheritance, and all the theology, laws, institutions and ethical imperatives that surrounded it.

The story of the monarchy, with the accompanying ministry and message of the prophets, would be equally illuminating, handled in both directions, as we have tried to do.

Matthew's opening genealogy, then, points us to one major way for us as Christians to take account of the Hebrew Bible in relation to Jesus and the New Testament, and that is as story – *the* story, with a multi-dimensional relevance culminating in the story of Jesus himself. Taken together, both Testmaments record the history of God's saving work for humanity. 'Salvation-history' is a term that has been used by many scholars to refer to this, and some would regard it as the primary point of continuity or relationship between the two testaments of the Christian Bible. As with most scholarly positions, this has been argued over, but it does seem unquestionable that history is one important aspect of the link between Old and New, and that Matthew's genealogy, with all its explicit and implicit levels of meaning, points to this very clearly.

A unique story

We have used the expression 'salvation history' about the Old Testament. This affirms that in the history of Israel God was acting for salvation in a way which was not true elsewhere. Now this claim is an embarrassment for some. Not everyone relishes the idea of one single chosen people of God enjoying a unique history of salvation, as over against all the rest of the nations who seem to get a rather poor deal on the whole. Surely, it is argued by some theologians, if we believe in one God who is, and always has been, the one universal God of all humanity, then we need to see all the varied histories of different nations and cultures as being also part of his work on the earth. And can those extra-biblical histories not also function as valid preparations for the fulness of his saving work in Jesus Christ? Obviously, the history of the Old Testament represents one way to Jesus – the history of his own people. But, it is said, we need not stress that particular history as far as other peoples are concerned who do not stand within the stream of the Judaeo-Christian historical heritage. Rather we should look within world-wide history for other preparatory routes to the knowledge of the Gospel of Christ. When

taken to the logical conclusion, this train of thought leads to
the view that we may in fact dispense with the Old Testament
(at least as far as any canonical authority is concerned) for
people who have their own religious and cultural history and
scriptural traditions.

Clearly, then, if we believe that the Christian church has
been right all through the ages to hold on to the Hebrew
Bible as a vital and integral part of the canon of Christian
scripture, then we must say something about this problem of
the relationship between Israel's history, or salvation history,
and the rest of human history. Otherwise we might as well
go on pretending that the New Testament really starts at
Matthew 1:18 and forget all he was trying to tell us in his
unique prologue. But, as we shall see, if we were to jettison
the Old Testament, we would lose most of the meaning of
Jesus himself. For his uniqueness was and is built upon the
foundation of the uniqueness of the story that prepared for
him.

Unfortunately, this is a link which is not often preserved
in the current debate about the relationship between Christianity and other faiths. Many discussions about the significance
of Jesus Christ within the context of world religions virtually
cut him off from his historical and scriptural roots and speak
of him as the founder of a new religion. Now, of course, if by
that is meant merely that Christianity has historically become
a separate religion from Judaism, that may be superficially
true. But certainly Jesus had no intention of launching another
'religion' as such. Who Jesus was and what he had come to
do were both already long prepared for through God's dealings with the people he belonged to and through their scriptures. It is the contention of this whole book that we must
clearly face up to the distinctive claims of the Hebrew scriptures if we are to get our understanding of Christ's uniqueness
straight also.

A UNIVERSAL GOAL

The proper place to begin our discussion of this issue is to repeat a point made earlier, namely that the Old Testament itself quite clearly intends us to see Israel's history, not as an end in itself or for the sake of Israel alone, but rather for the sake of the rest of the nations of humanity. The order of the biblical story itself makes this clear. Just as the New Testament withholds our introduction to Jesus until we have been reminded of what went before, so the Old Testament brings Israel on stage (in the loins of Abraham) in Genesis 12, only after an extensive introduction to the dilemma of the whole human race. Genesis 1–11 is entirely occupied with humanity as a whole, the world of all nations, and with the apparently insoluble problem of their corporate evil. So the story of Israel which begins at chapter 12 is actually God's answer to the problem of humanity. All God's dealings with Israel in particular are to be seen as the pursuit of his unfinished business with the nations.

This, as we have seen, is the explicit purpose of God's covenant promise to Abraham, first expressed in Genesis 12:3 and repeated several times throughout the book:

'All peoples on earth will be blessed through you.'

It is then echoed in many various ways in other parts of the Old Testament. At Mount Sinai, for example, at the very point where God is impressing on Israel their unique identity and role in the midst of the nations, he leaves no doubt that he is far from being a minor local deity or even your average national god. The scope of his concern and his sovereignty is universal: 'the whole earth is mine' (Ex. 19:5). He had already tried, with less success, to establish the same point with Pharaoh, whose resistance afforded the opportunity for a display of God's power and a proclamation of his name 'in all the earth'. The purpose of the plagues and the liberation to follow was:

so that you may know there is no one like me in all
the earth . . .

that my name might be proclaimed in all the earth
. . .

so that you may know that the earth is the LORD's.

(Ex. 9:14, 16, 29)

The same universal dimension of Israel's role is alluded to by
the prophets at times. Jeremiah, for example, looking back
nostalgically to Israel's comparative faithfulness to God in the
wilderness (compared, that is, with their apostasy in his own
day), says:

Israel was holy to the LORD,
the firstfruits of his harvest.

(Jer. 2:3)

What harvest? Presumably his harvest among the nations.
Israel was not the sum and limit of God's interest, precious
though they were, as the context emphasizes. They were
rather the first fruits that guaranteed a much larger ingathering. Later the same prophet envisages what would happen if
only Israel could be brought to true repentance:

And if in a truthful, just and righteous way you swear,
'as surely as the LORD lives',
then the nations will be blessed by him
and in him they will glory.

(Jer. 4:2)

This is not only an echo of the universal promise to Abraham
in Genesis 12:3, but also of its expansion in Genesis 18:18-19,
where God says:

Abraham will surely become a great and powerful
nation and all the nations on earth will be blessed
through him. For I have chosen him, so that he will

direct his children and his household after him to keep the way of the LORD by doing righteousness and justice, so that the LORD will bring about for Abraham what he has promised him.

God's promise – the blessing of all nations – is here linked to the ethical demand on Abraham's descendants. They were to be a community committed to the way of Yahweh, namely, to righteousness and justice. Only thus could their mission be fulfilled. Jeremiah picks up this condition to the promise and builds it into his plea for genuine repentancè. If Israel would only come back to living as they were created to, with social life and public worship both grounded in 'truth, justice and righteousness', then God could get on with his wider and greater purpose – blessing the rest of humanity. Jeremiah, called to be a 'prophet to the nations' (not merely Israel), was aware of the universal dimension of his mission. Much more was at stake if Israel would or would not change her ways, than the fate of Israel alone.

In the Psalms also a universal note is often heard. We have already pointed out Psalm 72:17, with its linking of the Davidic heir to this same blessing of all nations. The participation of the nations of the earth in the blessings of Israel is also a common theme in those Psalms which celebrate the kingship of Yahweh, as we shall see shortly.

So we need to keep this perspective in our minds at all times when reading the Old Testament and its very particular history. It is like keeping a wide-angle lens viewpoint, alongside the more close-up picture. The particularism of Israel's history is a *particular means* for a *universal goal*. So we should not be tempted to give in to the accusation that by holding on to the Hebrew Bible and its history as vitally and indispensibly linked to the New Testament (as Matthew's genealogy requires us to) we are somehow being narrow and exclusivist in our theology or our attitudes. Quite the opposite is the case. The rest of the world was not absent from the mind and purpose of God in all his dealings with Israel. Indeed, to borrow a not unfamiliar phrase from John's Gospel: God so loved the *world* that he chose *Israel*.

A UNIQUE EXPERIENCE

Having made the point above, it still has to be maintained that according to the Old Testament itself no other nation experienced what Israel did of the grace and power of God. God's action in and through Israel was unique. The story of election, redemption, covenant and inheritance, outlined in the historical survey above, was a story shared by no other people. Now this does *not* mean that God was in no way active in the histories of other peoples. The Old Testament explicitly asserts that he was, and we shall look at that below. It does mean that only in Israel did God work within the terms of a covenant of redemption, initiated and sustained by his saving grace. Deuteronomy presents the events of Israel's previous history as unparallelled in all of time and space.

Ask now about the former days, long before your time, from the day God created man on the earth; ask from one end of the heavens to the other. Has anything so great as this ever happened, or has anything like it ever been heard of? Has any other people heard the voice of God speaking out of fire, as you have, and lived? Has any god ever tried to take for himself one nation out of another nation, by testings, by miraculous signs and wonders, by war, by a mighty hand and an outstretched arm, or by great and awesome deeds, like all the things the LORD your God did for you in Egypt before your very eyes? . . . Because he loved your forefathers and chose their descendants after them, he brought you out of Egypt by his Presence and his great

strength, to drive out before you nations greater and
stronger than you and to bring you into their land to
give it to you for your inheritance, as it is today.

(Deut. 4:32–4,37–8)

This passage includes all four elements of the redemptive
history referred to above: election, redemption, covenant and
inheritance. The passage then goes on to draw a theological
implication, namely that the uniqueness of Israel's historical
experience points to the uniqueness of Yahweh himself as
God:

You were shown these things so that you might know
that the LORD is God; beside him there is no other.

(Deut. 4:35)

Thus, the revelation of the character of God and the nature
of his redemptive work for humanity are bound together with
the history of Israel. Their uniqueness is tied to his. To put
it simply, God did things in and for Israel which he did not
do in the history of any other nation.

This uniqueness of Israel's historical experience, however,
was because of their special role and function in the world.
They were to facilitate God's promise of blessing to the
nations. They were to be his priesthood in the midst of the
nations (Ex. 19:6) – representing him to the rest of mankind,
and being the means of bringing the nations to saving knowledge of the living God. To fulfil that destiny they were to be
a holy nation (different from the rest), characterized by walking in the way of Yahweh in justice and righteousness (as we
saw in Gen. 18:19). That is why the text from Deuteronomy
above draws out not only a *theological* implication about God,
but also a *moral* implication about what is required of *Israel*
in the light of their unique experience:

Acknowledge and take to heart this day that the LORD
is God in heaven above and on the earth below. There

is no other. Keep his decrees and commands, which I
am giving you today, so that it may go well with you
. . .   (Deut. 4:39-40)

So Israel's unique historical experience was not a ticket to a
cosy state of privileged favouritism. Rather it laid upon them
a missionary task and a moral responsibility. If they failed in
these, then in a sense they fell back to the level of any other
nation. They stood, like all nations and all humanity, before
the bar of God's judgement, and their history by itself gave
them no guaranteed protection.

Amos was a prophet who perceived very clearly how Israel's
unique history, like a double-edged sword, cut both ways. He
recounts the critical stages of Israel's redemptive history, from
the exodus, through the wilderness, victoriously into the land,
up to the rise of the prophets. But he uses it, not in order to
congratulate Israel on their blessings and privilege, but as a
stark contrast to their present behaviour. By rampant injustice
and social corruption they were denying all that their history
was meant to have made them. Their unique experience of
God's salvation thus exposed them to even more severe penalty for their rebellion (Amos 2:6–16, 3:2).

So Amos predicted the unthinkable: Israel would be
destroyed and her land left deserted. But, surely, his hearers
must have protested, God cannot treat his own people so!
Are we not those whom he brought up out of Egypt? Yes
indeed, came the reply. But so what, if you have reduced
your moral standards of social life to the lowest common
denominator of the rest of humanity? Your history by itself
gives you neither excuse nor protection.

Are not you Israelites the same to me as the Cushites?
    declares the Lord.
Did I not bring Israel up from Egypt,

the Philistines from Caphtor and the Arameans from Kir?
(Amos 9:7)

This devastating word must have rocked Israel to the core –
even more than the fierce words of destructive doom which
surround it on both sides. Israel, the same to God as remote
foreigners on the very edge of the known world (Cush was
roughly Sudan/Ethiopia)!? God, as sovereign in the movements of Israel's traditional enemies as of Israel herself!?
Precisely, says God through Amos, if by your disobedience
you forfeit all that your own history entitled and prepared
you for.

We ought to be careful in handling this verse not to make
it say more than it does. It has been used by some scholars
to argue that other nations stood on a level with Israel in
God's sight and that he had been *savingly* active in their
history also. This then can be used as part of an argument for
various forms of religious universalism or pluralism. But Amos
did not say that other nations were like Israel, but that Israel
had become like them, in God's sight, because of their sinfulness and his imminent judgement.

Similarly, the fact that Amos affirms the sovereignty of Yahweh over the national histories of other peoples – including
their 'exoduses' and migrations – cannot mean that he believed
that God had 'redeemed' those nations through those events,
or that they stood in the same covenant relationship with God
as Israel did. Such a view flatly contradicts what Amos himself
had very emphatically stated a few chapters earlier:

> Hear this word the LORD has spoken against you, O
> people of Israel – against the whole family I brought
> up out of Egypt:
> 'You only have I "known" of all the families of the
> earth;
> therefore I will punish you for all your sins'.
> (Amos 3:1–2)

'Known', here, is a technical word which the Hebrew Bible sometimes uses to express the belief that God had chosen Israel and made a covenant relationship with them. As far as *that* is concerned, the text says, Israel alone had experienced it, whatever God may have done in the histories of other peoples. But as the verse also says in its last line, with that brilliant twist of the unexpected so characteristic of the rhetorical skill of Amos, this very uniqueness was no comfortable privilege, but the reason why they were facing God's judgement.

So then, the uniqueness of the history of Israel, as a history of the redemptive acts of God in his dealings with a people in covenant relationship with himself, is clearly part of the teaching of the Old Testament. Amos's unambiguous affirmation of it in 3:1–2 is even sharper when we notice that he knew that God was certainly active in other histories, and that Yahweh the God of Israel was also morally sovereign over the activities of other nations (1:2–2:3).

To remember and stress this truth about Israel does not take away from the other truth, namely that God's purpose was ultimately universal in scope. Israel existed at all only because of God's desire to redeem people from every nation. But in his sovereign freedom he chose to do so by this particular and historical means. The tension between the universal goal and the particular means is found throughout the Bible and cannot be reduced to either pole alone. What it comes down to is that, while God has every nation in view in his redemptive purpose, in no other nation did he act as he did in Israel, for the sake of the nations. That was their uniqueness, which can be seen to be both exclusive (in the sense that no other nation experienced what they did of God's revelation and redemption), and inclusive (in the sense that they were created, called and set in the midst of the nations for the sake of ultimately bringing salvation to the nations).

Now when we consider Jesus in the light of this, the vitally important fact is that the New Testament presents him to us as the *Messiah*, Jesus the *Christ*. And the Messiah 'was' Israel. That is, the Messiah was Israel representatively and personified. The Messiah was the completion of all that Israel had been put in the world for – i.e. God's self-revelation and his work of human redemption. For this reason, Jesus shares in the uniqueness of Israel. What God had been doing through no other nation he now completed through no other person than the Messiah Jesus. The paradox is that precisely through the narrowing down of his redemptive work to the unique particularity of the single man, Jesus, God opened the way to the universalizing of his redemptive grace to all nations. Israel was unique because God had a universal goal through them. Jesus embodied that uniqueness and achieved that universal goal. As the Messiah of Israel he could be the saviour of the world. Or as Paul reflected, going further back, by fulfilling God's purpose in choosing Abraham, Jesus became a second Adam, the head of a new humanity (Rom. 4–5, Gal. 3).

Israel and other stories

GOD IN CONTROL OF ALL HISTORY

Although the history of Israel is the unique story of God's saving acts, the Bible also clearly affirms that Yahweh was in control of the histories of all other peoples as well. Sometimes this was a control exercised in direct relationship to how those other nations impinged upon Israel. But in other cases it was not directly so. The migration of the Philistines from the Aegean, or of the Syrians from northern Mesopotamia had no connection with the Israelites at the time, but, says Amos 9:7, it was Yahweh who 'brought them up'. And whoever the Emites were, or the Horites, or the Avites, not to mention the dreaded Zamzummites, they had nothing to do with the Israelites! Yet their movements and destinies were under the disposition of Yahweh just as much as Israel's own historic migration, according to some fascinating bits of ancient geography and history in Deuteronomy 2:10–12, 20–23.

Mostly, however, it is the case that other nations are said to be under Yahweh's control in relation to how their history interacts with Israel's. That is to say, God fits them into his purpose for his own people Israel – sometimes for Israel's benefit, sometimes as agents of God's punishment on his own people. But then, God's purpose for Israel was ultimately the blessing and redemption of humanity as a whole. So it can be said that God's activity in the history of other nations also fits into that wider redemptive purpose.

In other words, we can make a theological distinction, but not a complete separation, between the history of Israel and other histories. Salvation history is real history. It must be seen as having happened within the flow of universal world history, all of which was under God's control. It is not some kind of extra-terrestrial, sacred or religious history, just because 'it's in the Bible'.

Some examples of God's activity in the historical affairs of nations other than Israel will help to illustrate this point. Some of these have been touched on already.

Egypt   God's activity there had the whole world in view (Ex. 9:13–16).

Assyria   The dominant world power for a century and a half, but to the prophetic eye, a mere stick in the hands of Yahweh (Isa. 10:5–19).

Babylon   Jeremiah owed much of his unpopularity in later life precisely to his conviction that Nebuchadnezzar had been raised up by Yahweh and entrusted with world dominion. He even went so far as to call him 'my servant' (Jer. 27:5–7).

Habbakuk was dumbfounded by the same revelation (Hab. 1).

According to the book of Daniel, this interpretation of current events was relayed even to Nebuchadnezzar himself (Dan. 2:37–8, 4:17, 25, 32).

Persia The central theme of Isaiah 40–48 was that the most burning topic of international alarm of the day – the sudden rise of Cyrus, king of the united Medes and Persians – was directly the work of Israel's God and no other. Such was God's involvement with the unwitting Cyrus that he could scandalize his own people by referring to him as 'my shepherd' and 'my anointed one' and by picturing him as led by God's own hand in all his victories (Is. 44:28–45:13).

The saving acts of God within or on behalf of Israel, then, most certainly did not take place in sterile, vacuum-sealed isolation, but within the turbulent cross-currents of international politics and the historical rise and fall of empires whose destinies Yahweh himself controlled.

THE NATIONS SHARE IN ISRAEL'S HISTORY

In the Old Testament it often seems as if the nations are the intended audience of what God is actually doing in Israel. They are presented almost as the spectators of the drama he is engaged in with his people. The nations will tremble, sings Moses, when they hear what Yahweh has done to the Egyptians on behalf of his people (Ex. 15:14–16). But, on the other hand, what would the Egyptians think of Yahweh, if he were to turn and destroy his rebellious people, as he threatened to do (Ex. 32:11–12)? Moses's intercession on their behalf at the time of the Golden Calf incident made much of God's reputation among the nations.

God had put Israel on an open stage. So if Israel would keep the laws God had given them, their national life would be so conspicuously righteous that other nations would notice and ask questions about their laws and their God (Deut. 4:6–8). But on the other hand, if they failed to do so and God kept his threat and acted in judgement upon his own people, destroying his own city, land and temple, then the nations would ask why such an incredible thing could have happened. The answer was ready in advance (Deut. 29:22–8).

But even if that judgement was fully deserved, such a state of affairs was a disgrace to God's own name. So when he acted to restore his people to their land, that too was for the purpose of reinstating his reputation among the nations (Ezek. 36:16–23).

More than this, however, there is in some of the Psalms a sense that the history of Israel is in some way actually available for the nations to appropriate for themselves. In the Psalms celebrating the kingship of Yahweh, the nations (plural), or the whole earth, are repeatedly called on to rejoice and praise God for his mighty acts in *Israel*. Read, for example, Psalms 47, 96:1–3, 98:1–3. Now if Israel's salvation history (which is referred to in these Psalms as the 'marvellous deeds', 'righteous acts', etc. of Yahweh) is to be a cause of *rejoicing* among the nations, then it must be that they in some sense benefit from it, or are included within the scope of its purpose, even though they have not personally experienced it.

How this could be so remains a mystery in the Old Testament. Indeed, I sometimes wonder what went on in the mind of the average Psalm-singing Israelite, let alone the average carol-singing Christian. What did he think when he sang words like:

> Clap your hands, *all you nations*;
> shout to God with cries of joy.
> How awesome is Yahweh Most High,
> the great King over all the earth!
> He subdued nations under *us*,
> peoples under our feet.
> He chose our inheritance for us,
> the pride of Jacob, whom he loved.
>
> (Ps. 47:1–4)

or this:

> Sing to Yahweh a new song;
> sing to Yahweh, *all the earth.*
> Sing to Yahweh, praise his name;
> proclaim his salvation day after day.
> Declare his glory among the nations,
> his marvellous deeds among all peoples.
>
> (Ps. 96:1–3)

For him, as an Israelite, Yahweh's *name, salvation, glory* and *marvellous deeds* meant only one thing – the incomparable history of his own people and all that God had done for them. Yet in his hymn he is heartily inviting all nations, peoples, all the earth no less, to join in the celebration and proclamation of those unique events. Mysterious as it may be, this universal and inclusive element in the worship of Israel is unmistakeably there. And it is very important to set it alongside the call for exclusive worship and loyalty to Yahweh alone, and the abhorrence of the religious practices of other nations, especially their idolatry, which is denounced in these very same Psalms.

THE NATIONS SHARE IN ISRAEL'S FUTURE

The Old Testament, however, goes further in its programme
for the nations than casting them in the role of spectators –
even clapping spectators. Psalm 47, which is really quite
breathtaking in its vista, moves the nations out of the audience
in verse 1, right on to the centre of the stage in verse 9:

> God reigns over the nations;
>> God is seated on his holy throne.
> The nobles of the nations assemble
>> *as the people of the God of Abraham*
> for the kings of the earth belong to God;
>> he is greatly exalted.

(Ps. 47: 8–9)

The nations before God's throne are there, not behind the
people of God, nor even just alongside them, but 'as' the
people of the God whose promise to Abraham had them in
mind from the beginning. It must have stretched the imagination of our Psalm-singing Israelite (if he had any to be
stretched, any more than our hymn-singing Christian), as to
when and how the words he had just sung could ever be a
reality. Yet there they are, to be sung with enthusiastic faith
and hope.

The prophets stretched the imagination even further.
Amos, in the same chapter that we read his devastating liken-
ing of Israel to the other nations, because of their sin and its
deserved doom, speaks of a future restoration of the house of
David, such that it will include 'nations that bear my name'
(Amos 9:11–12). This indeed is the very passage quoted by
James as scriptural authority for the inclusion of the Gentiles
in the young Christian church (Acts 15:13ff.). We shall look
at the significance of that event in chapter four.

James could easily have chosen several other prophetic
texts to support his understanding of the event. Isaiah 19,
for example, after a comprehensive oracle of judgement on

contemporary Egypt, raises one's eyebrows in a concluding
vision of both Egypt and Assyria gathering to worship God
alongside Israel, being blessed by God and a blessing on the
earth. They will be transformed from enemies into 'my
people', by a process of healing and restoration which has
deliberate echoes of the very exodus itself. A saving exodus
for the Egyptians?! (Is. 19:19–25).

Jeremiah holds out to the nations the same hope, in virtually the same terms, that he had held out to his own people.
They stand under God's judgement, and he will punish them
for what they do to Israel, but for them also repentance is
the road to restoration – *and inclusion:*

> After I uproot them [the nations], I will again have
> compassion and bring each of them back to his own
> inheritance and his own country. And if they learn
> well the ways of my people and swear by my name,
> saying 'As surely as the LORD lives' [notice the echo
> of 4:2] – even as they once taught my people to swear
> by Baal – then they will be established *among my*
> *people.*
>
> (Jer.12:15–16)

The link between belonging to the people of God and
acknowledging the name of Yahweh as the one true and living
God, is even more clearly forged in a beautiful picture of the
conversion of outsiders as the result of the outpouring of
God's spirit and blessing, like fertilizing, life-giving water, in
Isaiah 44:3–5:

> One will say, 'I belong to *Yahweh*';
>   and another will call himself by the name of *Jacob*;
> still another will write on his hand '*Yahweh's*';
>   and will take the name *Israel*.

The same prophet moves far beyond this individual picture
to a climactic vision of the saving work of God extending to

all nations on earth. The same saving, liberating justice as God had manifested on Israel's behalf will be activated for the nations:

> The law will go out from me;
>> my justice will become a light to the nations.
> My righteousness draws near speedily,
>> my salvation is on the way,
> and my arm will bring justice to the nations.
>
>> (Is. 51:4–5).

God is the speaker in that passage, but the mission is elsewhere committed to the servant of Yahweh, who, in the power of the Spirit,

> will bring justice to the nations . . .
> and establish justice on earth (Is. 42:1–4).

In view of his mission, which God lays upon him,

> I will make you a light for the Gentiles,
>> that you may bring my salvation to the ends of the earth (49:6),

the appeal can go out universally:

> Turn to me and be saved, all you ends of the earth (45:22).

In chapter four we shall look at how these particular texts and the figure of the servant of the Lord are taken up into the identity and mission of Jesus.

This, then, is the 'end of the story', to which the Old Testament points, but which is never reached within its pages, and indeed still awaits us. The eschatological future hope of Israel saw their own history ultimately flowing into the universal history of the nations, in order that the nations should be granted salvation and inclusion within the people of God. This confluence was achieved, as we have seen, without abandoning the uniqueness of the history of Israel as a history of saving acts of God unparalleled in any other history, but equally without denying the activity and interest of God within all human history. On the contrary, the eschatological vision includes the sight of the achievements of the nations being brought into the new age and new creation. The economic and cultural history of the nations, coming as it does within the creation mandate to all humanity to use and steward the resources of the earth, is seen eventually to flow into the substance of the people of God. Isaiah 23:18, for example, after the declaration of historical judgement on the economic oppressions of Tyre, foresees all the profits of the great trading empire as ultimately destined for the people of God. Haggai 2:6–9 envisages the wealth of the nations returning to its rightful owner – the LORD himself, in his temple. This expectation is endorsed in the vision of Revelation 21:24. In other words, human history 'beyond' salvation history, the history of the rest of humanity who live by God's grace on the face of God's earth, also has its meaning and value and will ultimately contribute in some way to the glory of the kingdom of God as he rules over his redeemed humanity in the new creation.

A unique history, then, with universal effects. This is where the story implicit in Matthew's genealogy leads. We shall look further at the theme of the ingathering of the nations in chapter four, but it is fitting to conclude this chapter by noticing how Paul, so conscious and defensive of his unique mission to the nations, binds together the two dimensions of history.

It had indeed been a 'mystery' (to use Paul's own word) all through the ages of Old Testament Israel as to *how* God could bring about for Abraham what he had promised him – namely blessing for all nations. But Paul saw very clearly how that mystery had been 'solved' through the tremendous achievement of God in Christ. He saw that it was paradoxically through the narrowing down of his redemptive acts to the unique particularity of one single man – the Messiah, Jesus, that God had opened the way to the universal offering of the grace of his Gospel to all nations. In Galatians 3 and Ephesians 2 and 3, he shows how it is that what the Gentiles had not had before (because it was at that time limited to the nation of Israel), is now available to them in the Messiah (and nowhere else – either for them or for the Jews). The great Old Testament hope that the nations would come to be part of Israel is then already being fulfilled through Jesus the Messiah.

But in Romans 9–11, he wrestles with the fact that it is happening in an an unexpected, and (from his own point of view as a Jew) undesirable, way. The majority of his contemporary Jews had in fact rejected Jesus as Messiah. But as a result of that rejection, the Gentile nations were being 'grafted in'. However, the Gentiles did not constitute a separate 'olive tree'. For Paul there was only one people of God – then, now or ever. No, the Gentiles were being grafted into the original stock. In other words, as in the Old Testament worship and prophecy, the nations were now participating in the saving work of God which he had initiated through the history of Israel. These were Gentiles from every conceivable background, even within the confines of Paul's missionary endeavours in the eastern Mediterranean basin. But they now shared the root and sap of Israel's sonship, glory, covenants, law, temple worship, promises, patriarchs – *and* ... 'the human ancestry of the Messiah' (Rom. 9:5). The Gentile Christian, therefore, is a person of two histories: on the one hand, his own national and cultural background, ancestry and heritage, which as we have seen is by no means to be despised, and on the other hand, his new spiritual, 'ingrafted' history – that of God's people descended from Abraham which he inherits through inclusion in Christ.

Perhaps, since the Apostle Paul is not so popular at Christmas, the average carol-singing Christian is not as aware of this as he should be – even when he puts himself, by whatever stretch of imagination he can muster, in the sandals of ancient

Israel while singing 'O come, O come Immanuel'. Nevertheless, it is true. He or she and the Psalm-singing Israelite are as much brothers and sisters in the Messiah as the rest of the church congregation are brothers and sisters in Christ. The genealogy of Jesus conceals a story which led up to Jesus, but which, as Luke also perceived, led up to a new beginning with him (Acts 1:1). The story goes on, until the promise to Abraham will finally be fulfilled, in a great multitude from every nation, tribe, people and language. That is the goal of all history, as it was of Israel's history, and in the church of the Messiah it is already being brought about in anticipation.

> There is neither Jew nor Greek, slave nor free, male
> nor female, for you are all one in the Messiah, Jesus.
>
> (Gal. 3:28)

One people, one story. The fact is, that whether we read Matthew 1:1–17 in our Christmas carol service or not, that story is our story as much as it is the story of Jesus. For through him, we have come to be, like him, the descendants of Abraham.

> If you belong to the Messiah, then you are Abraham's
> seed, and heirs according to the promise.
>
> (Gal. 3: 29)

CHAPTER TWO

Jesus and the Old Testament Promise

'And so was fulfilled . . . '

Even if Matthew's genealogy is understandably omitted from the readings at our Christmas service, the list will undoubtedly include other portions from the rest of Matthew 1 and 2, for they are among the most familiar of the infancy stories. Matthew weaves together five scenes from the conception, birth and early childhood of Jesus. And then, perhaps for the benefit of those who missed the point of his genealogy (or more likely skipped it altogether), he ties up each of those five scenes to a quotation from the Hebrew scriptures which, he claims, has been 'fulfilled' by the event described.

FIVE SCENES FROM JESUS'S CHILDHOOD

The five scenes and their scriptural links are as follows:

i) The assurance to Joseph concerning the child conceived in Mary:
1:18–25 'to fulfil' *Isaiah 7:14* which was the Immanuel sign, given by Isaiah to King Ahaz.

ii) The fact that Jesus was born in Bethlehem: 2:1–12 'to fulfil' *Micah 5:2* in which it is prophesied that a ruler of Israel will come from Bethlehem.

iii) The escape to Egypt, and then the return from there:

2:13–15 'to fulfil' *Hosea 11:1*, which is a reference to God
having brought Israel, his son, out of Egypt, at the exodus.

iv) The murder by Herod of the boys in Bethlehem:
2:16–18 'to fulfil' *Jeremiah 31:15*, which is a lament for
the Israelites who were going into exile.

v) The settlement of Jesus's family in Nazareth:
2:19–23 'to fulfil' 'the prophets . . . ' which is a bit of a
puzzle, because there is no text which says exactly what
Matthew records here. It seems to be a reflection of several
possible allusions which needn't detain us here.

The five scenes thus cover the early life of Jesus, from
conception, through his birth in Bethleham, his temporary
stay in Egypt, up to his settling in Nazareth. And in all of it
Matthew 'sees' Old Testament reflections. By repeated use
of the fulfilment phrase, Matthew clearly wants his readers
to see that Jesus was not only the *completion* of the Old
Testament story at a historical level, as his genealogy portrays,
but also that he was in a deeper sense its *fulfilment*. This
gives us another way of looking at the Old Testament in
relation to Jesus. Not only does the Old Testament *tell the
story which Jesus completes*, it also *declares the promise
which Jesus fulfils*.

A destination is not just the end of a journey, it is also the
point of a journey. The journey is undertaken because of some
purpose or commitment, which is fulfilled when the journey
reaches its destination. Similarly, in the Old Testament journey, God has declared his purpose, shown his commitment
to redemption, and made it known in all kinds of ways to and
through Israel – especially in the prophets. This purpose or
commitment has been fulfilled in the arrival of this child,
Jesus. And by his five Old Testament quotations in quick
succession, Matthew makes sure we don't miss the point.

Now various questions can be raised about Matthew's tactics here – if not by the average carol-singing Christian, cer-

tainly by more scholarly folks. Is he not just 'proof-texting'? That is, just matching up a few Old Testament predictions with some stories that seem to fit them. Or is it even worse, according to some, that he has invented stories to make the predictions 'come true'? This idea that the infancy narratives are pious fiction, produced by a scripture-fired imagination, has become quite popular in some quarters, but it really does not stand up to the evidence. There are two solid objections.

First of all, why did Matthew pick such obscure texts? If his purpose was to start from Messianic prophecies and create stories to fulfil them, there are any number of texts which, already in Matthew's day, were far better known and much more detailed regarding the coming Messiah. Any of them could have produced good narratives, if the 'facts' were negotiable.

Secondly, it is clearly mistaken to say that the narratives Matthew tells are fulfilments of Old Testament *predictions*, because only one of the texts he quotes is in fact a recognized Messianic prediction at all, and that is Micah 5:2, predicting that the Messiah will be born in Bethlehem. The 'Immanuel' prophecy was a sign given to King Ahaz in his own historical context, not (originally) a long-range prediction. In any case it would be odd as a straight prediction, since the child was actually given the name Jesus, not Immanuel – a fact which hardly escaped Matthew's notice, so he cannot have regarded his story as a neat prediction-fulfilment. Hosea 11:1 was no prediction but a past reference to the exodus. Jeremiah 31:15 is a figurative picture of the mourning of Rachel at the time of the exile of her descendants in 587 BC after the fall of Jerusalem. It was not predictive and had nothing to do with the Messiah in its context. The concluding comment related to Nazareth is so obscure that it has neither explicit Old Testament reference nor undisputed interpretation – hardly compatible with the view that Matthew was making up stories to fulfil Messianic predictions.

It seems altogether much more probable that Matthew is doing exactly what he says – that is, working back from actual events which happened in the early life of Jesus to certain Hebrew scriptures in which he now sees a deeper significance than they could have had before. It is the events, the narratives, which suggest the scriptures, not the other way around. And since the scriptures are not obvious predictions of the events recorded, Matthew must have meant more by his affirmation that the scriptures were being fulfilled by Jesus than just that predictions had come true. But then, a *promise* is much more than a *prediction*, as we shall discuss shortly.

GEOGRAPHY AND HISTORY

So then, what *was* Matthew's intention in his choice of scriptures to punctuate his narrative? Probably there is more than one level of meaning in his mind. On the surface, the passages 'accompany' Jesus in a geographical sense. That is, they are linked up to the fact that the Messiah, born in Bethlehem, ended up in Nazareth, after a stay in Egypt. This in itself was probably a form of explanation as to why the one claimed by Christians as the Messiah had come from Nazareth – a point of conflict between Christians and Jews which went back to the days of Jesus himself (cf. John 1:46, 7:41ff.). Matthew is pointing out that he was actually born in Bethlehem, and that this fact, along with the subsequent movements of his childhood which brought him to Galilee, fitted in with the scriptures. So the point is that the prophet of Nazareth could be claimed as the Messiah because not only had he actually been born in Bethlehem, as the scriptures foretold, but also the movements by which he ended up a resident of Galilee were also consistent with the fulfilment of scripture. This, the scripture-fulfilment motif in the infancy narratives, serves the same purpose as the genealogy in chapter 1 – to portray Jesus as the Messiah, the completion of a story and the fulfilment of a promise.

But even in this geographical dimension there lies a deeper significance, to be picked up by those with a little more awareness of the scriptures. There is, in fact, rather a lot of geography in Matthew 2–4. Either by his travels or by his reputation Jesus had an effective ministry which spans the whole of the classical area of ancient Israel – particularly the boundaries of the old Davidic kingdom (note especially the places referred to in 4:24-25). The one who was the son of David and the Davidic Messiah of the line of Davidic kings appropriately has a ministry as wide as the kingdom of David itself. The focal point of that ministry in the region of Galilee is further vindicated by scripture when Matthew quotes from Isaiah 9:1–2, (Matt. 4:13–16), which introduces one of the outstanding Messianic and Davidic prophecies in that book.

> In the past God humbled the land of Zebulun and the land of Naphthali, but in the future he will honour Galilee of the Gentiles, by the way of the sea, along the Jordan
>
> The people walking in darkness
>   have seen a great light,
> on those living in the land of the shadow of death
>   a light has dawned.

So, the point of the *history* lesson in the genealogy of chapter 1 is corroborated by the *geography* lesson in chapters 2–4. 'Great David's greater Son' is claiming his Kingdom.

The genealogy, however, has a wider scope than David, as we saw in our first chapter. There is the implicit universal scope connected with Abraham, and the explicit inclusion of Gentiles among the female ancestors of Jesus. This historical dimension also has its geographical counterpart in what follows. After the birth of Jesus, the first story Matthew recounts is the visit of 'Magi *from the east';* and the second is the visit of Jesus himself *to Egypt,* in the west. The stories thus embrace both extremes of the biblical world – expecially in Old Testament times – east and west. Furthermore, both regions are included within various Old Testament prophecies concerning the extent of God's work of salvation (most notably, Isa. 19:23–5). God's purpose for Israel, and for the Messiah who would embody Israel, was the blessing of all nations.

Matthew then, though he wrote the most Jewish of the Gospels, wastes no time at all before getting to the point that when the Messiah came he had visitors, gifts and worship from the east, and was personally, if temporarily, resident in Egypt. Furthermore, the worship of the Magi is almost certainly intended as an echo of Psalm 72:10, which in turn echoes the visit of the Queen of Sheba to Solomon, while the gifts of gold and frankincense recall Isaiah 60:1–6, where they are brought by kings, from Arabia, to greet the dawning of God's new light in Zion. So the geographical ripples spread even wider in Matthew's allusive and suggestive narrative. By showing Jesus in relation to the wider Gentile world so early in his Gospel, Matthew clearly wants us to see him as more than merely Israel's Messiah, but as the fulfilment of God's saving purpose for the nations beyond Israel. And that is a fundamental part of what the Old Testament is all about.

There is yet another level of meaning in the scriptures linked to these stories. Talking about Egypt on the one hand and Mesopotamia (Assyria, Babylon, 'the East') on the other, would never leave any Jew thinking only of geography. He or she would inevitably revert to history, as Jews characteristically do. As we saw in the first chapter, the bulk of the history recorded in the Hebrew Bible is slung like a great hammock between the two poles of Egypt and Babylon, more specifically between the exodus from oppression in Egypt, and the exile to Babylon and the return. And that indeed is what is in the mind of Matthew as he reflects on the infancy of the Messiah, for he puts together two quotations from the scriptures, one of which refers to the exodus from Egypt, and the other to the exile to Babylon.

Hosea 11:1, quoted in Matthew 2:15, looked back to the exodus. Jesus has been taken to Egypt, but he will return, and so Matthew sees a correspondence with the experience of Israel itself.

Out of Egypt I called my son (meaning Israel, cf. Ex. 4:22).

He is not suggesting that the Hosea text was a prediction. His point is simply that what God had done for his people Israel – in fact the greatest thing he had done for them – had its counterpart, even in a purely physical sense, in the life of Jesus.

Then Matthew records Herod's slaughter of boys under two years old in Bethlehem. This he links to Jeremiah 31:15 about Rachel weeping and mourning for her children. Now you don't need biblical chapter and verse to prove that parents whose children are killed will tend to mourn and grieve. So the meaning of Matthew's quotation from Jeremiah lies a bit deeper than that. The verse in fact refers to the events immediately after the fall of Jerusalem to the armies of Nebuchadnezzar in 587 BC, when the defeated Israelites had been marshalled at Ramah for their long trudge into exile in Babylon. This was the cause of Rachel's 'mourning', since there was a tradition that Rachel was buried at Ramah (cf. Jer. 40:1). So Matthew observes that Jesus's 'exile' to Egypt was followed by an outburst of grief and mourning, and he likens it to the grief that accompanied Israel's exile to Babylon. But the context of his quotation puts it in a more positive light, for all the rest of Jeremiah 31 is in fact a message of hope that out of the tragedy and grief would come future blessing. The very next words after Matthew's quotation run on:

Restrain your voice from weeping
   and your eyes from tears . . .
They will return . . .
   So there is hope for your future.

So then, in his reflection on the single event of Jesus's going to
Egypt and returning (and the linked massacre at Bethlehem),
Matthew sees a double historical analogy, which he brings
out by the use of two scriptures, one referring to the exodus,
the other referring to the exile, key points in the history and
theology of Israel in the Old Testament.

But of course, the exodus and the exile (and return) were
key points in the Old Testament precisely because they were
indeed much more than mere history. Both events were
utterly saturated in *promise*. And that is what makes them
specially significant for Matthew who is here presenting Jesus
as the fulfilment of Old Testament promise. The exodus is
described from the very beginning as the result of God acting
in faithfulness to his own promise (cf. Ex. 2:24, 3:16ff., 6:5–8,
etc.). Even the text Matthew quotes from Hosea, with its
designation of Israel as God's son, implies this, for God could
not allow his son and heir to languish further in slavery. The
exodus proved his commitment to them and his purpose for
them.

Likewise, the exile was predicted by the prophets for two
centuries, and the return from exile and future hope was built
into those predictions from an early period. But especially in
the prophecies of Jeremiah, Ezekiel and Isaiah 40–55, the
note of promise and hope became a symphony of expectation.
Significantly, the original exodus itself was used as a pattern
for God's future action, just as Matthew uses both exodus and
return from exile as patterns for what he sees in the life of
Jesus.

Furthermore, by taking a text which describes *Israel* as
God's son (as was fairly common in the Old Testament), and

applying it to *Jesus*, Matthew is obviously also setting up a Jesus-Israel correspondence, which is even more suggestive for the thoughtful reader. After all, Israel were the people of promise, fruit of a promise to Abraham miraculously fulfilled, inheritors of a promised land, and vehicles of a universal promise for the human race. What a legacy Matthew pins on this little toddler being hurriedly carried off to Egypt by his anxious parents!

Now we could go deeper still. These early chapters of Matthew are so full of direct and indirect allusions to the Old Testament that scholars never tire of finding more and more – some more plausible than others. Certainly there is a clear intention to echo the Moses story: the hostile king; the threat to the child's life; the flight amidst the suffering of others; the death of the hostile king; the return (cf. Ex. 4:19ff.). And this only adds to the picture of imminent salvation, for Moses was the liberator *par excellence*, and 'Jesus' (the same name as 'Joshua', in Hebrew) has already been explained as the one who will deliver his people.

Our purpose here, however, is not primarily to expound Matthew's Gospel, but rather to see from it how Jesus is perceived in relation to the Old Testament. And it stands out clearly that the Old Testament is seen to have declared a promise which Jesus fulfils. What Matthew does in these opening chapters about the childhood of Jesus is programmatic for the rest of his Gospel, in which repeatedly he comes back to this note of fulfilment, whether in some action or some teaching of Jesus, and supremely of course in his suffering and death.

But it is not just, as we have observed, a matter of predictions coming true. Rather Matthew sees the whole Old Testament as the embodiment of promise – in the sense of presenting to us a God of gracious and saving purpose, liberating action, and covenant faithfulness to his people. That generates a tremendous sense of expectation and hope, reflected in all parts of the Hebrew canon. Hence, all kinds of Old Testament writing (not just prophecies) can be drawn on in relating that promise to Jesus. The dynamic reality of Jesus was plugged into the no less dynamic potential of the Old Testament's future hope. For Matthew, as for other New Testament authors, their Hebrew scriptures stood before them rather like the words of a song I once heard a child sing, a song composed presumably by understandably optimistic parents:

> I am a promise, I am a possibility,
> I am a promise with a capital 'P',
> I am a great big bundle of potentiality ...

The promise declared

Now that we have reached some understanding of what is meant by saying that Jesus fulfils the Old Testament promise, we can move on to explore how the concept of promise helps us to a better understanding of the Old Testament itself, which is part of our overall purpose in this book. A good starting point for that will be to point out in more detail the difference between promise and mere prediction. Even in everyday life, promise is a much deeper and more significant thing than prediction. It is one thing to predict a marriage between two people. It is quite another thing to promise to marry a particular person! That is a good illustration of the first major difference which is very clear in the Bible.

PROMISE INVOLVES COMMITMENT TO A RELATIONSHIP

A promise is made between two people, as an 'I-Thou' matter. It presupposes a relationship between them, indeed it may cement or forward that relationship, or depend upon it. A prediction, on the other hand, may be quite impersonal, or 'third-personal', and does not require any relationship between the predictor and the person or persons about whom the prediction is made. A promise may involve some degree of prediction (or expectation), but a prediction need not have anything to do with a promise. A promise is made *to* someone, whereas a prediction is made *about* someone.

Now in the Old Testament there are plenty of predictions involving the nations beyond Israel. Some of them are surprisingly detailed, and even more surprisingly fulfilled in the course of ancient history. But they do not indicate a relationship or any commitment between God and those nations, in terms of those predictions. In most cases the nations concerned were most probably unaware of the predictions. So in those cases predictions could be made and fulfilled without any on-going relationship involved.

It was totally different in the case of the promises God made concerning Israel. There, the very existence of Israel at all was the substance of the promise, as it had been first declared to Abraham, and the promise itself was the immoveable foundation on which the relationship between God and Israel survived in spite of all that threatened it. To say that the Old Testament declares God's promise, is another way of saying that at a particular time in history God entered into a commitment to a particular man and his descendants, a commitment to a relationship between himself and them which involved growth, blessing and protection.

But it involved something else as well, of course – namely, the universal goal of blessing to all nations through the descendants of Abraham. Indeed, sometimes this is emphasized as the very thing which God had promised Abraham. For example, in Genesis 18, the immediate promise that Abraham and Sarah would have a son within a year is quickly subsumed under the much more long-term and ultimate promise that God would bless all nations through the community which was as yet to emerge from the loins of Abraham. (cf. Gen. 18:19).

In that sense, God's promise to Abraham is in fact a commitment to *humanity*, not just to Israel. So although, as has just been said, the predictions concerning the nations during Israel's contemporary history in the Old Testament do not entail any promise or relationship with those nations at that time, the promise of God to Abraham does ultimately encompass humanity, precisely by envisaging the nations entering into the same saving and covenant relationship with God which Israel currently enjoyed – enjoyed for the purpose of bringing it to them. So it is perfectly appropriate that when the New Testament authors speak of Jesus as the fulfilment of the promise of the Old Testament, they think not just of Israel, but see Jesus as the saviour of the world, or rather see God saving the world through Jesus.

For Paul, the whole of his theology of mission hinged on his understanding of the crucial importance of the promise to Abraham and its universal significance. Galatians 3 is a clear witness to this. For Paul, the very Gospel itself began, not just with Jesus, but with Abraham. For what, after all, *was* the Good News? Nothing other than God's commitment to bring blessing to all nations of humanity, as announced to Abraham.

> The Scripture foresaw that God would justify the Gentiles by faith, and announced the Gospel in advance to Abraham: 'All nations will be blessed through you.'
>
> (Gal. 3:8)

The redeeming work of the Messiah Jesus was therefore:

> in order that the blessing given to Abraham might come to the Gentiles through Christ Jesus, so that by faith we might receive the promise of the Spirit.
>
> (v. 14)

Then after further discussion of the relationship between this fundamental promise based on grace and other aspects of the Old Testament, specifically the law, Paul concludes his words to these very Gentile believers:

> If you belong to Christ (the Messiah), then you are Abraham's seed, and heirs *according to the promise.*
>
> (v. 29)

Today, just as much as back then in the days of the Apostle Paul, every Gentile believer who enjoys his *relationship* of sonship to God as Father, does so as a living proof of the fulfilment of the Old Testament *promise* in Jesus the Messiah.

PROMISE REQUIRES A RESPONSE OF ACCEPTANCE

A prediction needs no response. It can be made and fulfilled without the persons concerned knowing anything about it, let alone doing anything about it. There are examples of this in the Old Testament also.

There is no evidence that Cyrus ever acknowledged Yahweh (Isa. 45:4, 'you do not know me', seems to rule it out), and although it is possible, it seems unlikely that he ever heard of the predictions concerning him made in Isaiah 40–45. Nevertheless, he fulfilled them remarkably, unwittingly confirming the sovereignty of the God who used him for his redemptive plans involving Israel. He proclaimed liberty to the exiles after their generation in Babylonian captivity.

This is an interesting example because in this case the prediction concerning Cyrus was *part* of a *promise* concerning Israel, and it helps to point up the difference. In fulfilling the prediction made concerning him, Cyrus was instrumental in fulfilling a promise concerning Israel, but he himself did not participate in it. His part required no response to God. He simply acted in the exercise of his own ambitions, thereby in the mystery of providence also carrying out God's promise.

But his action carved out the historical and political space within which the promise of God for the future of his people could operate, and *that* most definitely called for *their* response. Indeed, the whole burden of the prophetic word of Isaiah 40–55 is to stir up that response among a people who had come to fear that they were finished for ever. There was no point in God having promised a return from exile if nobody actually got up and returned! And that meant exercising faith in His word, uprooting from a generation of settled life in Babylon, and setting out on the long journey back to Jerusalem. Without that faith and action, the promise was pointless in itself.

This, of course, is the pattern we find from the start. The promise to Abraham was effective because he believed it and acted upon it, continuing to do so long after it had become humanly impossible. The exodus was promised by God, but it would not have happened if the Israelites had not responded to the leading of Moses, and even then some of them did so reluctantly. The same people received the promise of the land, but because their faith and obedience failed at the crucial point, they never received it and perished in the wilderness. And so it goes on all the way through scripture. The promise comes as the initiative of God's grace and always depends on his grace. But that grace has to be accepted and responded to by faith and obedience.

This way of regarding the Old Testament, as *promise*, thus has two effects. First it helps us realize that salvation is, and always was, a matter of God's grace and promise. The idea that the difference between the Old and New Testaments is that in the Old salvation is by the law whereas in the New it is by grace, sets up a totally false contrast. In the Old as in the New, it is God who takes the initiative of grace and calls people to faith and obedient response. In the book of Exodus, eighteen chapters describing God's mighty act of redemption, in fulfilment of his own love and promise, come *before* the giving of the law to a people already redeemed. Israel, in the

Psalms and elsewhere, regarded the law itself as a further gift of grace to those already redeemed by grace. Far from setting aside the promise, it was given to enable the recipients of the promise to live accordingly, within a discipline acceptable to God. Paul saw this clearly and argued it strongly against those who wished to build everything on Moses and the law. Don't forget, he points out, that Abraham and the promise came *first* – chronologically and theologically, and that is what our 'inheritance' of blessing and salvation depends on (Gal 3:16ff.).

Secondly, it reinforces that there is a conditional element to the promise, inasmuch as its fulfilment requires the response of faith and obedience from the recipients of the promise. The prophets ruthlessly demolished Israel's confidence in the very things that were replete with attached promises of God, whenever that confidence was not linked to moral response. Amos, faced with a people who were living in blatant disobedience to God's social demands, turned the fundamental promises upside down. Neither election itself (3:2), nor the exodus itself (9:7), nor the land itself (2:10–16, 5:2), were any guarantee of immunity from God's judgement. Jeremiah, in Jerusalem a century later, took an axe to the complacent trust in the promises concerning the very temple on Mount Zion by a people living in contempt for the demands of Mount Sinai. (Jer. 7:1–15). That temple was indeed destroyed, but in the courts of the one that replaced it, Jesus himself fought the same battle with those who were proud of their election in Abraham but failed to '*do* as Abraham *did*' (John 8:31–41). And the author of Hebrews, with the highest possible doctrine of the eternity and assurance of God's promise, has the sternest warnings in the New Testament about the danger of not responding to that promise by faith and obedient action – using Old Testament Israel for his object lessons (Heb. 3:7–4:11 [esp. 4:1ff.), 6, 10:19ff.).

Both of these two points will receive some fuller discussion in chapter five.

The message is clear and consistent throughout the Bible. The covenant promise of God is axiomatic and fundamental and all our hope of salvation hangs upon it. But no doctrine of election, no covenant theology, no personal testimony of redemption, can relieve us of the imperative necessity of faith proving itself in active obedience.

So, when we talk about the Old Testament declaring the promise which Jesus fulfils, it does not mean that the Old Testament is declared redundant because Jesus fulfilled it. If it were merely a book of predictions, that would be so, because once a prediction comes true, it has no further useful function. Rather it means that in the Old Testament God has both proclaimed and proved his purpose of redemption. And that initiative of his grace (promise) calls forth a response of obedient faith, as much from us as from the Israelites.

PROMISE INVOLVES ONGOING LEVELS OF FULFILMENT

A prediction is a fairly flat affair. It comes true or it doesn't. If it does, that's the end of it. If it doesn't you can either say the prediction was mistaken, or try to say it wasn't properly understood, and may yet come true in some redefined way. That is why the biggest prediction industry of all – astrology – is so notoriously vague or ambiguous in its pronouncements. They can hardly fail to come true! By the same token, that is why it is so remarkable that predictions which are in the Bible, in such specific detail sometimes, did in fact come true.

A promise is different. Because it involves personal relationship and commitment, it has a dynamic quality that goes beyond the external details involved, that is if we are talking about promises a little beyond the level of 'I promise to give you back the book I borrowed.'

When a young man and woman commit themselves to marrying each other, a promise is involved in the betrothal or engagement. At one level, that specific promise is fulfilled on the day of the wedding itself. But it is then taken up and surpassed by a fresh exchange of promises which launches their married life. In those promises, words such as 'for better, for worse; for richer, for poorer; in sickness and in health' are included. This is because the promise 'to have and to hold, to love and to cherish' looks far beyond the honeymoon. Fulfilling the promise will take different forms and make different demands and call for different responses as life and circumstances proceed. The promise remains, and the words don't need to be changed, but it is the *relationship* which dictates how the promise is fulfilled in any given situation.

Another significant point about promise is that, because it is the relationship behind it that really matters, the material form in which it is fulfilled may be quite different from the literal form in which it was originally made, and yet it is no less a valid fulfilment of the promise.

Imagine a father who, in the days before mechanized transport, promises his son, aged 5, that when he is 21 he will give him a horse for himself. Meanwhile the motor car is invented. So on his 21st birthday the son awakes to find a motor car outside, 'with love from Dad'. It would be a strange son who would accuse his father of breaking his promise just because there was no horse. And even stranger if, in spite of having received the far superior motor car, the son insisted that the promise would only be fulfilled if a horse *also* materialized, since that was the literal promise. It is obvious that with the change in circumstances, unknown at the time the promise was made, the father has more than kept his promise. In fact he has done so in a way that *surpasses* the original words of the promise which were necessarily limited by the mode of transport available at that time. The promise was made in terms understood at the time. It was fulfilled in the light of new historical events.

Coming back to the Old Testament promise, I hope the relevance of these illustrations can be seen. God's relationship with Israel through all the centuries was founded on the specific promise to Abraham. But in the Old Testament itself that promise is seen in different levels of fulfilment. In one sense, the promise to Abraham of 'seed' was fulfilled the moment Isaac was born. But of course it went further than that. A major theme of Genesis is how from such small and threatened beginnings, the posterity of Abraham grows to a community of seventy people. Hardly yet a great nation. But the book of Exodus opens with those seventy having been 'fruitful and multiplied greatly and becoming exceedingly numerous' (Ex. 1:7), thus fulfilling the promise at another level. The New Testament can see yet another level of fulfilment in referring to Jesus, singular, as the 'seed' of Abraham (Gal.3:16, 19), and still another in regarding the believing Gentiles of all nations as the sons of Abraham, in fulfilment of the same promise. One promise, but several levels of fulfilment as history proceeds.

Another dimension of the Old Testament promise is the way it leads to a recurring pattern of promise-fulfilment-fresh promise-fresh fulfilment, repeating and amplifying itself through history. Like some science-fiction, time-travelling rocket, the promise is launched, returning to earth at some later point of history in a partial fulfilment, only to be relaunched with a fresh load of fuel and cargo for yet another historical destination, and so on.

Launched at the time of Abraham, God's promise receives its first specific fulfilment at the time of the exodus. The references back to the patriarchs in the exodus narratives are frequent. At that point the promise of posterity is indeed kept, for Israel are not only a great nation, but they have been freed to live as such.

But the promise also included a special relationship between God and this people, and that becomes the focal point at Mount Sinai. 'Let my people go that they may serve me', God challenged Pharaoh, and when at last they reached

Sinai, as God had promised Moses they would when he commissioned him there (Ex. 3:12), God says 'I have brought you to myself for the purpose of entering into a covenant with you' (Ex. 19:4–6).

Launched from Mount Sinai the people of the promise head for its next stage of fulfilment – the gift of the land. After the failure initially at Kadesh Barnea, the next generation realize the promise under Joshua's leadership. But, as Hebrews observes, even Joshua did not give them 'rest' in the land. That is, they were *in* the land but not yet fully in possession and control of it. The promise lurches precariously forward during the two centuries of tribal federation and infighting and judges, until at last under David there emerges a unified Israel in possession of the whole of the land as promised to Abraham.

At that point the promise receives a fresh launch with the promise to David that God would give him an heir (deliberately echoing the Isaac promise), and that his descendants would reign over Israel for ever. That promise appeared to have crashed to earth amid the ruins of Jerusalem which ended the Davidic monarchy in 587. But already it had been given a fresh impetus which survived and transcended that catastrophe, by the prophetic vision of a future true son of David who would reign over his people in an age of justice and peace. And additionally, out of the wreckage of the exile arose the promise of future redemption, but still fuelled by the original ingredients of the promise – a new *exodus*, a new *covenant*, a fresh appropriation of the *land* under the blessing and presence of God himself.

The historical flight path of the promise looks a bit like this:

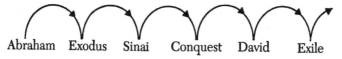

Abraham   Exodus   Sinai   Conquest   David   Exile

There is, then, a clear pattern of promise-fulfilment-fresh promise in the Old Testament, built into the ongoing historical relationship between God and Israel over the centuries. This means that when the New Testament talks about Jesus fulfilling the Old Testament promise it is not doing something new or unprecedented. Rather it sees Jesus as the final destination of an already well recognized pattern of promise-fulfilment.

The repeated 'refuelling' of the promise for fresh application also prepares us for the expectation that the final fulfilment will not be in terms of the literal details of the original promise, like the horse and motor-car analogy. The New Testament delights to portray Jesus as the one in whom the reality of the scripture promises is found, even in surprising ways. Even Jesus played on that surprise element, teasing the learned with questions about who the Messiah could be if, though David's son, David called him lord; tantalizing them with apparent claims to be the Son of Man – did it mean all that Daniel 7 implied? Never mind his enemies, even those who believed in him had difficulty recognizing the fulfilment of promises in his person and ministry. John the Baptist was baffled. His disciples took offence. If he was the Messianic king, where was his kingdom? When would it really be seen in power?

It was only as the church reflected on their experience of Jesus in the light of the resurrection that they came to see, as Paul put it, that *all* the promises of God are 'Yes' in Christ'. He was the singular seed of Abraham, through whom that seed would become universal and multi-national. He was the one in whom all nations would be blessed. To be 'in Christ' was to be 'in Abraham', and therefore to share in the inheritance of God's people. And that inheritance now far transcended the national territory, and included rather all the blessings and responsibilities of the fellowship of God's people. He was the passover lamb protecting God's people from his wrath. His death and resurrection had achieved a new exodus. He was the mediator of a new covenant. His sacrifical death and risen life fulfilled and surpassed all that were signified in the tabernacle, the sacrifices and the priesthood. He was the temple not made with hands, indeed he was Mount Zion itself, as the focus of the name and presence of God. He was the son of David, but his Messianic kingship was concealed behind the basin and towel of servanthood and the necessity of obedience unto death.

In the next two chapters we shall look further at the meaning of some of these pictures and patterns which the New Testament uses to portray all that Jesus meant. Our point here is simply that in terms of the original promise in the Old Testament, all these features were quite naturally literal or physical, in relation to the historical nationhood of Israel. So promises concerning God's actions in the *future* had to be made in terms already within the experience and comprehension of those who received them (just as a five-year-old before mechanization could understand the reality and the usefulness of a horse). But the *fulfilment* of the promise, with all these varied forms, through what God actually did in Christ, is at a different level of reality. A different level, but still with continuity of meaning and function in line with the original promise (just as a motor car is a quite different 'level of reality' from a horse, but has the same function and purpose as a means of transport).

Of course, even in the age of motor cars, there are those who would prefer horses. The writer to the Hebrews addresses those who, having come to faith in Jesus as Messiah, had not fully understood what that meant in terms of the complete fulfilment of all that their scriptural, Old Testament, faith had meant to them as Jews. So he sets out to demonstrate that in Christ we *have* all that the great institutions and promises of Israel signified, only *'better'*. He wanted Jewish Christians to recognize that they had not *lost* anything of their

Jewish, scriptural, inheritance by putting their faith in Jesus as Messiah. In Christ they *have* it all still, but enriched, enhanced and fulfilled. So much so that to want to go back to the previous era would be not merely retrograde, but a denial of what they possessed in reality in Christ. To hanker after the original forms of the promise would be like preferring shadows to real objects. Or like wanting four legs when you've been given four wheels.

In our own day, there are those who look for future fulfilments of Old Testament promises in a manner as literal as the original terms themselves. They expect to see things happening literally in the land of Israel, with a tribal division like Ezekiel describes. From the same prophet, they look for a rebuilding of the temple and reconstitution of the priesthood and sacrificial system. Or a battle between biblically identifiable enemies. Or Gentile nations on actual pilgrimage to the present physical Jerusalem. Or a revival of the throne of David.

There is a wide variety of such interpretations of prophecy held by many sincere Christian people. However, such expectations seem quite wide of the mark. Sometimes they simply make the mistake of taking literally what the Bible always intended figuratively even in its original form. But at other times they fail to see the living and 'transformable' quality of promises which were probably understood quite literally at the time of their giving. Just because the gift turns out to be a motor car doesn't mean we should try to argue that the promise of a horse was only meant figuratively. A horse was meant and a horse was expected. But the changed circumstances and the progress of history enabled the promises to be fulfilled in a different and superior way, without emptying the promise either of its purpose (to give a means of transport), or of its basis in a relationship of fatherly love.

To expect that all the details of Old Testament prophecies have to be literally fulfilled is to classify them all in the category of flat *predictions* which have to 'come true', or be judged to have failed. Certainly, as we saw right at the beginning of the chapter, the Old Testament did make predictions and they were fulfilled with remarkable accuracy – as in the case of Jesus's birth in Bethlehem. But as we also saw, Matthew's understanding of promise and fulfilment goes way beyond mere prediction. To insist on literal fulfilment of prophecies can be to overlook their actual nature within the category of *promise*, with the potential of different and progressively superior levels of fulfilment. To look for direct fulfilments of, say, Ezekiel in the 20th-century Middle East is to bypass and short-circuit the reality and the finality of what we already have in Christ as the fulfilment of those great assurances. It is like taking delivery of the motor car but still expecting to receive a horse.

The promise guaranteed

To speak of 'the Old Testament promise' is almost a repetition. The word 'testament' would actually be better called 'covenant', for that is the word used in the Hebrew Bible, and it is the word used by the New Testament when referring to the Old. And the idea of promise is very much at the heart of the word covenant.

THE FEATURES OF BIBLICAL COVENANTS

In the world of biblical times, covenants of all kinds were common in secular life. There were international treaties between a superior, imperial power, and its vassal states, in which the 'benefits', protection and services of the conqueror were granted in exchange for political and military loyalty and allegiance. Such treaty covenants were sanctioned by threats of dire punishment from the gods or men or both. In everyday life there were simple covenantal oaths in which promises were elevated to a very solemn and binding form. There were 'parity' covenants, entered into by equal partners who swore mutual obligations and responsibilities to each other, similar to what we call contracts.

When the term is used in the Old Testament as a means of describing the relationship between God and human beings, it is somewhat flexible – that is, it does not conform wholly or neatly to any of the existing secular models, but draws from different features of them, some more than others. Among the 'standard' features of covenants made between God and people, the following are important:

i) God's initiative.
It is God who takes the initiative in making the covenant. Sometimes this may come 'out of the blue', as with Abraham; sometimes as a sequel to what he himself has done, as at Sinai after the exodus; sometimes in response to some human act or attitude, as in the case of Noah's righteous obedience, or David's desire to build a house for God. In all cases, it is God himself who says, 'I will make a covenant with you.' To that extent, although there is a human response and obligation, the biblical covenants involving God are not 'parity' ones – that is, between equal partners. God is the sovereign initiator – the Lord of the covenant.

ii) God's promises.
In declaring his initiation of a covenant, God undertakes some specific commitment which constitutes the substance of the covenant. God, of course, remains soverign and free (he is not 'bound' in the sense of being under constraint to any authority higher than himself), but he chooses to bind himself to his own word, and bases the security of that word on his own name and character – 'by myself have I sworn . . .' The effect of the covenant, therefore, is to put the promises of

God under guarantee, since they issue from the truthfulness and eternity of God himself.

iii) Human response.

In all of the divine-human covenants in the Bible, there is a required response. We have already taken note of this in the last section. Sometimes there is argument between different theological schools of thought as to whether certain covenants are 'unconditional' or 'conditional'. Actually, in my view, the words aren't really adequate either way. The covenants are all 'unconditional' in the sense that they issue from the redemptive intention of God to act in blessing for human beings, who neither deserve such action, nor could fulfil any condition to deserve it. They *call* for human response, but they are not *based* on it, nor motivated by it.

Yet in another sense, they are all 'conditional' in that some clear stipulations are laid down for those who are to benefit from the covenant relationship. This is clearly so in the Sinai covenant, with the commandments and laws written into it. But the continuance of the covenant itself is not conditional on those laws. If the survival of the covenant had *depended* on Israel's obedience, they would never have left Sinai, let alone have made it into the promised land, for they broke the most fundamental commandments within weeks of receiving them. As the story of the golden calf, Moses' intercession, and the renewal of the covenant, in Exodus 32–4, makes clear, the covenant was not only initiated by God's grace, it was also sustained by God's grace. It can be called 'conditional' if one thinks of any given generation of Israelites, for whom the blessings of the covenant were indeed dependent on their obedience. Many a generation suffered the curses and threats of the covenant by their disobedience. But the *covenant itself* continued, grounded as it was in the grace of God's redemptive purpose for humanity, not just the obedience or blessing of Israel.

In our first chapter we did a rapid survey of Old Testament history, along the three section analysis of Matthew's genealogy. Earlier in this chapter, we reviewed it again as the 'flight-path' of God's promise, in its constant pattern of fulfilment and re-interpretation. It is worth surveying the route one last time, through a brief summary of the successive major covenants in the Old Testament, seeing how each is related to the others, and how all eventually lead towards the New Covenant inaugurated by Jesus himself.

Some books talk about an Adamic or an Edenic covenant, between God and Adam and Eve in the garden of Eden. Certainly there were instructions, permissions and warnings in the narrative of creation and the garden of Eden, but the text itself never speaks of a covenant, and it is not described that way anywhere else in the Old or New Testament. Even after the fall, there are certainly marks of God's grace: the provision of skins for clothing; the naming of Eve (mother of living – life would go on, in spite of the disobedience); and the prediction that the seed of the woman would ultimately crush the head of the serpent. This verse (Gen. 3:15), sometimes called the 'proto-evangelium' – or 'first Gospel' – is taken in some quarters as the first messianic prophecy in the Old Testament. Looked at retrospectively, of course, it is possible to see that Jesus did indeed crush Satan and will finally destroy him. But it is reading a lot into the verse in its own context to regard it as 'messianic'. It simply predicts that there will be unceasing conflict between the serpent and the human race, but that in the end, it will be humanity that wins – as indeed it was, in the man Jesus, representative of new humanity. So there are rays of hope in the engulfing darkness of the fall and the curse. But there is no reference to any covenant as such in Eden, either before or after the fall.

THE COVENANT WITH NOAH

Genesis 6:18–21, 8:21–9:17

The **scope** of this covenant is universal. It is explicitly a commitment by God to the whole of his creation – not just the human race, but every living creature. It comes in two parts – first of all his promise to preserve Noah in the midst of the judgement of the flood, but that in itself was for the purpose of preserving the human race beyond the flood. After the flood, the commitment is extended to all humans and all creatures.

The **substance** of the promise is both negative and positive. Negatively God promises never again to destroy the earth with a flood, in spite of the continuing wickedness of humanity. There will be no global destructive judgement in the course of human history itself (this does not of course rule out the reality of a final, universal and destructive judgement. Peter uses the flood as a prototype of that, 2 Peter 3:3ff.). Positively, God promises to preserve the conditions necessary for life on earth – the seasons, the regularity of nature, the provision of harvests.

The ongoing history of the human race is based on the endurance of this Noachic covenant. As all development agencies point out, the hunger of many and the starvation of some of the human race is not because of an overall shortage of food in the earth, or the inability of the earth to produce food for its current (or future) population. The productive resources of the earth's crust and the oceans seem almost limitless in their resilient renewability. God has kept his covenant. It is *human* incompetence, greed, injustice and aggression which deny the benefits of it to so many. God gives us the means to live and let live. Humanity chooses to live and let die.

The **response** stipulated to this covenant is very appropriate to its substance. God promises to *preserve* life. He calls on humanity to *respect* life. Though animals may be eaten, their 'lifeblood' is exempt. And the lifeblood of human beings is to be held in highest sanctity, because God made human beings in his own image (Gen. 9:3–6).

The Noachic covenant is the broad context of the biblical view of God's providence. It is not limited to a people or a place, but explicitly includes all life in the whole earth. It also illustrates quite well the inadequacy of asking whether it is unconditional or conditional. On the one hand, God asks for a response from humanity, yet clearly he has continued to keep this covenant in spite of humanity's failure to maintain the sanctity of life. But on the other hand, where human beings have shown utter disregard for life, human and animal, they tend to reap consequences of great severity in the natural world also – eventually. Not all deserts, famines and droughts are the result of purely 'natural' causes. There is a close connection between human behaviour and ecological health or disaster. Hosea observed this long before twentieth century environmentalists, when he complained about the degraded human behaviour that accompanies ignorance of God:

> There is only cursing, lying and murder,
>   stealing and adultery;
> They break all bounds,
>   and bloodshed follows bloodshed.
> Because of this the land mourns,
>   and all who live in it waste away;
> The beasts of the field and the birds of the air
>   and the fish of the sea are dying.
>
> (Hos. 4:2–3)

THE COVENANT WITH ABRAHAM

Genesis 12:1–3, 15:1–21, 17:1–27

The **scope** of this covenant is also universal, but in a different
sense from the Noachic covenant. The earlier covenant is the
basis of God's *providential* preservation of all life throughout
the span of human history. This is sometimes referred to as
God's 'common grace' – the indiscriminate good will of the
creator, by which 'he causes his sun to rise on the evil and
the good, and sends rain on the just and the unjust' (Matt.
5:45).

The covenant with Abraham, on the other hand, is the
basis of God's *redemptive* work within human history. The
universality is expressed in the goal of the covenant, that is
to bring God's redemptive blessing to all nations. The 'all'
clearly does not mean every human being who ever lived,
but has a representative sense. God's redemptive purpose will
ultimately be as global in its scope as the current sinfulness of
the human race, as typified in the nations at Babel. People
of every nation will share in the blessing covenanted to and
through Abraham.

The **substance** of the covenant is seen in what was specifically promised to Abraham and his descendants, in pursuance
of that ultimate, universal goal. It was threefold:

posterity:	From Abraham would come descendants who would be a great nation.
relationship:	With them God would have a special relationship of blessing and protection: 'I will be their God; they will be my people'.
land:	To them God would give the land of Abraham's own wanderings as an inheritance that would prove his faithfulness and their relationship to him.

The **response** required by God is first specified as circumcision, in Genesis 17. Superficially this might seem a rather undemanding sort of response. But that would be just that – superficial. Even in its own context, the command to circumcise comes after the summons to Abraham to 'walk before me and be blameless' – an obviously ethical injunction. Chapter 17 then describes how Abraham circumcised his whole household. Immediately following, in chapter 18:19, God affirms that the very purpose for which he had chosen Abraham was so that he will direct his children and his household after him (i.e. the precise ones he had circumcised) to keep the way of the LORD by doing what is right and just.

The expressions, 'the way of the LORD' and 'righteousness and justice' would come in the top five most significant and content-rich ethical expressions in the Hebrew Bible. Here they occur as the very purpose of the election of Abraham, and as the means by which the promise will be fulfilled (see the last expression of purpose in the same verse, 'so that the LORD will bring about for Abraham what he has promised him.') The ethical nature of the response required from Abraham is very clear and stands out in stark contrast to the context of this section of Genesis, which describes the wickedness of Sodom and Gomorrah and God's judgement upon them. In the midst of a world going the *way of Sodom*, God wants a community characterized by the *way of the Lord*, and that is the response he is looking for in Abraham and the covenant community yet to emerge.

That circumcision was more than just an outward ritual, but involved the commitment of the heart to practical obedience, was a truth well perceived in the Old Testament itself. It did not need Paul to point it out for the first time (Rom 2:25–9). Moses had done so emphatically before the people even reached the land of promise. In Deuteronomy 10:12–22, the command 'circumcise *your hearts*' is preceded by reference to the ancestors of Israel, and is therefore clearly intended to recall the fact that circumcision was essentially the sign of the covenant with Abraham. And it is followed by specific ethical instruction to imitate God in his compassion and justice, since that is what it means to 'walk in his ways'.

When we put together the universal, 'missiological' goal of the covenant with Abraham ('blessing to all nations'), and this practical, socio-ethical response required of Abraham and his descendants ('walking in the way of the Lord'), it produces an interesting double link between the election of the people of God, their ultimate role and mission for the sake of all nations, and the ethical characteristics that are required of them as a community in order that such a role and mission may be fulfilled. We shall develop this further in the next chapters.

THE SINAI COVENANT

Exodus 19:3–6, 24, and Deuteronomy

The **scope** of this covenant was national. God initiated it between himself and the national community of Israel after their deliverance from Egypt. But the explicit links with the Abraham covenant prevent it from being national in an exclusive or narrow sense. First of all, the whole sequence of events from Egypt to Sinai is repeatedly said to be in fulfilment of God's promise to Abraham. God will act in redemption for this people because he is the God of Abraham, Isaac and Jacob, whose descendants they are. Thus they are the people through whom his promise of blessing to all nations will be forwarded. The initiation of a new and covenanted relationship with them is thus neither unprecedented nor an end in itself. It is simply the next step on the road of his ultimate purpose in history for all nations.

Secondly, in his 'preface' to the making of the covenant, recorded in the key verses of Exodus 19:3–6, God gave Israel an identity and role which was explicitly related to the rest of the nations. In the midst of all the nations, in the 'whole earth' which belongs to God (v. 5), Israel were to be a priestly people and a holy nation. The function of priesthood in Israel itself was to stand between God and the rest of the people – representing God to the people (by their teaching function), and representing and bringing the people to God (by their sacrificial function). Through the priesthood, God was made known to the people, and the people could come into acceptable relationship to God. So God assigns to his people as a whole community the role of priesthood for the nations. As their priests stood in relation to God and the rest of *Israel*, so they as a whole community were to stand in relation to God and the rest of *the nations*.

There is, therefore, a missiological dimension to the Sinai covenant also, linked to the ultimate goal of the Abrahamic covenant. It is not greatly stressed in the covenant arrangements and the laws, but it is unmistakeably there (cf. Deut. 4:5–8), and comes into focus again in some prophetic passages which reflect on Israel's failure to keep the covenant as being a failure in their mission to the nations.

The **substance** of the Sinai covenant was largely the ratification and filling out of what had been promised to Abraham for the sake of the nation as a whole. A useful summary is given in the 'programme' God sets before Moses just before the onslaught of the plagues, in Exodus 6:6–8. God promises to accomplish four things:

The *redemption* of Israel from their oppressors (6);

The special *relationship* between God and Israel: 'I will take you as my own people, and I will be your God' (7a);

The *knowledge of Yahweh*: 'You will know that I am the LORD your God' (7b);

The gift of the promised *land*: 'I will bring you to the land

86

I swore with uplifted hand to give to Abraham, to Isaac and to Jacob' (8).

As these themes are developed in the rest of the Pentateuch, especially in the blessing and curse sections at the end of Leviticus and Deuteronomy, it can be seen that the special relationship includes the promise of well-being and protection, on condition of obedience; the knowledge of Yahweh as the unique and living God is a responsibility as well as a privilege entrusted to them through their unique experience of his saving power (Deut. 4:32–9); and similarly, the land is not a gift to be taken for granted and squandered in forgetful complacency, but a place to live responsibly before God with a lifestyle that will ensure prolonged enjoyment of the gift itself (Deut. 8).

Appropriately, therefore, the **response** stipulated within this covenant is total and exclusive loyalty to Yahweh. This involves not only the worship of Yahweh alone, to the exclusion of all other gods, but also moral commitment to the values and character of Yahweh. The commandments and laws stress both. The instinct by which Jesus selected the two-fold love for the LORD God (Deut. 6:5), and for one's neighbour (Lev. 19:18) as the heart of the law, or the hook from which it all was suspended, is fully borne out by the converse, negative emphasis in the law itself (especially Deut. 4–11) on the twin evils of idolatry and injustice.

This is sometimes aptly described as the perpendicular of covenant obligation. There is the vertical line of loyalty and obedience to God alone. And there is the horizontal line of love, compassion, justice and brotherhood to other human beings. The two are inseparable. In the law this is sometimes seen in the way social legislation is motivated by gratitude and loyalty to the God who delivered them. Such gracious action by God requires comparable compassion and justice towards the weak, poor or vulnerable in their own society.

This feature of Hebrew law was very influential on Jesus, as we shall examine in chapter five.

Looking again, then, at the relationship between the Sinai covenant and the covenant with Abraham, we can see a definite link between the required *response* to the Sinai covenant and the ultimate *goal* of the Abraham covenant. That is, Israel's loyalty to Yahweh and obedience to the law were the major means by which they would enable God to fulfil his goal of bringing blessing to the nations. The Sinai covenant was not an end in itself, to make Israel into a separate nation for their own exclusive sake and benefit. It was a means towards the achievement of God's ultimately universal purpose for humanity. The prophets perceived this in passages such as Jeremiah 4:1–2 and Isaiah 48:17–19. In the Old Testament, ethics is linked to mission as means is to end.

THE COVENANT WITH DAVID

2 Samuel 7, 23:1–7, Psalms 89, 132

The **scope** of the covenant with David was primarily the house of David itself – and that indeed was the **substance** of the covenant also, i.e., that there *would be* a house of David to continue on the throne of Israel.

As we saw in the historical survey in chapter one, the arrival of monarchy was a major change in the nature of Israel as a people. After the loose federation of tribes, with their internal fragmentation and the external pressures from Canaanites and other enemies, the Israelites were finally bound together into a single state not only occupying the territory promised to Abraham, but also controlling a number of subject states on their borders. And so at that point of change in the nation's life, even though it was initiated by human desires and compromises which God himself, through

Samuel, disapproved of, God renewed his commitment to their future by pledging yet another covenant with the king he had given them. So although the scope of the promise was the house of David itself, it was in fact a covenant for the whole nation, because the promise of permanence to the Davidic line was by implication a promise of a future for the people of Israel also.

The context in which the covenant with David is recorded also makes this link clear. The chapter immediately before it (2 Sam. 6) records how David brought the ark of the covenant into Jerusalem. David had recently captured Jerusalem and made it his capital city. From Jerusalem he reigned over all the tribes of Israel, having previously reigned for seven years over the tribe of Judah alone at Hebron. The ark, more than anything else, symbolized the ancient historical tradition and faith of Israel as the people of Yahweh. It was constructed at Sinai and represented all that the Sinai covenant meant to Israel – the law, the holiness of Yahweh, his approachability through the blood of sacrifice at the mercy-seat, and his presence in the midst of his people. David's action in bringing the ark of the covenant into Jerusalem, therefore, was clearly a deliberate move to demonstrate his allegiance to the ancient traditions of Israel's historical faith in Yahweh, to show that his understanding of his kingship was founded on the same covenantal basis as the old tribal federation.

In God's oracle to David through the prophet Nathan, we likewise find that the substance of this promise was both for the house of David and also for Israel, to whom God promised continued security and 'rest' (i.e. peace from enemies, 2 Sam. 7:10ff.). And in the prayer of response which David offered after hearing God's promise through Nathan, the editor of the books of Samuel obviously wishes his readers to hear clear echoes of the exodus-Sinai theme. (Read 2 Samuel 7:22–4, and compare it with Deuteronomy 4:32–8). The covenant with David is thus presented in the historical record, not as something utterly new or as a break with the past, but as an extension of God's covenant relationship with his people to the line of Davidic kings who would now reign over them.

The Davidic covenant not only has these explicit links with the Sinai covenant, but also seems deliberately framed in such a way as to recall the Abrahamic covenant also. We have already seen that it was David, in fact, who first achieved for Israel the possession of all the territory promised to Abraham. Other parallels include the promise to make *David* great, to make his *name* great, to maintain a special *relationship of blessing* with him and his offspring, and especially the promise of *a son* and heir.

These echoes of the Abraham tradition in the historical narrative are greatly amplified in the poetic materials concerning the link between the throne of David and God's purpose for the nations beyond Israel. There are some Psalms, for example, known as 'royal psalms', which celebrate different features of the Davidic kingship and its base in Zion. Characteristic of these royal Psalms is the idea that David, or his descendant on the throne, rules over all the nations of the earth. Now, whoever wrote hymns like that (e.g. Ps. 2:8ff., 72:8–11, 110:6) knew perfectly well that such worldwide dominion had never been the privilege of any historical king of David's line. And as the history of the monarchy dragged onwards and downwards, it would have been absurd to imagine that it ever would be. Yet they wrote such hymns, and people sang them, and presumably meant something by them.

We might say that perhaps it was just typical oriental flattery of monarchs with exaggerated claims for their imperial ambitions, and that maybe nobody took it seriously, (or literally at least). But there are times when it is clear that the Psalmists had more in mind than just the historical or geographical statistics of the Davidic kingdom itself. Rather they saw that behind the throne of David stood the throne of

Yahweh himself (this is clearest in Psalm 2), and that God's purpose in and through Israel's king was the same as his purpose for Israel itself – i.e. to be the vehicle of his intentions for all nations. Psalm 72, one of the most notable of the royal Psalms has this to say about the son of David:

> May his name endure for ever;
> may it continue as long as the sun.
> *All nations will be blessed through him,*
> *and they will call him blessed* (v. 17).

The echo of the promise to Abraham could scarcely be more loud and clear.

When we observe the **response** that is written into the Davidic covenant, it reinforces the links that we have already pointed out with the Sinai and Abrahamic covenants. It is the same fundamental demand for loyalty and obedience, and in this case grounded on the relationship of son to father, which God grants to David and his descendants on the throne. The son-father relationship of the Davidic king to God is recorded both in the historical record (2 Sam. 7:14), and also in the poetic celebration (e.g. Ps. 2:7, 89:26ff.). Among other things it points to the way the king in a sense 'embodied' Israel, since Israel was also designated Yahweh's 'firstborn son' (Ex. 4:22). But in the context of the Davidic covenant it has a double purpose: to emphasize God's love (i.e. his unbreakable commitment) on the one hand, and the requirement of obedience (the primary duty of sonship) on the other. We shall see in the next chapter how both of these were fundamental to Jesus's self-consciousness as the Son of God.

The moral response expected of the Davidic king existed, in a sense, before there even was one. The Deuteronomic law of the king (Deut. 17:14–20) very carefully makes the point that the king is not to consider himself above his fellows, nor above the law. On the contrary, he is to be exemplary in paying heed to the law and obeying it. The king was not to be a super-Israelite, but a model Israelite. Psalm 72, written by or for a Davidic king, with the covenant much in mind, goes to the heart of the law's concern, and expects the king to act for the special interest of the poor and needy:

> He will defend the afflicted among the people
>   and save the children of the needy;
> he will crush the oppressor ...   (v. 4, cf. vv. 12–14).

This standard was not forgotten, even (especially, perhaps) in later days when the monarchy in Jerusalem had become a matter of royal wealth and power, exercised on behalf of the wealthy and powerful elite in society, not on behalf of the 'afflicted and needy'. Jeremiah saw some of the worst of that kind of kingship, and he placarded the neglected duties of Davidic kings in the very gates of the palace itself.

> Hear the word of the LORD, O king of Judah, you who sit on
> David's throne ... This is what the LORD says: Do what is just and right (cf. Gen. 18:19). Rescue from the hand of his oppressor the one who has been robbed. Do no wrong or violence to the alien, the fatherless or the widow, and do not shed innocent blood in this place.
>
> (Jer. 22:2ff.)

This is very clearly the language of the Sinai covenant law. It shows that even after the inauguration of the Davidic covenant and all its accompanying theology about Mount Zion, the prophets still gave priority to the fundamental moral demands of the Sinai covenant. On these scales Jeremiah weighed king Jehoiakim and found him wanting on all points (Jer. 23:13, 17), especially as compared with his godly father, the great reforming king Josiah (vv. 15ff.).

So once again, we find the same combination: the universal, missiological dimension of the covenant, in its ultimate scope, for the blessing of all nations through Israel; and the explicit moral conditions of obedience and practical, social justice, which are here laid as a duty not solely on the nation as a whole as in the Sinai covenant but also on those who were entrusted with leadership and authority within it.

THE NEW COVENANT

Ceremonies of covenant renewal are scattered through the history of Israel in the Hebrew Bible. The first happened less than two months after the Sinai covenant was made, while Israel were still at Mount Sinai (Ex. 34). After then we could mention occasions of renewal by Moses, on the plains of Moab (Deuteronomy), by Joshua, after the conquest (Josh. 23–4), by Samuel at the institution of the monarchy, (1 Sam. 12), by Hezekiah (2 Chron. 29–31), and by Josiah (2 Kgs 22–3).

The last of these, at the time of Josiah, was the greatest of them all. It involved a major religious, social and political reformation that radically reversed the direction of Judah's life as it had proceeded for the previous half-century. And Jeremiah witnessed it. In fact, Jeremiah's call to be a prophet as a youth came when the reforms of Josiah had been going for about two years. About five years later, the book of the law (probably Deuteronomy) was discovered in the temple during repairs, and that led to an even more stringent reformation and the actual covenant renewal.

It was all most impressive, externally. But Jeremiah saw beneath the surface, and observed that the heart of the people was not really changed. The religious purges had not purged the deep-seated idolatry, nor the rampant social curruption (see especially Jer. 2 and 5, and his comments, probably, on Josiah's covenant renewal, in ch. 11). Something much more transforming was needed not so much a *renewal* of the covenant, as a *new covenant* altogether. For his own generation, Jeremiah could see nothing but judgement – the fulfilment of the curses and threats inherent in the Sinai covenant. But beyond that judgement, he had a vision for the future of his people, part of which was his portrait of a new covenant (Jer. 31:31–4).

Because it is quoted twice in the letter to the Hebrews (8:9–13, 10:15–18), it is Jeremiah's picture of the new covenant which is commonly meant when the expression 'new covenant' is used. However, it was not unique to Jeremiah, though it may have originated with him. Ezekiel was a prophet among those who suffered the exile Jeremiah had predicted, and he also held out hope of a new covenant. And the idea is also found in the rousing words of encouragement to the exiles in Isaiah 40–55.

This breadth of material about a new covenant makes it more difficult to analyse in quite the same way as we did for the previous historical covenants, especially since this one is in the realm of visionary expectation, not precise historical detail. But it is well worth the attempt, if the reader will take the time to look up the passages as we go along. A most interesting fact that will emerge as we do so, is that these prophets have drawn in items from all the earlier historical covenants in their rich and allusive portrayal of the new covenant of their future hope.

The **scope** of the new covenant is at first very clearly national. In both Jeremiah and Ezekiel, the major thrust is the hope of the restoration of Israel itself. Jeremiah's new covenant saying comes in the midst of two chapters (30 and 31) wholly taken up with this comforting hope (these chapters are sometimes called 'The Book of Consolation', in contrast to the bulk of Jeremiah's oracles of doom and judgement). The contours of Jeremiah's own ministry are echoed in 31:27–8 (cf. 1:10), when God says he plans 'to build and plant' his people. Accordingly, the covenant will be one which God will make 'with the house of Israel and the house of Judah'.

Ezekiel's vision of the future restoration of Israel, with a new covenant relationship between God and his people, is spread mainly over chapters 34, 36 and 37. Again, the scope is predominantly national, in the terms described. God promises a restoration of the theocracy – i.e. he himself will be the true 'shepherd' – king of Israel, but at the same time, 'David' will be prince over them (34:11–24). In chapter 36 the restoration of Israel will be a marvel in the sight of the nations, which will vindicate the reputation of Yahweh, their God. The reunification of the nation is the theme in Ezekiel 37:15–28 (following hard on the resurrection of the nation in the first part of the chapter). Again, 'David' will be king of the unified nation.

In Ezekiel's vision, the nations are referred to rather in the role of spectators. When God acts to restore Israel, then the nations will see, and hear, and know who really is God. So there is a universal dimension, but it is not integrated into the covenant itself. In Isaiah, however, the universal inclusion of the nations is worked into the covenant idea from the start. The scope of the new covenant in Isaiah 40–55 is as wide as the scope of salvation itself in those chapters, and that is 'to the ends of the earth'. The identity of the 'servant of God' figure in these chapters is much debated (and we shall add to the debate in chapter four), but it is clear that he is sometimes identical with Israel (cf. 41:8, 42:19, etc.) and sometimes apparently distinct from Israel. In the so-called 'servant songs', it appears that an individual, called and anointed by God, will fulfil the role and mission of Israel – enduring great suffering as he does so. His mission, as it was Israel's mission in terms of the Abraham covenant, will be to bring God's salvation to all nations. And this idea is first expressed in 42:6, using covenant language:

> I will make you to be a covenant for the people
> and a light for the nations.

The creation-wide context of the immediately preceding verse

(Isa. 42:5) shows who is in the prophet's mind – all those who breathe and walk on the earth. The same point is made in 49:6 (a verse used by Paul to sanction his own decision to take the Gospel to the Gentiles, in Acts 13:47), and 49:8. In 54:9–10, the 'covenant of peace' (an expression also favoured by Ezekiel) is primarily again made with a restored Israel. But the explicit comparison with the Noah covenant shows that the universal aspect is not lost from sight. It comes back into full view in chapter 55, the great 'evangelistic' conclusion to this section of prophecy. There the 'everlasting covenant' is equated with God's 'unfailing kindness promised to David' – i.e. his covenant commitment. And that in turn is filled out by envisaging peoples and nations coming to Israel and to their God (55:3–5), which is a link between the Davidic and the Abrahamic covenants that we noticed before.

The echoes of all four historical covenants should have been audible in that brief survey, but here is a replay in case you missed any of the notes.

Noah gets his explicit mention in Isaiah 54:9f. But there are other places where the idea of all creation being involved in God's future covenant blessing is present. Ezekiel's covenant of peace included God's promise to restrain the ravages of nature and instead to give his people such an abundance of harvest that comparisons were forthcoming with Eden itself (Ezek. 34:25–27a, 29, 36:30, 33–35). Jeremiah, also, uses the regularity and unfailing consistency of nature (which was a feature of the Noachic covenant) as a way of guaranteeing God's own intention to maintain his covenant with his people (Jer. 31:35–7 and 33:19–26).

Abraham is to be heard in the resounding universalism of Isaiah 40–55, and the extension of God's salvation to the ends of the earth, through one who will be a covenant and a light for the nations.

Sinai is to be heard in almost all the passages: Jeremiah's emphasis on the law being written in the heart and on the knowledge of God; Ezekiel's emphasis on the cleansing of sin, and the dwelling of God among his people; Isaiah's expectation of new exodus, liberation from all kinds of bondage, and the administration of justice for the nations.

David is also to be found in all three prophetic visions of the new covenant: Jeremiah's 'Righteous Branch' who will 'do righteousness and justice' as the Davidic king was supposed to (Jer. 33:15ff., 23:1–6); Ezekiel's true shepherd, ruling again over a united Israel of God (Ezek. 34); and Isaiah's witness, leader and commander for the peoples (Isa. 55:3–4).

The **substance** of the new covenant is also complex, and ideally we should analyse each of the prophetic passages separately, in its own context. But for sake of gaining an overall view, we can isolate several key themes which are common.

i) A new relationship with God
'You will be my people and I shall be your God.' These words formed the very essence of the covenant relationship between God and Israel from the beginning. The new covenant would reaffirm that central, warm and possessive relationship. One people, one God, forever (Jer. 31:33b, 32:38–40, Ezek. 37:23, 27). Isaiah expresses it in terms of a restored marriage (Isa. 54:5–10).

ii) A new experience of forgiveness
So much of the prophets' message had been accusation of the people for their accumulating sins. Judgement was inevitable. But they also saw that God's capacity for forgiveness was not bounded by the people's capacity for sin. It was his divine desire and intention to 'solve the sin problem' for good. He would remember it no more (Jer. 31:34b). Characteristic of his priestly imagery, Ezekiel envisages it as a complete cleansing (Ezek. 36:25, 37:23). Isaiah invites the sinner to an abundant pardon that surpasses human reasoning (Isa. 55:6–9).

iii) *A new obedience to the law*

If even the reform of a Josiah, in which the law was read and publicaly assented to, brought little change in the people's behaviour, then more than external pledges of obedience were needed. So Jeremiah writes into his new covenant that God's intention is:

> I will put my law in their minds
> and write it on their hearts. (31:33)

The result will be that knowledge of God will no longer need to be 'taught', because it will be an inner characteristic.

> They will all know me,
> from the least of them to the greatest.

This is sometimes regarded as a picture of the individualizing and personalizing of the knowledge of God, with the assumption that previously it had only been thought of in corporate or national terms. Certainly it does imply that every person will know him. But on the other occasions that Jeremiah uses the phrase 'from the least of them to the greatest', it is a way of portraying a whole community by a single common characteristic (6:13, 8:10). That is probably its intention here also. The people of God *as a whole* will be characterized as a community who know him.

Now if we go on to ask what it means to know God, Jeremiah allows us no sentimental feelings of private spiritual piety. He is absolutely clear. To know God is to delight in faithful love, justice and righteousness, as God himself does (9:24). More than that, it means not only to *delight* in such things, but actually to *do* righteousness and justice by defending the rights of the poor and needy – that is to know God. Jeremiah defines the knowledge of God in one of the most challenging verses in the Bible.

'Your father (i.e. Josiah) did what was right and just.
He defended the cause of the poor and needy
 and so all went well.
Is that not what it means to know me?' declares the Lord.

(Jer. 22:15–16)

These things were the heart of the law, the law which would
now, in the new covenant, be written in the heart.

'The law written in the heart' means much more than a
new upsurge of sincerity in keeping it. We have already seen
that the Old Testament from the beginning had called for
obedience from the heart. The popular parody of the Old
Testament as a religion of external legalism is far from the
truth. The heart, as the seat of the will and intelligence (not
just emotions), was of great importance, in the law, in the
Psalms and in the book of Proverbs. Ezekiel goes further in
emphasizing that such obedience of the heart involves not just
a new law, but a new heart itself, a veritable heart transplant
performed by the Spirit of God. Only such a spiritual miracle
will produce the obedience called for (Ezek. 36:26ff.). True
obedience would be the gift of the same Spirit who could
turn dead bones into a living army in the mighty act of
resurrection pictured in Ezekiel 37:1–14.

The book of Isaiah does not include this dimension in its
sayings about the covenant itself, but there is a strong emphasis on the full acceptance of the law and the reign of justice
in its visions of the mission of the servant to the nations, as
the agent of God's purpose for humanity (42:1–4, 51:4–8).
This is very similar to the prophecies of the messianic age
under the future anointed son of David, found in the earlier
chapters of Isaiah (cf. 9:7, 11:1–5). It will be an age ruled by
a new David, but ruled according the law and justice of God.

iv) A new Davidic king

Jeremiah includes this element in his future hope, as we saw (23:5f., 33:15–26), though his famous new covenant passage is entirely Sinaitic in flavour. Ezekiel looks to a future 'David' as the agent of theocracy and of the unity of the people. It is possible, though scholars are not agreed on it, that the 'David' referred to in Isaiah 55:3ff. is actually an identity for the servant figure, previously anonymous and mysterious. If that were so, it would certainly link up the expectations associated with the coming 'David' with the mission of bringing God's law and justice to the nations.

v) A new abundance of nature

Abundance and fruitfulness were part of the promised bless-ings for obedience to the Sinai covenant (Lev. 26:3–13 – language which recalls the bounty of Genesis 2; Deut. 28:1–14). If the covenant were to be restored, on the farther side of the fulfilment of its curses in God's judgement, then it is not surprising that we find as part of that hope of renewal the expectation of restoration to the land, secure settlement, freedom from the traditional perils of wild beasts and human enemies, and abundant fertility of crops and herds.

Old Testament hope was no pie in the sky when you die, but the living reality of God's blessing on his creation here and now for his renewed and obedient people. The recollection of Eden is also not out of place, since the hope of humanity since the fall, so poignantly expressed by Lamech at the birth of his son Noah, was that God would lift the curse from the *earth*, and return to dwell once more with humanity *in the earth* (Gen. 5:28f.). This is also the hope which brings the whole Bible to a close, with a vision of its fulfilment in a new heaven and new earth (Rev. 21:1–3). A foretaste of that new creation is seen in the otherwise extravagant language with which the prophets look forward to the renewal of the land of Israel itself (Jer. 31:11–14, Ezek. 34:26–9, 36:8–12). As elsewhere in the Bible, the land of Israel functions in part as a token of the future new creation, as the place of God's presence and unhindered blessing.

CONCLUSION

It has been a long journey (involving horses, cars and space shuttles!) through the historical span of the Old Testament, and its rich array of promise. We need to finish off by stepping back for a moment to survey the way we have come.

To change metaphors yet again, the Old Testament, considered as promise, is like a great river. Along the way, several streams flow into it, from different starting points, and with different individual courses. These are the different streams of tradition, law, narratives, poetry, prophecy, wisdom, etc. But in the end, they all combine into a single current, flowing deep and strong – the ongoing, irresistible promise of God. Scholars, particularly those involved in traditio-historical criticism, can map each stream of tradition, indicating its distinctiveness, the route it takes through the Old Testament literature, and the individuals or groups responsible for preserving its flow. Our survey has been only a very rough sketch map, because our aim has not been the minute details of Old Testament history and literature, but to feel the full force of the great current of promise, fed by all its many streams.

The overwhelming impression that makes itself felt through all this study of promise and covenant, is *God's unwavering intention to bless.* His covenant with Noah proclaims his blessing, through the promise to preserve the conditions of life for all his creation. His covenant with Abraham proclaims his purpose of blessing all humanity in and through the descendants of Abraham. And that remains the constant background to all God's subsequent dealings and promises involving Israel. His commitment to that intention for humanity is what motivates and sustains his commitment to Israel, in the midst of all the ups and downs of their chequered historical relationship.

So, when the writers of the new Testament witnessed God's climactic discharge of that commitment to humanity in the life, death and resurrection of Jesus of Nazareth, they checked what they had experienced with what they already knew through their Hebrew scriptures. They looked at all the events surrounding Jesus, and they understood them, illuminated them, explained and finally recorded them, all in the light of the whole sweep of Old Testament promise. God had made a commitment. And God had kept his word. The Old Testament had declared the promise which Jesus fulfilled.

CHAPTER THREE

Jesus and his Old Testament Identity

So Jesus came, then, as the completion of the story which the Old Testament had told, and as the fulfilment of the promise which the Old Testament had declared. That much has been made abundantly clear by the way Matthew uses his Hebrew Bible even before we have got beyond chapter two of his Gospel. But who was Jesus himself?

Mark, whose Gospel gets us into the action of Jesus's ministry faster than any of the others, punctuates his narrative with a whole series of questions that were raised by the impact of Jesus.

The demons started it: 'What do you want with us? Have you come to destroy us?' (1:24) Too true!

Then the crowds took it up: 'What is this? A new teaching, a new authority?' (1:27) True again!

The religious leaders took offence: 'Why does this fellow talk like this? Who can forgive sins but God alone?' (2:7) Truer than they realized.

'Why does he eat with sinners?' (2:16)

'Why does he not keep the rules on the Sabbath?' (2:24)

'Where did he get all this from?' (6:2)

'Isn't this just the carpenter's son?' (6:3)

Finally, his disciples got to the real point, as they sat trembling in a gently rocking boat that a few moments before had been tossing and on the brink of swamping in a storm which Jesus had simply snuffed out with a word.

'Who is this man?' (4:41) That was the real issue. Who was *he?*

Coming back to Matthew's Gospel, we remember that Matthew 2 ended with Jesus growing up as a child in Nazareth. Nazareth the insignificant. Nazareth in Galilee of the Gentiles. Nazareth from which no good thing was expected to come. How could a local boy from such a background have the kind of significance that Matthew's first two chapters have prepared the reader to expect? This very question dogged Jesus in his own lifetime. It has been suggested that the word 'Nazarene', the mystery term of Matthew's list of fulfilments in chapter two, may actually be a nickname meaning something like 'the insignificant'. Not the most promising identity for one born to be the very pivot of history.

'This is my Son'

Perhaps that is why Matthew's next chapter leads up to a climax with a very different assessment of the identity of Jesus. Matthew 3 describes the ministry of John the Baptist and how he was persuaded, reluctantly, to baptize Jesus. This event, the baptism of Jesus, was so important that it is included in all four Gospels, and is frequently also the starting point of the apostles' preaching in Acts. It was obviously important to God as well, because here we have God the Holy Spirit coming down visibly on God the Son with an audible declaration by God the Father:

> This is my Son, whom I love, the one in whom I delight
> (Matt. 3:17).

And it was important to Satan, since the three synoptic Gospels all record that immediately after this event, Satan threw all his effort into getting Jesus to cash in on his identity as the Son of God in ways that would divert him from his real mission (a mission in which Satan saw his own defeat and destruction): '*If* you are the Son of God . . .

And clearly it was important to Jesus. As a boy he had been aware of a special relationship with God as his Father (which Luke, not Matthew, tells us about, Luke 2:49). But through his baptism, in his adult maturity at the age of about thirty, he receives the full confirmation of his true identity and mission from the mouth of his Father himself. So awesome was the sense of identity and the implications that it carried, that it led to a period of intense struggle in desert solitude. But immediately after he had survived that and proved his loyalty to his Father, by resisting Satan with the very scriptures he cunningly used, he entered on his ministry with immediate, stunning, effect.

So there is a contrast between what other people thought of Jesus (at least in the beginning) and what God his Father thought of him. Luke brings this out in a rather clever way by putting *his* version of the genealogy of Jesus immediately after his baptism. So, just after we have read that God declared 'You are *my* Son', Luke begins his next paragraph,

> Now Jesus himself was about thirty years old when he began his ministry. He was the son, *so it was thought*, of Joseph . . . (3:23).

In other words, to human eyes, Jesus was the son of an unimportant carpenter in insignificant Nazareth. In God's sight, however, he was 'My beloved Son in whom I delight'. That was his real identity.

For such an important occasion as the baptism of his Son, you might have thought that God would have come up with something wholly new. Words never heard before by human ears. A fresh burst of divine speech, such as launched the ministry of Moses or Isaiah. But no. Whether history repeats itself or not, God certainly does. The words that meant so much to Jesus at this critical moment in his life were actually echoes of at least two and probably three different passages in the Old Testament. Presumably God the Father knew that his Son, by age thirty, was so steeped in his Hebrew scriptures that he would not only recognize the texts but also understand all that they meant for his own self-identity. The words themselves were not new. What *was* new was the way the three passages are brought together and related to a single person with a unique identity and mission. The three texts echoed here are Psalm 2:7, Isaiah 42:1, and Genesis 22:2.

This is/You are my Son

This is an echo of Psalm 2:7 which was originally a Psalm about king David and then any king descended from him. He need not fear the posturings and antagonism of his enemies because it is God himself who has anointed him king and who protects him. The declaration: 'You are my son; today I have begotten you', was probably said at the coronation or enthronement of Davidic kings as God's way of endorsing their legitimacy and authority. However, the fall of Jerusalem and the exile in 587 BC was the end of the line for the Davidic kings. So this Psalm was given a future look and applied to the expected, messianic, son of David who would reign when God would restore Israel. The heavenly voice at his baptism identified Jesus as that very one.

My loved one, in whom I delight

This is an echo of Isaiah 42:1 which is the opening verse of a series of 'songs' in Isaiah 40–55 about one called the servant of the Lord. He is introduced rather like a king, but as the songs develop (42:1–9, 49:1–6, 50:4–10, 52:13–53:12) it becomes clear that this servant will accomplish his calling, not by kingly power as we know it, but through frustration, suffering, rejection and death. By willingly paying that cost, however, the servant will not only bring restoration to Israel, but also be the instrument of bringing God's salvation to the ends of the earth.

My son, my beloved one

Many scholars find in this phrase a third echo from the Hebrew Bible, Genesis 22:2, where God told Abraham, 'Take your son, your only son Isaac, whom you love', and sacrifice him to the Lord. In the end, Isaac was spared, but Abraham was commended for his willingness to trust and obey God even to that ultimate extent. The story, known in later Jewish lore as 'The Binding of Isaac', was deeply studied and reflected on for its double theme of Abraham's willingness as a father to sacrifice his son, and Isaac's willingness as a son to be sacrificed.

Paul probably had this story in mind when he wrote Romans 8:32, 'He who did not spare his own Son, but gave him up for us all – how will he not also, along with him, graciously give us all things?' And almost certainly it was in the mind of God the Father as he identified Jesus at his baptism as his only Son whom he loved, but whom he was willing to sacrifice for the salvation of the world. Only this time it would be for real. There would be no ram to substitute at the last minute. Was Jesus, like Isaac, willing for that? No wonder Jesus, now fully aware in his adult manhood of the identity being laid on him, went from this experience into a time of intense and prolonged personal struggle and testing (which we shall look at more closely in chapter five).

Old Testament pictures and patterns

Later in this chapter and the next, we shall look at these terms for Jesus in more depth. The point to observe for the moment is how the Old Testament is being used here in relation to him. This moment of baptism, as we have seen, was of immense significance for Jesus. At the threshold of his public ministry he needed to be absolutely sure of who he was and what he had come to do. Both his identity and his mission were involved in his coming for baptism by this prophetic herald of the coming kingdom of God – John the Baptist. And how did his Father declare and confirm that identity? By quoting the Scriptures. By using figures, events and prophecies from the Old Testament as a way of 'colouring in' the reality of who Jesus was.

Matthew has shown us how the Old Testament tells the story which Jesus completed. Then he showed us how the Old Testament declares the promise which Jesus fulfilled. Now he opens up the Old Testament as a store house which provides images, precedents, patterns and ideas to help us understand who Jesus was.

Indeed, to step further back, it was the Old Testament which helped *Jesus* to understand Jesus. Who did he think he was? What did he think he was to do? The answers came from his Bible, the Hebrew scriptures in which he found a rich tapestry of figures, historical persons, prophetic pictures and symbols of worship. And in this tapestry, where others saw only a fragmented collection of various figures and hopes, Jesus saw his own face. His Hebrew Bible provided the shape of his own identity. By pointing this out to us in connection with Jesus's baptism, Matthew shows that this was not some arbitrary, fanciful use of the Bible by later romantic admirers of Jesus. Rather, it was God's own way of declaring the identity of his Son. Jesus's self-identity was based on his Father's explicit identification of him. And that in turn was based on the the Hebrew scriptures of our Old Testament.

This point has brought us a step further in our purpose in this book. Our conviction has been that the more you understand the Old Testament, the closer you will come to the heart of Jesus. In our first two chapters we were seeing that fact 'externally', so to speak. They described how the observers and interpreters of Jesus understood and explained him in relation to the Old Testament story and promise. But here we are reaching into the 'internal' self-identity of Jesus himself. We are no longer talking about a new-born baby or a migrant child, or even about an abstract concept of messiahship. Here we have an adult man, at one level indistinguishable among the crowds of those who flocked to John for baptism and in any case otherwise unknown except as a carpenter's son from Nazareth, who takes upon himself a staggering identity with awesome personal consequences. And he does so by accepting and internalizing three Old Testament figures.

He has the authority of the Davidic king, with a special relationship of sonship to God, the divine King. This means that from the beginning of his ministry Jesus was conscious of his identity as the Son of God and Davidic Messiah, even though later on he sought to play it down among his followers because of its political misunderstandings. He chose to emphasize a dimension of Davidic sonship which we looked at in the last chapter – namely obedience to God. Obedience was a requirement of sonship which Israel prized – literally, for actual children, and metaphorically when describing themselves as the son or sons of Yahweh (e.g. Mal. 1:6). And it was the particular calling of the Davidic king (2 Sam. 7:14f., Jer. 22:1–5). How much more then for the Son of God himself, who later affirmed that obedience to his Father's will was his very meat and drink (John 4:34).

Obedience was also the link between Davidic sonship and the otherwise unexpected Servant figure. This was not an association that contemporary Jewish traditions had drawn. It seems to have been an insight originating from the ministry of Jesus himself to see the messianic role of the Davidic king in the light of the suffering, obedient, servant of the Lord. Similarly, obedience was the link with the allusion to Isaac, as the one willing to be sacrificed, even as the only son of a loving father.

Sovereignty, servanthood, sacrifice. All three are built into the calling of Jesus. All three are given depth and meaning by the Old Testament characters whose identities are merged in Jesus. His personal identity, the shape of his mission and the pattern of his life are all, so to speak, programmed by the intricate spiral patterns of a genetic code provided by the Old Testament scriptures.

The 'genetic' metaphor is not meant to suggest that somehow Jesus himself was 'programmed', or that it was possible simply to 'read off' from the Old Testament the 'genetic fingerprints' of Jesus of Nazareth. In the Gospels, it was those with the closest familiarity with the Hebrew scriptures who did not or would not recognize him as the Messiah. And Jesus's own use of the scriptures in relation to himself was creative and sometimes surprising. As we have already seen in chapter two, it was no simple matter of matching predictions to fulfilments in a kind of messianic identity parade.

However, what the genetic metaphor *is* trying to emphasize is that Jesus was not some new and exotic species. Especially he was not, as so many want us to think, the 'founder of a new religion'. Yes, of course, he was unique in so many ways, which we shall discover as we go on. But for those with eyes and ears and memories, the Hebrew scriptures had already provided the patterns and models by which he could be understood, and by which he could understand and explain himself and his goals to others.

'THAT'S JUST TYPICAL'

The word *typology* is sometimes used to describe this way of viewing the relationship between the Old Testament and Jesus. The images, patterns and models that the Old Testament provides for understanding him are called *types*. The

New Testament equivalents or parallels are then called *anti-types*. This used to be a very popular way of handling the Old Testament in former generations, but it has fallen into disfavour among many scholars recently. Typological interpretation remains a traditional way of using the Old Testament, however, in some quarters of the Christian church. It is worth explaining a bit about it, for the benefit of those who have never heard of it, and also for the sake of those who may have been exposed to unbalanced or fanciful uses of it.

i) Biblically, typology is not a theological or technical term

The English word *type* comes directly from the Greek word *typos*, which means an example, pattern or model. It is found in the New Testament with that loose range of meaning – sometimes applied to Christ but often to others. For example, Paul speaks of the events in the history of Israel as 'warnings' or 'examples' for us (1 Cor. 10:6, 11). In several places, it means an example to be followed, either the apostles themselves, or certain churches, or pastors for their flock (Phil. 3:17, 1 Thes. 1:7, 2 Thes. 3:9, Tit. 2:7, 1 Pet. 5:3). In Romans 5:14, we find Adam described as a pattern for Christ. In 1 Peter 3:21, we find an analogy being drawn between the flood and the ark on the one hand and Christian baptism on the other. So *typology*, then, is not a hard and fast method of tying the Old to the New Testament. Biblically, it still just means a range of examples, models and patterns of correspondence. It is not a major interpretive key to unlock the mysteries of the Old Testament.

ii) Typology is a normal and common way of knowing and understanding things

There is really nothing fanciful about typology. We use it every day when trying to learn or teach something new or as yet unknown. Any teacher knows that in introducing new ideas or skills, you have to work by analogy or correspondence from what is already known and familiar – either past events, or experience, or pre-understandings. Even at the most advanced level, scientific knowledge progresses within what are called *'paradigms'* in the trade – i.e. accepted models or patterns of how physical reality is believed to function. Often one proven scientific result will act as a 'type' or model for attacking as yet unsolved puzzles. And in the whole world of law and law courts, we build steadily on the power of *'precedents'*. A judgement which was made in one specific case will function as a model or 'type' in future cases in which corresponding issues are at stake. And even in everyday speech, when we exclaim, 'That's just typical!' about somebody's action, what we mean is that we are not really surprised by it because it fits in with a pattern of behaviour which we have come to expect from previous experience of that person.

iii) Typology was already a feature of the Old Testament itself
Already, in our survey of the Old Testament in the last two chapters, we have seen how the Old Testament itself has a kind of internal typology. Many events and persons are picked out and seen as 'typical'. That is, they illustrate something characteristic about the way God does things. So those particular cases can then be used to help understand something new which God has done or is threatening or promising to do. Sodom and Gomorrah become proverbial for God's judgement against human sin. What God had done in destroying Shiloh is used by Jeremiah as a graphic type of what he intends to do to Jerusalem (Jer. 7:12–15). Hosea and Jeremiah use the wilderness period as a picture for the future purification of Israel (Hos. 2:16ff., Jer. 32:2). The exodus is repeatedly used as a model for subsequent historical acts of deliverance. Even individuals can take on this 'typical' dimension. David, of course, as the ideal king; but also Abraham as the model of faith and obedience (Gen. 15:6), and Moses as the model prophet (Deut. 18:15, 18).

iv) Typology is a matter of analogy

I said that the word *typos* itself is not used in a technical or formal sense in the New Testament. But there are many ways in which the writers of the New Testament draw our attention to analogies between the Old and the New, where the word *typos* may or may not be used. In the midst of the obvious differences between the Testaments, there are also real points of correspondence.

We find, for example, correspondence between the word of God in creation in Genesis and the beginning of the new creation with Jesus, the Word, in John 1. The birth of Jesus as the beginning of the Gospel of redemption in the New Testament is parallelled to the birth of Isaac as the child of promise in the Old (Gal. 3–4, Rom. 4). The shedding of the blood of Jesus can be understood by analogy with the exodus, the passover lamb, and the crossing of the Red Sea all rolled into one! There are definite analogies between the community that Jesus gathered around him as the Messiah and a restored Israel, which we shall look at later. Paul draws heavily on the analogy of land and kinship to describe the new status of the formerly excluded Gentiles once they have been reconciled to God through Christ (Eph. 2:11–22). The same passage makes comparisons between the temple and the church (meaning people, not a building, of course). Peter has the same combination of ideas in 1 Peter 2:4–12. There are other analogies, some of which we have noted already, such as between the New Covenant in Christ and all the previous covenants in the Hebrew Bible; between the kingship of Yahweh and of Israel's kings and the kingdom of God; between God's concern for all nations and the whole world in the primal history of Genesis 1–11 and the scope of the Gentile mission and our future hope of all creation being redeemed and united in Christ.

So there is good biblical justification for seeing analogy as a valid feature of biblical interpretation, because the Bible itself uses it. The Old Testament uses analogy to speak of what was as yet future. '*That* (the future) will be like *this* (the present).' And the New Testament uses analogy to explain present events by reference to the past. When Peter stood up to preach on the day of Pentecost, the sun was not darkened and the moon was not blood, but he could confidently relate the significance of what was happening at that moment to the famous vision of Joel in Joel 2:28–32 and assert, '*This* is *that* . . . (Acts 2:16ff.).

v) Typology is a matter of history
The correspondence between the Old and New Testament is not merely analogous, but points to the repeating patterns of God's actual activity in history. 'Salvation-history' as we have already seen, is a shorthand expression for the belief that God has acted through specific events in history to accomplish salvation. In the last two chapters we saw in some detail how that action followed patterns of promise and fulfilment and then fresh promise. Observing this helps us to grasp both God's sovereign control over history and also his consistency in action.

God behaves typically as God. That is, there is something characteristic, something predictable about what he does, once you know his previous actions. As I once heard a new Christian put it, in sheer wonder at her fresh experience of God's constant and consistent action, 'God is always Godding!'

Now, of course, this is not at all saying that God is bound to a boring repetition of the past. He is also the master of surprise and could even exclaim triumphantly through Isaiah, 'Forget the past! Look, I am doing a new thing!' But even then, his 'new thing' could be described in terms of the original thing – new exodus or new creation or new covenant. So when the New Testament witnesses saw who Jesus was and what he had achieved, they said in effect, 'That's just typical of God. What he has done in Jesus Christ is just like all that he actually did in the past, only it surpasses and completes it all.'

vi) Typology is not just prefiguring or foreshadowing
The older view of typology fell into disfavour because it was solely concerned with finding 'prefigurations' of Christ all over the Old Testament. The idea was that the central feature of a 'type' was that it prefigured Christ. But this was handled, not as something observed *afterwards* in the light of Christ, but rather as the very reason for existence of whatever was being regarded as a 'type'. So a 'type', on this view, was any event, institution or person in the Old Testament which had been ordained by God for the *primary purpose* of foreshadowing Christ. This had two unfortunate side effects.

First, it usually meant that the interpreter of the Old Testament failed to find much reality and meaning in the events and persons of the Old Testament in themselves. There was no need to spend time exegeting and interpreting the texts in their own Israelite historical context and background or to ask what they meant then. You could just jump straight to Christ, because that is where you would find the supposed 'real' meaning. This ends up with a very 'Platonic' view of the Old Testament. That is, it is really only a collection of 'shadows' of something else. It thus devalues the historical reality and validity of Israel and all that God did in and through and for them.

Secondly, this kind of typology had a tendency to indulge in fanciful attempts to interpret every detail of an Old Testament 'type' as in some way a foreshadowing of some other obscure detail about Jesus. Once you had severed the event, institution or person from their actual historical roots in Israel, then the details could not be allowed to be just incidental to the Old Testament text, i.e. simply part of the story as the narrator told it. Since the 'real meaning' was actually to be found in Jesus and the New Testament, all the details must have some hidden significance that could be applied to him. It was up to the skill or imagination of the writer or preacher to bring such meanings out, like a magician bringing rabbits out of a hat, to the astonished gasps of admiring readers or listeners. This way of handling the Hebrew text is quite rightly now regarded as invalid and subjective. Unfortunately it is still around in certain kinds of preaching especially.

Typology, then, to sum up, properly handled, is a way of understanding Christ and the various events and experiences surrounding him in the New Testament by analogy or correspondence with the historical realities of the Old Testament seen as patterns or models. It is based on the consistency of God in salvation-history. It has the backing of Christ himself who, on the authority of his Father, saw himself in this way.

But typology is not *the* way of interpreting the Old Testament for itself. This is partly because it is selective in the texts it uses from the Old Testament (i.e. those which particularly help us to understand Christ), whereas the New Testament itself tells us emphatically that the *whole* of the scriptures are written for our profit (2 Tim, 3:16f.) and partly because it is limited in the meaning it extracts from those selected texts (i.e. again, meanings which specifically relate to Christ). To come back to our three texts in the declaration at Jesus's baptism, it is clear that each of them helps us to understand great truths about the identity and mission of Jesus. But when we go back and read the whole of Psalm 2, Isaiah 42 and Genesis 22, it is equally true that they have enormous depths of truth and meaning for us to explore which are not *directly* related to Jesus himself. Typology is a way of helping us understand Jesus in the light of the Old Testament. It is not the exclusive way to understand the full meaning of the Old Testament itself.

Jesus as the Son of God

Having come back, then, to Jesus and his baptism after our detour through the meaning of typology, let us look more closely at the sense of identity and purpose which he derived from his baptismal experience. We shall check out the Old Testament background a bit more thoroughly and see how it influenced the way Jesus thought of himself. But we shall also discover that Jesus was not just an identikit figure pasted together from bits of the Old Testament. He transcended and transformed the ancient models. He filled them with fresh meaning in relation to his own unique person, his example, teaching and experience of God. So that, for his followers, what began as a shaft of recognition and understanding of *Jesus* in the light of their Scriptures, ended up as a deepening and surprising new understanding of their *Scriptures* in the light of Jesus. That was certainly the experience of the disciples on the Emmaus road in Luke 24.

So we go back, then, to the baptismal voice and its first phrase, 'You are my son'. The awareness of God being his Father and himself being God's Son is probably the deepest foundation of Jesus's selfhood. This is something on which most New Testament scholars would agree. Even those who sift the texts of the Gospels with rigorous suspicion as to what may be regarded as authentically from Jesus himself, agree that the Father-Son language regarding God and himself survives the most acid scepticism. And they would also point out that for Jesus, God's fatherhood and his own sonship were not merely concepts or titles. Nor were they merely part of his teaching curriculum. They were living realities in his own life. Jesus *experienced* a relationship with God, of such personal intimacy and dependence, that only the language of Father and Son could describe it. It was deepest in his prayer life, and that was also where his closest friends observed it, as they heard him habitually use '*Abba*', the intimate Jewish

117

family word for father, in personal address to God. This was something new and unprecedented that Jesus brought to the meaning of being children of God.

Let us then turn back to the Scriptures from which Jesus would have soaked up his preliminary understanding of what it meant to call God Father and what it meant to be a son of God. For Israel also called God Father and he called them his son.

God as Father – Israel as son

In order to understand Jesus we have to look at more than just the titles by which he was addressed or which he used for himself. In fact, Jesus tended to avoid titles, with the single exception of the Son of Man. And even if we take those titles that we find in the New Testament and go back to the Hebrew scriptures, we have to do more than just look up a concordance and check out the phrases there. This is especially so of this expression 'son of God' in its Old Testament usage. If we only look it up in the concordance, we may end up very confused, for the expression has a bewildering elasticity. It can, for example, refer to angels (probably, Gen. 6:2, 4, Ps. 89:6). Even Satan is called one of the sons of God (Job 1:6, 2:1). It can be used to describe human rulers and judges (Ps. 82:6). Even the pagan king Nebuchadnezzar used it to describe the mysterious fourth man in his fiery furnace (Dan. 3:25). And, of course, we have already seen that it was applied especially to the Davidic king.

Rather, what we must do is look at the whole range of material that was associated with sonship in relation to God as Father in the Hebrew Bible. The idea was not, of course, anywhere near as dominant as the idea of covenant relationship between God and Israel, but it is much more extensive than many Christians think. And it also began early.

It is found in Deuteronomy 32, the Song of Moses, which

is universally acknowledged to be amongst the oldest of the poetic texts in the Hebrew Bible. This poem is therefore a very ancient witness to the faith of Israel and rules out the idea that the fatherhood of God was a late development in Israel's history, or that it was a brand new teaching by Jesus. Actually in Deuteronomy 32 it would be better to talk about the *parenthood* of God, since it uses the imagery of mother as well as father to describe God. This parenthood of God is linked to his creation of his people (v.6); Yahweh's own uniqueness as God (vv. 15–18, 39); and his corrective discipline of his people (vv. 19–20).

We shall look at the metaphor in four ways. First, we shall check up what the parent-child relationship actually meant in Israel's society, since that will clarify what it meant when transferred to God and Israel. Secondly, we shall see how the metaphor undergirded the covenant concept, which we have already studied in some depth in chapter two. Thirdly, we shall see how sonship was a relationship that generated hope and expectation. Fourthly, we shall see how the idea was broadened and given a universal and eschatological flavour. In each case we shall find significant links with Christ which illuminate his sense of identity and destiny.

FATHERS AND SONS IN ISRAELITE SOCIETY

Obviously, to use the language of fatherhood and sonship is to draw from the human experience of family life, and then to apply the parent-child experience metaphorically to God and to human relationship to him. (This is to look at the matter from the human perspective. Ultimately, our own human experience of parenthood and family is a reflection of God, for we are made in *his* image. That is probably what Paul is getting at in Ephesians 3:14f.)

In Israel we find evidence of the metaphor in common life in the use of the Hebrew word '*Ab*' (father) in '*theophoric*' names (ie. personal names which include all or part of the name of God). Names such as Joab, Abijah, Eliab, etc, mean Yahweh (or God) is father. It is arguable whether the implication is 'my father' (personally), or 'the father' (i.e. of the family, or tribe or nation). But either way, the bearer or giver of such a name was making a statement about God in relationship to himself or his people. This shows that the idea of the fatherhood of God was common enough in the popular life of Israel, even if it did not achieve a prominent place in their major theology.

The metaphor has two fairly well defined, complementary meanings.

i) *The attitude of God as Father towards Israel*

This is one of concern, love, pity and patience with the son. But it also a desire for his best interests, which therefore includes discipline.

> The LORD your God carried you, as a father carries his son (Deut. 1:31).
> Know then in your heart that as a man disciplines his son, so the LORD your God disciplines you. (Deut. 8:5)

Other examples of this would include: Psalm 103:13; Proverbs 3:12; 2 Samuel 7:14.

ii) *The expectation of God as Father from Israel*

He is to be viewed as a trustworthy, protective authority to be respected and obeyed. This aspect can be seen negatively when God complains or grieves that his fatherly care is being scorned, abused or ignored.

> 'A son honours his father and a servant his master. If I am a father, where is the honour due to me? If I am a master, where is the respect due to me?', says the LORD Almighty.
>
> (Mal. 1:6)

Other examples of this include: Deuteronomy 14:1, Isaiah 1:2f., Jeremiah 3:19 and Hosea 1:11f. These show how God felt towards his son and what was expected of his son in return.

At the human level these dimensions are seen clearly in the laws related to parental authority which were unusually strict in Israel because of the vital importance of the stability of the family within the covenant basis of the nation (e.g. Ex. 20:12, 21:15, 17; Deut. 21:18–21, 27:16; Prov. 30:17). At the sociological level the Israelite father in Israel was the head of the household ('head of a father's house' was his technical title in Hebrew). That is, he had domestic, judicial, educational, spiritual and even military authority over a quite sizeable community of people, including his adult sons and their families and all dependent persons – i.e. the extended family. He was, in short, a figure of considerable power, social importance, and protective responsibility. This is illustrated positively in Joab's protection of his adult son, Gideon, in Judges 6, and negatively in Job's lament of what he had lost as a result of the calamity which had deprived him of family and substance, in Job 29–30. It was almost certainly these heads of households who functioned plurally as 'the elders' whom we read of in many Hebrew stories.

The fatherhood of Yahweh was not, then, primarily an emotional metaphor. Rather it was a matter of authority on the one hand and obedience on the other, within the framework of a trusting, providing and protective relationship. Already we can see the matching outline shape of Jesus's personal awareness of God as his Father. For authority, willing obedience and complete trust were the hallmarks of that intimate relationship as he enjoyed and expressed it.

ISRAEL'S SONSHIP AND THE COVENANT

Although the idea of the fatherhood of Yahweh is over-shadowed by the covenant concept in the Hebrew Bible, there is a close link between the two. When you analyse the texts where father-son language is used for God and Israel, they show up an interesting dual aspect which is quite similar to the dual nature of the covenant itself, namely that the relationship between Israel and God was both a fact which God had achieved, and also a demand which Israel must fulfil. The covenant was both a statement and a claim; in technical terms, an indicative and an imperative. As regards sonship, this same dual aspect emerges when we notice the difference between passages where Israel is referred to as 'son' in the singular and those where Israelites are addressed as 'sons' or 'children' in the plural:

i) National level
There are some passages where Israel as a whole is called Yahweh's son, or Yahweh is portrayed as father of the whole nation. These would include: Exodus 4:22; Deuteronomy 32:6, 18; Hosea 11:1; Jeremiah 31:9, Isaiah 63:15–16, 64:8.

The point here is that Israel owes its national existence to the creative or 'procreative' action of Yahweh. Yahweh was father and Israel was his son because he had brought them into existence. It was not by Israel's choice or action or merits that they enjoyed the status of being Yahweh's son. In this respect, Israel's sonship is a *given* which corresponds with the unconditional givenness of Israel's election and the coven-ant. It was entirely a matter of divine initiative. Israel was the 'first-born son of Yahweh' for no other reason than that he had brought them into existence as a nation, just as they were the 'people of Yahweh' for no other reason than that he had 'set his love upon them' and chosen them for himself (Deut. 7:6ff.). Sonship here is very much a matter of privilege.

ii) *The personal level*

There are other passages where Israelites are addressed as sons of Yahweh in the plural. These would include Deuteronomy 14:1, Isaiah 1:2, Jeremiah 3:22, Isaiah 30:9.

Here the focus is on the Israelites' responsibility before Yahweh to show the loyalty and obedience required of sons. Thus Deuteronomy 14:1 argues that the 'sons of Yahweh', a holy God, must themselves be holy. Most of the prophetic passages which use the metaphor are in this plural category, accusing Israelites of failing in their duty as sons to live in ethical obedience to God. In the texts above, for example, they are 'rebellious sons', 'faithless sons', or 'lying sons'. This second aspect of Israel's sonship thus clearly corresponds to the other side of the covenant relationship , namely the imperative demand for obedience – a demand which applied to all individual members of the nation.

So what we find then, is that both poles of the covenant (God's initiative and Israel's obedience) are held together within the same relational metaphor of father and son.

Deuteronomy adds two other ideas to enrich the metaphor still further. First, there is its use of *'inheritance'* language. This is a prominent feature of Deuteronomy. It repeatedly describes the whole land as Israel's inheritance. This is another way of expressing and reinforcing the point that Israel is Yahweh's son, for it is the first-born son who inherits. This inheritance image corresponds precisely with the first aspect of Israel's sonship, namely that it is something unconditional and simply given, for that is exactly what Deuteronomy stresses again and again as regards the gift of the land to Israel.

Secondly there is Deuteronomy's use of *'love'* language. Deuteronomy is very fond of love! It highlights Yahweh's love for Israel (e.g. 7:7ff. and elsewhere). And it was Deuteronomy that Jesus quoted when asked what was the greatest commandment in the law: 'Love the Lord your God with all your heart and with all your soul and with all your strength' (6:5, cf. 10:12.). Now 'love', in Deuteronomy, is a love which can be commanded, and therefore means much more just the emotion or affection that father and son share. It is rather a matter of faithfulness and obedience within the discipline of the father-son relationship. In fact, some scholars have argued that in Deuteronomy filial love is synonymous with covenant obedience. That is, to love God as son to father is the same thing as to obey God and keep the covenant.

Now, when we turn back to the New Testament, we can detect some of these covenantal patterns in the ways it speaks of Jesus as Son of God. We saw in the last chapter that the successive covenants of the Old Testament converge on Jesus as the inaugurator of the New Covenant. In several ways Jesus was aware of being the one who represented Israel. In referring to himself, for example, as 'the true vine' (John 15:1ff.) he was drawing on the Old Testament imagery of Israel as Yahweh's vine or vineyard. In a related image, he described himself as the heir (Mark 12:7)., and the language of inheritance entered into Christian vocabulary to describe aspects of Christian experience through Jesus Christ who is 'heir of all things' (Heb. 1:2).

On the shoulders of Jesus as the Son of God lay the responsibility of being the true son, succeeding where Israel had failed, submitting to God's will where they had rebelled, obeying where they had disobeyed. This was certainly a dimension of his temptations in the wilderness after his baptism, which we shall look at more fully in the next chapter.

The author of Hebrews, who more than any other New Testament writer, glories in the exalted status of Jesus as the unique Son of God, also links his sonship with his suffering and obedience. 'Though he was a son, he learned obedience from what he suffered' (Heb. 5:8). This of course does not mean that Jesus had to be compelled by suffering to be obedient after being otherwise disobedient. It is simply underlining that sonship for Jesus, as for Israel, was tied to obedience and that for him, obedience to his Father's will involved suffering. Perhaps the author of Hebrews had the temptations in mind, or perhaps more particularly the final great spiritual battle of Jesus in Gethsemane. There, as he faced the extremity of what obedience would cost him, he chose finally and fully to submit his own will to that of his Father, as he had done all his life to this point. There, too, we find on his lips the intimate word 'Abba', as he struggled to hold together his lifelong experience of his Father's loving presence and protective care on the one hand, with the immediate prospect of abandonment to death on the cross as the price of obedience on the other (Mark 14:36).

SONSHIP AS THE FOUNDATION FOR HOPE

Jesus, Gethsemane shows us, shrank back from suffering and death, like any other human being. Yet the Gospels also tell us that he went to his death with the confidence of resurrection. Earlier, during his ministry, as soon as his disciples had begun, however dimly, to grasp who he truly was and to articulate it in terms of messiahship, Jesus immediately began to prepare them for his rejection, suffering and death (Matt. 16:21). He seems to have done this repeatedly. But all the Gospel accounts add that he said he would be raised again on the third day. Apparently this made little impression on the disciples in their shock and bewilderment over a suffering messiah, but they remembered after it happened that Jesus had indeed said it. We must not think, of course, that having this confidence concerning his resurrection in any way lessened the horror of the cross for Jesus. Gethsemane itself wipes out any facile idea that the expectation of resurrection somehow neutralized the depths of pain and suffering he endured in bearing the sin of the world. So does the agonized cry of dereliction and abandonment from the cross. However, the question arises, how and why could Jesus have been so sure of his resurrection?

One clue in the Caesarea Philippi passages is that Jesus, while accepting Peter's recognition that he was the *Messiah*, redirected his teaching in terms of the *Son of Man* (Mark 8:31). As we shall see in the next chapter, the Son of Man was a term Jesus used for himself which was derived from Daniel 7. And one marked feature of the imagery in that text is that the Son of Man figure apparently is vindicated and endowed with great glory and authority. Another clue is that Jesus identified himself with the suffering servant figure of Isaiah 40–55. We saw that that was part of the identity he had confirmed for him at his baptism. And again, the servant was a figure who, beyond suffering and death, would see vindication, victory and the positive achievements of his ministry (Isa. 52:12, 53:10–12).

But in my view the strongest reason for Jesus's confidence in the face of death lies in his self-conscious identity as the Son of God. For as such he embodied and represented Israel, the son of God in the scriptures. And the father-son relationship between Yahweh and Israel was a ground for hope and permanence, even when Israel stood among the wreckage of a broken covenant – a covenant, that is, broken by their own disobedience. The sonship relationship was something that survived the greatest disaster.

In the narrative texts, the declaration that Israel was Yahweh's first-born son came *before* the exodus and the making of the Sinai covenant (Ex. 4:22). And in the prophetic texts, the relationship of sonship not only survived even *after* the judgement of exile had fallen on the nation, but could be appealed to as the basis for a fresh act of redemption and a restored relationship. So, in Isaiah 63 and 64, Israel cries to God as their Father in the expectation of his loving care after discipline, and his forgiving, restoring power. As Father, he

will be their champion, defender and redeemer, even if he
has had to exercise parental discipline on them also.

> Yet Yahweh, you are our Father.
> We are the clay, you are the potter;
> We are all the work of your hands. (Isa. 64:8)

> You, Yahweh are our Father,
> Our redeemer from of old is your name. (Isa. 63:16)

The same combination of ideas is found in Jeremiah
31:18–20.

The father-son relationship between God and Israel, therefore, contained within itself an element of permanence which
injected hope into an otherwise hopeless situation amidst the
ruins of the Sinai covenant. Israel's relationship to Yahweh
could continue to be affirmed in spite of alienation from the
land and in spite of the experienced wrath of God. Yahweh
still had a future for his people. He could not abandon them.
The Father could not ultimately disown his son.

If this had been so for Israel as the rebellious son of
Yahweh, then how much more must it be true for the sinless
Son of God himself? If God would not abandon or utterly
destroy his son Israel, whose sufferings were the result of
their own sin and God's judgement upon them, then he would
certainly not abandon the Son whose sufferings were not for
his own sin but for the sin of the world, including Israel itself
(cf. Acts 2:24–8). Jesus went to his death confident in his
Father, because he knew his history (God had always proved
his covenant faithfulness to Israel), and because he knew his
identity (as Son of God he embodied Israel and would therefore prove that faithfulness of God, even in death).

Another small clue to this understanding of Jesus's confidence lies in his prediction of a 'third day' resurrection. The
texts in which he told his disciples that he would be rejected
and put to death add that he would rise again 'on the third

day' (Matt 16:21, Mark 8:31, Luke 9:22). He repeated this detail when explaining the whole event to the disciples after his Emmaus encounter (Luke 24:46). It even entered into the Christian tradition, since Paul summarizes the Gospel as he had received it with the phrases:

> that Christ died for our sins according to the scriptures, that he was buried, that he was was raised on the third day, according to the scriptures.
>
> (1 Cor. 15:3f.).

Now the only scripture which makes any reference to a third day in relation to resurrection is Hosea 6:1f.

> Come, let us return to the LORD.
>   He has torn us to pieces but he will heal us;
>   he has injured us but he will bind up our wounds.
> After two days he will revive us;
>   on the third day he will restore us
>   that we may live in his presence.

The meaning here is is unquestionably national. That is to say, it is the people of Israel who, in the midst of God's judgement, look forward in repentance to him raising them up again. By taking up that detail of the prophecy, Jesus links his own expected resurrection to Israel. In his resurrection lay their restoration. We shall come examine that point in the next chapter. For the moment we recall, from chapter one, that Matthew has already made the connection between Jesus as the Son of God and Hosea's description of Israel as God's son. (Hos. 11:1). The Father who brought his son out of Egypt, in the face of threat and death, would not abandon the same son to the power of death for ever (cf. Acts. 2:24–8). Sonship meant hope and confidence.

ISRAEL'S SONSHIP AND GOD'S UNIVERSAL PURPOSE

This inextinguishable hope that Israel always maintained was based, then, on the unique relationship which they had with God, a relationship pictured on the one hand as a father-son relationship and on the other hand as a covenant which bound them both together. But their hope was also linked to their understanding of their role in the fulfilment of God's great purpose for all the nations and the world. There was a future for Israel because, by God's grace and promise, there was a future for the world.

We saw already, in the first two chapters, that from the start, Israel was aware that its very existence was for the sake of the rest of humanity. This had been explicit in the covenant with Abraham (Gen. 12:3b., 18:18, etc.). It had been recalled in the prelude to Sinai, when Israel was given its identity and mission as God's priesthood in the midst of the whole earth, which belongs to Yahweh (Ex. 19:4–6). God's dealings with Israel, as one missiologist has put it, were simply carrying forward his unfinished business with the nations.

So, when you examine key Old Testament concepts, which in their immediate reference seem to apply only to Israel, you find that they have also got this universal dimension or vision. *Election* obviously meant the choice of Israel, but not to status, rather for servanthood and for the sake of the nations, as Isaiah 40–55 points out. *Covenant*, likewise, indicated God's unique relationship to Israel, but that too was to enable them to be a 'covenant to the nations' and to bring the knowledge of Yahweh's law and justice to the ends of the earth (Isa. 42:4–6, 51:4f.). *The kingship of Yahweh* was acknowledged in Israel, but in the Psalms which celebrate it, it is also clearly universal in an eschatological sense (e.g. Pss. 47:7–9, 96, 98).

It is worth asking, then, whether the idea of Israel as son and Yahweh as Father also had or led to a more universal, eschatological dimension. Because if it did, this would clearly be another important thing to include as we explore what sonship meant for Jesus.

'Israel is my first-born son', declared God (Ex. 4:22, cf. Jer. 31:9). The expression *first-born son* implies the existence or the expectation of other sons. This cannot mean that Yahweh is somehow the father of all other nations or of their gods. The earliest use of Yahweh as Father of Israel in Deuteronomy 32 actually distinguishes between Israel and the rest of the nations on the grounds of Israel's unique relationship to 'the Rock who fathered you'. Nevertheless, the idea of Israel being Yahweh's first-born son certainly envisages the possibility, indeed the definite expectation, that other nations will become sons. But that expectation in turn depended on Israel fulfilling the demands of *its own* sonship – i.e. that they should live in loyalty and obedience to Yahweh. From this point of view, the sonship of Israel can be understood as a 'missionary' concept. If Israel, as Yahweh's first-born son, would live by his standards and obey his laws, then God could pursue his goal of bringing blessing to the nations.

We have seen already that there is in the Old Testament a very strong link between Israel's ethical obedience, especially social righteousness and justice, and God's fulfilment of his promise to Abraham to bless all nations. In Genesis 18:18–20, especially v. 19, we saw that the very purpose of election is that Abraham and his descendants should keep the way of the Lord in righteousness and justice, in order that God would be able to keep his promise – that is, blessing all nations. Ethical obedience stands as the middle term between election and mission. But, as we have seen, ethical obedience was the primary significance of the son-father relationship of Israel to Yahweh.

Jeremiah 3–4 gives us an interesting combination of these ideas. The overall thrust of the passage is an appeal for true repentance, a genuine turning back to God with practical evidence and not mere words. The father-son motif is used several times (as well as Jeremiah's more familiar husband-wife motif). In 3:4 Jeremiah pictures Israel appealing to Yahweh as father to let them off and not be angry any more. But it is clear that it is just superficial talk and not a true ethical repentance. 'This is how you *talk*,' says God, 'but you *do* all the evil you can. (3:5)'

Later we find God himself yearning for a real father-son relationship between himself and Israel, with an inheritance gift from him and obedience from them. There is a real pathos in his words.

> How gladly would I treat you like sons
>   and give you a desirable land,
>   the most beautiful inheritance of any nation.
> I thought you would call me 'Father'
>   and not turn away from following me. (3:19)

Finally, God appeals for a genuine repentance from Israel, and goes on to point out what will happen if they do as he asks.

> If you will return, O Israel, return to me,
>   declares the LORD.
> If you put your detestable idols out of my sight
>   and no longer go astray,
> and if in truth, justice and righteousness, you swear
>   'as the LORD lives'
> *then the nations will be blessed* by him
>   and in him they will glory. (4:1-2)

Here we find a clear allusion to the universal promise of the Abraham covenant, and it is linked to the requirement of ethical obedience on the part of Israel, using three of the 'biggest' ethical words in the OT vocabulary: truth, justice and righteousness. If Israel, as the son of God, would turn back to a quality of living that was true to God's moral desire for them, then the consequences would be wider than just the forgiveness of Israel itself. God would be able to get on with his ultimate purpose of bringing blessing to the nations. Similar thinking lies behind Isaiah 43:6f. and 48:1, 18f.

'If you are the Son of God . . .

Now we can see what an awesome responsibility lay on the shoulders of Jesus as he faced up to the task of being the Son of God. As the representative or embodiment of Israel, he was called to obedience. But what was at stake in that obedience was not merely Jesus's own conscience and his relationship with God his Father – vital though that was. Nor was it even just a matter of proving, in his own person, that Israel could be obedient after all, and thus satisfy the longing of God's heart as expressed in the prophecies above.

More than both of these, the obedience of Jesus as Son of God opened the way for the fulfilment of God's universal purpose for all humanity, the purpose for which he had called Israel his first-born son. His obedient sonship fulfilled the mission which their sonship had prepared for but had failed in disobedience. The saying attributed to David Livingstone, 'God had only one Son and he made him a missionary', has more depths of truth than perhaps the old explorer himself appreciated.

For that reason, because so much was at stake – no less than the salvation of the world – the Devil's onslaught on Jesus's sonship tried so desperately to deflect him from obedience to his Father's will. Aware that Jesus, through his obedience, would win the world for God, the Devil offered him the world in advance if he would sell out to him. But Jesus resisted and set himself deliberately on the path of loyal obedience to his Father, in full awareness that it would lead to suffering and death. There was no other way. But it was the way by which he, the first-born Son, would 'bring many sons to glory'. Very probably it was this combination of Jesus's sonship, obedience, suffering, humanity, temptation and victory which underlies the profound meditation of Hebrews 2:10–18 and 5:8f.

The Apostle Paul was appointed as 'apostle to the Gentiles [the nations]' and thus had a special personal interest in the effect for all nations of what God had done through his Son. At the beginning of his letter to the Romans he summarizes the Gospel in an interesting way which combines the human and divine sonship of Jesus with the opening up of salvation to all the nations.

> ... the gospel he promised beforehand through his prophets in the holy scriptures regarding his Son, who as to his human nature was a descendant of David, and who through the Spirit of holiness was declared with power to be the Son of God by his resurrection from the dead: Jesus Christ our Lord. Through him and for his name's sake, we received grace and apostleship to call people from among all the nations to the obedience that comes from faith.
>
> (Rom. 1:2–5)

Later on, when he is exploring the mystery of how it is that current rejection of Jesus by most (but not all) Jews had led to the ingathering of the non-Jewish believers, he picks up a prophecy of Hosea which talked about the sons of God (one of Hosea's favourite metaphors, as we have already seen):

> Yet the Israelites will be like the sand on the sea shore,
>   which cannot be measured or counted.
> In the place where it was said to them ' you are not my people'
>   they will be called 'sons of the living God'.
>
> (Hos. 1:10)

Now, Hosea was talking about the restoration of Israel after judgement and envisaged it in the language of the father-son relationship. But in the first part of the verse he alludes to the Abraham promise of the expansion of Israel into a great nation beyond the possibility of numbering (Gen. 13:16, 15:5). This reference to Abraham, as we have seen so often already, 'opens up' the prophecy to a wider future scope than the restoration of Israel alone. It breathes in the air of God's universal promise of blessing.

So although Hosea undoubtedly had *Israel* alone in mind, Paul, when he quotes the verse in Romans 9:26, picks out the wider implication and applies it to the fruit of his own missionary work. It is the *Gentiles* who are now becoming 'sons of the living God' through their believing response to Jesus. The expression 'not my people' had originally, in Hosea's prophecy, been a term of judgement on Israel. But Paul uses it here to describe those who had previously had no share in the blessings of Israel – i.e. the Gentiles. It is *they* who have now been called to belong to the people of God and *they* who thereby enter into a relationship of sonship to God as Father. Paul has taken the Old Testament terminology for Israel as God's people and God's son and transposed it into his own missionary vocabulary in order to explain what was going on as a result of his own evangelistic work.

What he says here in Romans is the theological expansion of what he had much earlier written to the Galatians – a church of Gentile believers. First of all he emphasizes that through the Messiah, Jesus, they are one with the Jews in relation to God – using the language of sonship.

> *You are all sons of God* through faith in Christ Jesus, for all of you who were baptized into Christ have clothed yourselves with Christ. There is neither Jew nor Greek, slave nor free, male nor female, for you are all one in Christ Jesus. If you belong to Christ,

then you are Abraham's seed and heirs according to the promise.

Then he goes on to show how this has come about through the work of God's own Son.

When the time had fully come, God sent his Son, born of a woman, born under law, to redeem those under the law, that we might receive the full rights of sons. Because you are sons, God sent the Spirit of his Son into our hearts, the Spirit who calls out *Abba*, Father. So you are no longer a slave, but a son; and since you are a son, God has made you also an heir.

(Gal. 3:26–9, 4:4–7)

We have come a long way from our starting point, the baptism of Jesus, and have already begun to jump ahead to the missionary theology of Paul and the early church. I hope it is clear from what has been said so far that this missionary theology was based on the identity of Jesus and that in turn was based on a deep understanding of the Hebrew scriptures. In the next chapter we shall look at Jesus's own sense of mission and how it both derived from his Hebrew scriptures on the one hand and shaped the mission of the New Testament church on the other.

What we have seen in this chapter is that the Old Testament provided the models, pictures and patterns by which Jesus understood his own essential identity and especially gave depth and colour to his primary self-awareness as the Son of his Father God.

CHAPTER FOUR

Jesus and his Old Testament Mission

'God sent his Son . . .' (Gal. 3:26)

One thing that is very clear about Jesus is that he knew he had been sent. He was no self-appointed saviour, no popularly elected leader. He had not just arrived. He was sent. This awareness of a purpose and a mission seems to have developed alongside his consciousness of being the Son of his Father, even from a young age, as Luke tells us (Luke 2:49). But it became crystal clear, as we have seen, at his baptism. It was knowledge of what his mission would entail that led to the struggle in the wilderness. No sooner, however, had he returned from that costly victory over the testings of Satan, than he declared the manifesto of his programme in the Nazareth synagogue with a word from the prophets, 'The Lord has anointed (commissioned) me . . .' From then on his driving purpose startled his friends and enemies alike. Nothing could stand in the way of what he was conscious of having been sent to do. To do his Father's will was his very meat and drink (John 4.34). What then was his mission? What did Jesus himself believe he was sent to achieve? What were his personal aims and objectives? What did he think he was doing?

Much scholarly ink has been used up answering these questions! There are two ways of approaching the problem. One way is to look at the kind of expectations that surrounded Jesus in the Jewish society of his day. If the Messiah were to come, what did people think would happen? Of course, as the Gospels make plain, Jesus did not fit all these expectations precisely. Nevertheless, he was as much aware of them as any of his contemporary Jews would have been. And in so far as they had scriptural roots, he must have been deeply influenced by them and would have sought to interpret his own ministry and mission in relation to them. The other way is to look at the sayings and the actions of Jesus himself to see how he portrayed his own identity and mission. Here again we will find that it is Jesus's creative and original way of handling his Hebrew scriptures that gives us the clearest clues to his mission. These two ways of approach, of course, interlock and overlap in many ways. But we shall take each in turn and see how they reinforce what we have been discovering already.

Jewish expectations at the time of Jesus

The sources for knowing what Jewish expectations were at the time of Jesus are found in what is known as the intertestamental literature. This includes a great variety of materials, poetic, narrative, apocalyptic, etc., from the centuries that lie between the end of the Old Testament era and the emergence of the Christian church. These writings come from many different ages and sources and are not at all homogeneous. But they are of very great importance in understanding the world of Jesus and the first disciples and therefore as background to the New Testament. Great amounts of scholarship, both Jewish and Christian, have been devoted to studying this literature.

By the time of Jesus the strongest strand of expectation, widely evident in these writings, was a looking forward with desperate hope to the restoration of Israel. God would intervene in world affairs to vindicate his people, liberate them from their oppressors and restore them to their rightful place as his redeemed people. They used the language of exile to describe their current situation. Even though the Jews had come back to their land after the Babylonian exile in the sixth century BC, many believed that in a sense the exile had not ended as long as they were still an oppressed people in their own land. In fact, Rome was regarded as the new Babylon and Babylon was used as a code name for Rome among resistance movements. So the hopes of restoration, originally expressed by the prophets in terms of return to the land, were re-applied to the hope of ultimate freedom from their enemies. This hope was sometimes based on God's direct action; sometimes linked with the arrival of the messiah – though that was not a clearly or unanimously defined figure; sometimes linked to the expectation of a new Jerusalem and/or a new temple. Whatever the accompanying details, the core of the hope was clear – Israel would be restored.

Alongside this central expectation was the belief that after, or as part of, the restoration of Israel there would be an ingathering of the nations to become part of the people of God with Israel. The fate of the nations has an ambiguity about it in Jewish expectations. On the one hand there were many predictions that they would be judged and destroyed as the enemies of God and his people. Yet on the other hand, there was the belief that the judgement of the nations, like the judgement of Israel itself, would be a purging judgement after which salvation would be extended to the nations as they would be gathered in to the future people of God.

Both these aspects of Jewish expectation at the time of Jesus – the restoration of Israel and the ingathering of the nations – had deep roots, of course, in the Old Testament itself. As regards Israel, even the prophets with the sternest words of judgement on Israel held out the hope of restoration beyond that judgement. And from the exile onwards, that hope grew stronger and clearer. It can be seen in Jeremiah's

'Book of Consolation' (Jer. 30–34), in Ezekiel's vision of the new land and temple (Ezek. 40–48), in the soaring vistas of new creation and redemption in Isaiah 40–55. And as regards the nations, we saw in chapter one that God's purpose for them was ultimately inclusion within his restored people. The coming of the king to Jerusalem would mean peace and universal rule for the nations (Zech. 9:9ff.). When God would act to restore Zion and reveal his glory, then the nations would also gather to worship him.

> You will arise and have compassion on Zion
>> for it is time to show favour to her;
>> the appointed time has come.
> For her stones are dear to your servants;
>> her very dust moves them to pity.
> The nations will fear the name of the LORD,
>> all the kings of the earth will revere your glory.
> For the LORD will rebuild Zion
>> and appear in his glory.
> He will respond to the prayer of the destitute;
>> he will not despise their plea.
> Let this be written for a future generation,
>> that a people not yet created may praise the LORD
> The LORD looked down from his sanctuary on high
>> from heaven he viewed the earth,
> to hear the groans of the prisoners
>> and release those condemned to death.
> So the name of the LORD will be declared in Zion
>> and his praise in Jerusalem
> when the peoples and the kingdoms
>> assemble to worship the LORD.
>> (Ps. 102:13–22. cf. also Isa. 49:5f., 56:1–8, 60:10–14, 66:18–24)

Old Testament prophecies concerning the future of Israel, then, are interwoven with prophecies about the future of the nations also. There is even a comparable 'ambiguity' of judgement and hope. Israel is to be sifted in judgement virtually to extinction; yet Israel will be redeemed and restored. (e.g. Isa. 26:9, Amos 9, Mic. 2 and 3, Isa. 35, Jer. 16, 25:15ff., 30–33.) Likewise, the nations are to be judged and destroyed as enemies of God; yet the nations are to be gathered in to share in the salvation and inheritance of the people of God (e.g. Isa. 24, 34, Mic. 4, Joel 3). In Zephaniah, the punishment of the nations is set parallel to the judgement on Jerusalem, and so, in chapter 3, the restoration of Jerusalem (vv. 14ff.) has universal overtones for the nations (v. 9). In other words, the dividing line between judgement and salvation is not a line that runs simply *between* the nations and Israel, but *through* both of them. Just as there will be a 'remnant of Israel', so there will be 'survivors of the nations' (Isa. 45:20ff., 66:19ff., Zech. 14:16ff.). And the Old Testament sees *both together* (the purified and believing, obedient remnant of Israel along with those of the nations who respond to the appeal to identify with Yahweh and his people) as the eschatological future people of God.

So Jewish hopes at the time of Jesus, then, focused primarily on the restoration of Israel, with the closely attached implications for the nations. The restoration of Israel and the ingathering of the nations were seen in eschatological terms as the final great act of God, the Day of the Lord. The two things would be part of the same final event that would usher in the new age, but the restoration of Israel was logically and in a sense chronologically expected first.

John the Baptist

Into this charged atmosphere of eschatological hopes, 'there was a man sent from God whose name was John'. It is indeed this framework of restoration hope which New Testament scholars use as the context for understanding the ministry and message of John the Baptist. As the records of his preaching show, he regarded his mission as one of winnowing and sifting the nation by his call to repentance so that they would be prepared for the coming purging and restoration. He consciously stood on the threshold of the fulfilment of Israel's hope. But not every child of Abraham by birth would enter into it. Only those who produced the 'fruit of repentance' in radically changed lives (Luke 3:8ff.) would escape the purging judgement and belong to the renewed people of God. His mission was to identify, through his call for repentance and baptism, the remnant of Israel who, by responding, were destined for cleansing and restoration as the true, eschatological people of God. His ministry would thus prepare the ground for the imminent intervention and arrival of God himself, as the quotations from Malachi 3:1 and Isaiah 40:3 make clear (Mark 1:2f.). That, indeed, was how his life's work was summed up in advance by the angel who announced his conception to his astonished father:

Many of the people of Israel will he bring back to the Lord their God. And he will go on before the Lord in the spirit and power of Elijah, to turn the hearts of the fathers to their children and the disobedient to the wisdom of the righteous – to make ready a people prepared for the Lord.

(Luke 1:16f.)

And the Lord, when he came, submitted himself to be baptized by John!

So we come back once again to our starting point in the last chapter. But now we can see it from a different perspective. We can see how Jesus, by accepting John's baptism, accepted and agreed with his message and recognized his significance for the fulfilment of the hope of Israel. Jesus queued up with the crowds of those coming to the Jordan. With no need of personal repentance or cleansing, he nevertheless identified himself with those who wanted to express their longing to be right with God, obedient to his will, and to see the coming of his Kingdom. He joined those who were longing for the restoration of Israel, for that was *his* hope too. Indeed, it was his personal mission.

All the Gospels begin their accounts of Jesus's ministry with his baptism by John. It was also a key point in the apostolic preaching about Jesus among Jews in the book of Acts. Scholars who have researched the aims of Jesus regard this as a vital piece of evidence. The fact that Jesus accepted and endorsed the ministry of John the Baptist and launched his own ministry from it (there were differences, of course, as observers noted at the time, but there was considerable overlap and continuity), shows that Jesus also saw his own mission in terms of the fulfilment of the great expectations of the restoration of Israel. If John was the one who had been sent to *prepare* Israel for its eschatological restoration by God himself, then Jesus was the one who had been sent to *accomplish* it.

The Messiah

We need to look again at the baptismal voice and the identity it conferred on Jesus. We saw that the first part of what the voice from heaven said identified Jesus as the Son of God in the sense of the Davidic king, whose rule was celebrated in Psalm 2. And we have noted that that Psalm was already interpreted messianically in the time of Jesus. Among the many varied ideas about who or what the messiah would be and do, it was popularly agreed that he would be the son of David. So much so, that Jesus could use that belief as the basis for a characteristic piece of brain-teasing which challenged people to think through the consequences of their beliefs in the light of scripture (Matt. 22:41–6).

Jesus and his Old Testament Mission

We are so used to calling Jesus 'Christ' (which is simply the Greek form of the Hebrew 'messiah') that it comes as something of a shock to realize that the word itself as a title is actually hardly ever found in the Old Testament. It is in fact ironic that we talk so much about 'messianic' ideas and hopes when not only is it not common in the Old Testament, but Jesus himself rarely used the word, told others not to use it, and preferred other titles. What can account for this?

The title, messiah, (*mashia*, in Hebrew), occurs in Daniel 9:25–6. It is part of Daniel's visionary prophecy of the long term future for his people. An 'anointed one' will come and will bring a climax to God's purpose, which is summed up in the words, 'to finish transgression, to put an end to sin, to atone for wickedness, to bring in everlasting righteousness, to seal up vision and prophecy and to anoint the most holy [place, or person]'. The idea of fulfilment and completion is very strong.

Before this, the word is not used in a predictive sense in the Old Testament. That is, there are no texts specifically predicting a future 'messiah' in so many words. But the idea of *anointing* certain people for specific tasks was common enough in Israel. To anoint someone with oil was symbolic of setting them apart for a particular role or duty with appropriate authorization for it. Priests were anointed with a very special sacred oil. Kings were anointed at their accession (or beforehand in some cases, as for example David himself as a lad). Prophets were also regarded as anointed ones, which may have been literal in some cases, or perhaps metaphorical. The basic idea was that the anointed person was set aside and equipped by God and for God, so that what he or she did was in God's name, with the help of God's Spirit, under God's protection and with God's authority.

A most interesting use of the word 'anointed one', which is not predictive but historical, occurs in Isaiah 45:1. There, to everyone's surprise, God himself uses it to describe the pagan king Cyrus, the newly rising star of the Persian empire.

This is what the Lord says to *his anointed*,
to Cyrus, whose right hand I take hold of . . .

Now Cyrus was not an Israelite, certainly not a king in the line of David. Nor was he 'The Messiah' in the later technical sense of the term. But God's description of him as 'his messiah' at this point in history tells us a lot about what the term meant at the time. And that in turn sheds light on what it later meant when applied to the expected 'coming one'.

First of all it was God who chose Cyrus and raised him up for the appointed task (41:2ff, 25). Secondly, therefore, Cyrus's accomplishments were really God's, for it was God who was acting through him as his agent (44:28, 45:1–5). Thirdly, Cyrus's specific task was the redemption and restoration of Israel from the hands of their enemies (44:28, 45:13) so that fourthly, all his worldwide victories and dominion actually were for the purpose of delivering and establishing the people of God (41:2–4, 45:1–4). And fifthly, beyond that Israelite context, his work would ultimately be a step on the way to the extension of God's salvation to the ends of the earth (45:21–5).

All of these were features in the developing messianic concept in post-Old Testament times, particularly as associated with the expectation of a coming son of David. The messiah would be God's agent to deliver and restore Israel, not a pagan king this time, but a true Israelite, the true son of David.

Why, then, did Jesus soft-pedal the idea? Not because he rejected it. His own Father's voice had confirmed his identity as the messianic son of David. He claimed, from his earliest preaching, to be anointed by the Spirit of God (Luke 4:18ff., quoting Isa. 61). He accepted Peter's half-understood confession of faith at Caesarea Philippi. He identified himself as such to the woman by the well in Samaria (John 4:25f.). And when challenged on the point in his trial he did not deny that he was the Messiah but went on to add further definition to it (Mark 14:61f.). Nevertheless it is striking that on several occasions when those he had healed or blessed in some way acknowledged that he was the Messiah, he urged them not to spread the rumour around – which most of them promptly did, of course, such is human nature. And it is equally striking that scholars who have studied Jesus's use of the 'messianic' scriptures most closely observe that, of all the figures and titles in the Old Testament relating to the coming eschatological deliverer of Israel, the one that Jesus used *least* was that of the Davidic, kingly, Messiah. Indeed, although it was used *about* him, he never used it of himself in his teaching.

So why this reticence? The most probable reason is that the term had become so loaded with the hopes of a national, political and even military, Jewish restoration that it could not carry the understanding of his messiahship which Jesus had derived from a deeper reading of his scriptures. A public proclamation of his own messiahship would have been 'heard' by his contemporaries with a load of associations that were not part of Jesus's concept of his mission.

Jesu' lived in the midst of a highly charged political atmosphere. In spite of the return from Babylon centuries before, the Jews had never known real freedom and sovereignty – apart from a relatively short period after the successful Maccabean revolt. Under the Persians, and then the Greeks and now the Romans, they were still in a kind of exile, even in their own land. The longings for national freedom, the murmurs of revolt and the apocalyptic, messianic hopes all bubbled close to the surface of national life. There were others who claimed to be messiahs before and after Jesus and ended up as tragic failed heroes. And it would unquestionably have been within that potent mixture of hopes and angry aspirations that any messianic claims (by Jesus or anyone else) would have been interpreted and evaluated. If Jesus really were the Messiah, then his Jewish contemporaries knew exactly what *they* expected of him. The trouble was that what *they* expected and what Jesus intended did not match. He had no intention of being a conquering king, militarily or politically. Which is not to say that he was not a king or indeed not a conqueror, but of a very different sort from popular hopes.

Now at this point we need to be very careful to understand what is *not* being said here. It is *not* being said that Jesus disassociated himself from Jewish hopes of restoration. We have seen that the whole thrust of both Old Testament and post-Old Testament expectation was that God would act to restore Israel. If Jesus had tried to buy out of that he would never have gone to the Jordan for baptism in the first place and he would have found no followers of his own either. We shall see shortly other features of his teaching and actions which clearly show that he believed passionately in the scriptural promises of the restoration of Israel and his own part in it. No, the difference between Jesus and his contemporaries was not *that* Israel must be restored, but *how* it would happen and what it would mean.

Nor is it being said that because Jesus did not initiate a socio-political movement or revolt he therefore had no interest in politics or that his message had no political implications. In the next chapter we shall look more fully at the ethical teaching of Jesus and take note of its political dimensions. But for the present it will be enough to say that if Jesus had intended only to talk about a purely spiritual revival in an otherworldly framework with no relevance to the seething politics of his day then he went about it in a very strange way. So many of his words and actions were so challenging to the political authorities that they executed him as a political threat. He did not, of course, advocate violent revolution against Rome. But to argue that because he did not preach violent politics he was therefore uninterested in politics at all is absurd. Non-violent is not simply non-political – now or then. No, the difference between Jesus and his contemporaries was not that he was purely spiritual while they were political (a modern kind of dichotomy which would probably not have made much sense in Jesus's world anyway). The problem was that his announcement of the arrival of the kingdom of God in the present had political and national consequences for the old order of Jewish society that were too radical and final for its leaders to tolerate.

The Messiah came to usher in the new age. But the new age meant the death of the old age. He came to achieve the restoration of Israel. But that could only come about after the fires of judgement and purging. As Jesus looked at his own society, he saw it heading for that terrifying judgement. So much of his preaching has that urgent note of warning and impending disaster. Like John he saw a 'wrath to come': the wrath of Rome as well as the wrath of God. But the deeper awareness of his own messiahship lay in this, that he believed himself called to take Israel's judgement on himself at another level. For the Messiah was a representative figure. He *was* Israel. Their destiny was therefore his, and his theirs. Yes, at one level, national and political Israel was heading for destruction. But at another level Israel, in the Messiah, would suffer judgement and then the restoration that *God*, not the politicians or the guerillas, planned.

That was why as soon as the disciples came to accept that Jesus was the Messiah he immediately began to teach them of his impending violent death and third day resurrection. That was how the Messiah they now haltingly recognized intended to accomplish the restoration they expected of him. It is not really surprising that they could not grasp his meaning until after the events of the cross and resurrection. Even then, it took a seven mile walk from Jerusalem to Emmaus to spell out to two of them what it all meant. Like everybody else in Palestine (except, presumably the Romans), they were hoping for the redemption of Israel. In Jesus they thought they had the answer to their dreams. Jesus told them that actually they had indeed got the answer – in him, the Messiah. But, just as Israel's restoration lay the other side of judgement, so, in his person, 'it was necessary for the Messiah to suffer *and then* enter his glory' (Luke 24). The Messiah's resurrection was Israel's redemption. God had done for Jesus the Messiah what they were expecting him to do for Israel. But in Jesus *as* the Messiah, he had at a deeper level actually done it for Israel. The new age had dawned.

So it is not surprising either, therefore, that whereas during his earthly ministry Jesus had muted his messiahship because of misunderstanding among even those who believed in it, *after* the resurrection the disciples went about enthusiastically proclaiming that Jesus was truly the Messiah, with a new understanding of what that meant. An understanding that was exciting, surprising, joyful – but still just as threatening to the Jewish establishment, as the early chapters of Acts show.

The Son of Man

Jesus, then, saw his messiahship in terms of taking on himself the identity and destiny of Israel. This is confirmed by his favourite term for himself, 'the Son of Man'. If Jesus was reticent about using the name of Messiah, then the reverse was true of this expression. He sprinkled it so freely into his conversations and teachings that people enquired in genuine puzzlement, 'Who is this Son of Man?' (John 12:34). Scholars have filled libraries asking and answering the same question!

In fact it was not really a title at all. In the Hebrew Bible it is an expression (*ben-'adam*) used frequently as a poetic alternative to the word 'man' in the general sense (e.g. Pss. 8:4, 80:17, Isa. 51:12 etc.). It simply means 'a human being', with an emphasis on human weakness and mortality often implied. In Ezekiel it is used ninety-three times as a way of addressing the prophet. It may be to suggest humility before the glory of God, or it may be in some sense a representative term – he as the individual prophet representing his people as a whole.

In the Galilean Aramaic that Jesus spoke, the equivalent expression (*bar nash*, or *bar nasha'*) had a similar sort of meaning and could also be used as a way of speaking of oneself, rather like the English use of 'one' instead of 'I' or 'me'. It probably had a self-effacing tone as an alternative for 'I'. Thus Matthew quite often changes the phrase 'Son of Man' in a passage in Mark into 'I' or 'he' in his own Gospel when referring to Jesus.

Most scholars are agreed that the 'Son of Man' was not a messianic title or figure in the inter-testamental Jewish writings. That is, the people of Jesus's day, whatever else they were hoping for in the way of a messiah, were not on the lookout for a 'Son of Man'. This meant that by using it of himself Jesus could avoid the package of misunderstandings surrounding other familiar messianic titles, and instead fill this term with meaning that was based on his own true perception of who he was and what he had come for.

On the other hand, because it did not have a pre-fixed meaning, people got confused! They asked Jesus about the Christ and he answered about the Son of Man! As we have seen, it was really only after the cross and resurrection that his messiahship could be fully understood. From then on, Jesus as the *Christ* and as the *Son of God* dominated the preaching of the church and the term Son of Man was scarcely heard again. In fact in the whole New Testament it is found almost exclusively on the lips of Jesus alone, the only exceptions being Stephen's vision on the point of his martyrdom (which echoes Jesus, Acts 7:56), Hebrews 2:6 (which quotes

Ps. 8:4), and Revelation 1:13, 14:14 (which are allusions to Daniel 7:13).

So what meaning then did Jesus fill into this unusual self-designation? Scholars have studied the sayings in which it occurs in great depth. There are plenty of them – 30 in Matthew, 14 in Mark, 25 in Luke, and 13 in John! There is general agreement that, apart from some distinctive uses in John, the Son of Man sayings fall into three broad categories. First there are those where Jesus uses it when he is talking about his then present, earthly ministry. These sayings tend to speak of his authority, over sin, or sickness or even nature (e.g. Mark 2:10, 28). Secondly, there is a larger group of Son of Man sayings, which speak of the Son of Man suffering rejection, dying and rising again, which significantly come after the disciples begin to recognize Jesus as Messiah (e.g. Mark 8:31, 9:31, Luke 9:44, etc.). And thirdly, the largest group of all, there are sayings which talk about the Son of Man coming in eschatological glory, sometimes with the clouds (which represent deity), sometimes to act as judge on God's behalf (e.g. Mark 14:62, Matt. 13:41f., 19:28 etc.).

Taken together, these three categories are remarkably comprehensive as a way of encapsulating how Jesus saw his own identity as well as how he envisaged his immediate and more long term destiny. He was the one, firstly, entrusted with authority in his ministry, which he exercised over sin, disease, death, nature and even such fundamental ordinances of the Law as the sabbath. It was a startling and unique authority which raised eyebrows, questions and hackles all around him. But as he exercised that 'unauthorized authority', it led him into conflict with the existing authorities. That conflict eventually engineered his rejection and death. We have already seen how he understood the mission of the Messiah in terms of suffering and also, in the last chapter, how he recognized that suffering would be the price of his obedience as the Son of

God. However, beyond suffering and death lay the vindication of resurrection and the exercise of heavenly authority.

Where did he get all this? (another question he himself had to cope with!). There is no doubt that the third of the categories above, the idea of future vindication and glory, is dependent on the description of 'one like a son of man' in Daniel 7, and many scholars would argue that it was the Danielic figure that substantially lay behind Jesus's choice of the Son of Man as a self-designation.

In Daniel 7, Daniel sees the kingdoms of this earth, portrayed as ravaging beasts from the sea, given the freedom to oppress and harass the people of God. The people of God, described as 'the saints of the Most High', are attacked and devoured almost to the point of extinction. But then the visionary scene changes dramatically in verse 9. Instead of a picture of human history at ground level, we are transported into the presence of God ('the Ancient of Days') seated on his throne. There, through the presence of a human figure described as 'one like a son of man', the tables are turned. This son of man comes into the presence of the Ancient of Days, the beasts are stripped of authority and destroyed, and dominion, kingdom and authority are given to the son of man and the saints for ever.

This 'son of man' figure in Daniel 7 has a curiously double point of reference. On the one hand, he appears to represent the saints – that is, the human people of God in history. The parallellism between verse 14 (where authority and kingdom are given to the son of man) and verse 18 (where the kingdom is given to the saints) shows this. The son of man, in the vision, represents or symbolizes the saints. It has been suggested that he may be an angelic figure, since in Daniel, nations can be represented in the spiritual domain by angels (e.g. 10:13, 20f.). Or perhaps he is simply a kind of corporate, representative human figure, embodying, in the vision, the people of God as a whole. From this point of view, the figure fitted in very well with Jesus's identification of himself with Israel. As the Son of Man he represented them. He shared their experience. His destiny was theirs and vice versa.

But on the other hand the son of man in Daniel 7 is closely associated with God himself. Daniel sees him 'coming with the clouds of heaven' (v.13). That was very much part of the 'ambience' of deity in the Old Testament. Furthermore, he is given authority, glory, power and worship and his kingdom is eternal (v. 14) – all rather more than the normal lot of any son of Adam. In fact, there are Greek versions of the text which translate Daniel 7:13 in such a way as to *identify* the son of man with the Ancient of Days. And this tradition finds a strong echo in Revelation, where the description of Jesus in glory is a combination of the reference to the son of man and a virtual direct quotation of the description of the Ancient of Days in Daniel 7:9f. (Rev. 1:7, 12–16). The two descriptions are conflated into one picture.

So there was an air of divinity about the son of man figure also. Indeed, it may have been this aspect of the Danielic figure which clinched the verdict against Jesus on the grounds of blasphemy at his trial. When asked whether he was the Messiah, Jesus did not deny it, but went on to claim that his accusers would see the Son of Man in divine glory 'coming on the clouds of heaven' – i.e. in the presence of God (Matt. 26:63f.). The shift from Messiah to Son of Man must be deliberate and the description is clearly Danielic.

Even if this saying of Jesus in the context of his trial was not heard as a claim to divine status, it was still a horrendously conflictual affirmation to make. By casting himself in the role of the Son of Man in the sense of Daniel 7, Jesus was claiming to represent the true people of God, the saints of the Most High. But he was standing in the presence of the High Priest, Caiaphas, who occupied that role. He was before the Sanhedrin, the representative court of Israel, in Jerusalem its holy city, near the Temple its most holy place. And in.the midst of all these people and places, dripping with holiness and the very essence of Israel, Jesus calmly claims to be the Son of Man in full Danielic symbolism, the one whom God will vindicate and entrust with supreme authority. He was claiming to inaugurate the salvation and restoration of the people of God, to be the one who would be presented on their behalf to the Ancient of Days. He was the one who would receive eternal dominion and authority to act in judgement (an impression strengthened by the other Old Testament echo in what Jesus said, namely Psalm 110:1).

Strong stuff from one who had just been arrested at dead of night and was himself on trial for his life. But there was worse. For in Daniel 7 the enemies of the son of man/saints of God were the beasts. Who then were these enemies of Jesus? As so often, Jesus did not need to spell out the implications of what he said to the Jewish authorities. His meaning and its implied threat were clear and quite intolerable. Chief Priest or Chief Beast? No wonder Caiaphas tore his robes, cried blasphemy, called for the death penalty, and permitted the spitting and beating. The claims of Jesus were enough to burst blood vessels as well as old wineskins.

The Servant of the Lord

To find Jesus talking about himself as the Son of Man at the very start of his passion is in one sense to be expected by any attentive reader of the Gospels. Ever since Caesarea Philippi he had repeatedly emphasized that 'The Son of Man must suffer many things and be killed'. Yet in another sense this whole emphasis on the suffering of the Son of Man is strange because it is not clearly part of the picture of the son of man in Daniel 7. Some would say that suffering is no part of the Danielic son of man at all. Others would say that it is only there by implication, inasmuch as he is a representative figure of the saints who certainly do suffer all the ravages of the beasts. Yet Jesus, who used this expression for himself more than any other, linked it repeatedly to his expectation of suffering, rejection and death. Why did he do so?

The answer is that Jesus drew on another figure from his Hebrew Bible and that was the Servant of the Lord. We saw in the last chapter that the baptismal voice, by alluding to Isaiah 42:1, identified Jesus as the Servant. The figure of the suffering servant in the book of Isaiah was understood messianically in Jesus's day. But it was not explicitly connected or identified with the Son of Man. It seems that it was Jesus himself who brought the two together. That is, he called himself the Son of Man, which pointed in a Danielic sense to future vindication and authority, but he insisted that the Son of Man 'must suffer' and he portrayed his coming death as fulfilling a mission which has its roots in the description of the Servant in Isaiah.

These two ideas, suffering and servanthood, come together in a key saying of Jesus, Mark 10:45.

> For even the Son of Man did not come to be served,
> but to serve, and to give his life as a ransom for many.

The saying comes as the climax of a lesson on servanthood which Jesus gave to his disciples in the wake of the request of James and John for privileged positions in Jesus's kingdom. To reinforce his point, he uses his own example of voluntary servanthood, proved through his self-sacrificial coming death. It is the last phrase which lifts the saying from talking about serving in general to showing clearly that Jesus had in mind the very special ministry of the Servant of the Lord. For it is clear from Isaiah 53 that the Servant would not only suffer, but he would die – or rather be brutally killed – and his death would be as a sacrifice for the sin of many (Isa. 53:10f.).

Later on Jesus makes an even clearer reference to Isaiah 53, in Luke 22:37. On the night of his arrest, Jesus warns the disciples of dangers ahead. (Incidentally, in my view the reference to buying a sword was probably proverbial rather than literal. There was scarcely time or opportunity in the middle of the night for selling shirts and buying swords. Jesus was warning his disciples what to expect, not telling them to fight, since he later prevented them from doing so. As so often, they misunderstood him, v. 36.) They were all going to face danger because Jesus was about to be treated like a criminal, for, he says,

> It is written, 'And he was numbered with the trans-gressors' (Isa. 53:12), and I tell you that this must be fulfilled in me. Yes, what is written about me is reaching fulfilment.

The emphatic repetition about fulfilment shows that this was not just a casual quotation for effect. Jesus here claims to be the one that Isaiah 53 was written about, the Servant of the Lord.

In fact, finding words from Isaiah 53 on the lips of Jesus as he and his disciples were leaving for the Mount of Olives is not surprising, because the chapter seems to have been much on his mind that night. Just a little while earlier, with them arguing again about their competing claims for greatness (what a situation, to be obsessed with *that* question!), Jesus had had to repeat his lesson on servanthood, with the words, 'I am among you as *the* one who serves' (Luke 22:27). And at the most solemn moment of all, at the end of the passover meal, he took the fourth cup of blessing with the words,

> This cup is the new covenant in my blood (1 Cor. 11:25), which is poured out for you (Luke 22:20); for many (Mark 14:24); for the forgiveness of sins.
>
> (Matt 26:28)

Scholars argue over the precise reconstruction of the exact words of Jesus at that moment, but the essence is clearly that

Jesus referred to the shedding of his own blood as a covenantal act and that it was for the benefit of others.

Several Old Testament passages seem to be combined in his meaning. The blood of covenant recalls Exodus 24, where sacrificial blood sealed the covenant between God and Israel at Mount Sinai. But the 'new covenant' recalls Jeremiah 31:31–4 which, as we saw in chapter two, was promised by God for his people and included complete forgiveness of sin. Then again, the expressions 'poured out' and 'for many' recall Isaiah 53:12 and the work of the Servant in his death. And finally, the Servant was told by God, in Isaiah 42:6 and 49:8, that he would be 'a covenant for the nations'.

It may well be that the reason for the variations in the different accounts of the words of Jesus on this solemn occasion of the last supper is simply that Jesus did not just speak one sentence and move on, as if he were reciting a liturgy at a church service. He had in fact interrupted the Passover liturgy with his own startling declaration, and he quite probably explained his words from different scriptures to make sure his disciples didn't miss his full meaning this time.

So there are good grounds for believing that Jesus saw himself as the Servant figure and interpreted his mission and especially his suffering and death in terms of Isaiah 53. Certainly the early church made this identification and it seems much more likely that they got the idea from Jesus than that they invented it themselves. One of the earliest terms for referring to Jesus among his followers in the book of Acts was 'God's holy servant' (Acts 3:13, 26, 4:27, 30). Peter, one of those who shared most closely in the private thoughts of Jesus, found his own mind turning to Isaiah 53 also when reflecting on how Jesus set an example of suffering without retaliation (1 Pet. 1:21–5). Matthew links Jesus with the Servant very clearly, not just in his record of the baptismal voice with its allusion to Isaiah 42:1, but by his full-length quotation of Isaiah 42:1–4 (Matt. 12:15–21), and of Isaiah 53:4 (Matt. 8:17). Both of these are in the context of Jesus's healing ministry.

If Jesus's mind was absorbed with Isaiah 53 in relation to his coming suffering and death, it seems that he thought of his prior ministry of teaching and healing in terms drawn from the other servant songs and related passages in Isaiah. In his famous 'sermon' at Nazareth right at the beginning of his public ministry, he read from Isaiah 61:1–2 and applied the words to himself as now fulfilled.

> The Spirit of the LORD is on me, because he has anointed me
> > to preach good news to the poor.
> He has sent me to proclaim freedom for the prisoners
> > and recovery of sight for the blind,
> to release the oppressed,
> > to proclaim the year of the LORD's favour.

The passage has many similarities with the mission of the Servant as described in Isaiah 42:7. Later, when answering the disciples of John, he points to the visible effects of his healing and preaching ministry in words that echo both Isaiah 35:5–6 and Isaiah 61:1.

> Go back and report to John what you hear and see:
> The blind receive sight, the lame walk, those who have leprosy are cured, the deaf hear, the dead are raised and the good news is preached to the poor.
>
> (Matt. 11:4–5)

So, then, it is clear from his baptism, through his public ministry, and especially in his suffering and death, that Jesus saw himself as fulfilling the mission of the Servant of God. In order to get the full value of this insight into the mind of Jesus, however, we must do the same as we did for the other figures that Jesus found in his Hebrew scriptures and applied to himself – especially the Son of God. That is, we must look back into the Old Testament and find out how the identity and mission of the Servant was described there. For, as we have said before, the more deeply we understand the scriptures Jesus used, the closer we shall come to the heart of Jesus himself. And what is more, we shall have a sharper understanding of our own mission in the light of his.

The mission of the Servant in the Old Testament

In the book of Isaiah, before we are introduced to the mysterious figure of the Servant of the Lord as an individual, the prophet first applies the term to Israel as a nation. *Israel* was God's servant.

> But you, O Israel, *my servant*, Jacob, whom I have chosen
>> you descendants of Abraham, my friend,
> I took you from the ends of the earth,
>> from its farthest corners I called you.
>> I said, 'You are *my servant*';
> I have chosen you and have not rejected you;
>> do not be dismayed, for I am your God.
> I will strengthen you and help you;
>> I will uphold you with my righteous right hand.
>
> (Isa. 41:8–10)

This means that when the Servant is announced in ch. 42:1, in terms which appear to describe an individual, there must be some connection with the identity of Israel. The Servant figure is never in fact given any name in these chapters *except* Israel or Jacob (cf. also 44:1–2, 45:4). More significantly, many of the things which are said about the Servant figure in the so-called Servant Songs are also said or implied about Israel as God's servant in a corporate sense. So, for example, we immediately notice that being chosen by God and upheld by God's right hand is said of both (see Isa. 42:1, 6). Both are called to be witnesses to God in the midst of and to the nations (42:6, 43:10,21, 49:3, 6).

So there is a definite continuity between Israel as the servant and the Servant figure who appears to be an individual. So much so, in fact, that there is a line of interpretation which takes *all* the passages about the servant as corporate – i.e. as referring to Israel. It is true that Israel is sometimes personified in the Hebrew Bible as an individual – for example, as a wife, or a son. But in those cases the metaphorical intention is clear. Some of the passages in Isaiah which describe the commission, experiences, words and feelings of the Servant, however, are so graphic that most scholars reckon that the prophet must have meant them to refer to an individual person. Some would see even an autobiographical element in some of the texts (e.g. 49:4–6, 50:4–9). In any case, it is not uncommon in the Hebrew Bible for writers like prophets and poets to move back and forth between corporate and individual categories. The nation as a whole could be spoken of in the collective singular, and particular individuals could represent or embody the wider community. So there is nothing impossible about the prophet in these chapters using the same idea – servant – to describe both the nation of Israel and also a particular individual.

At this point, however, things get somewhat more complex! Not everything that the prophet has to say about Israel as the servant is as warm and positive as the verses quoted above. The historical context in which these prophecies of Isaiah 40–55 were heard was the exile. The whole section is a tremendous word of challenge and encouragement to the Jews who had survived the destruction of Jerusalem in 587 BC and were now into the second generation of captivity in Babylon. And they were there because of the judgement of God upon the sin, disobedience and failure of the nation which had been so denounced by the pre-exilic prophets. Israel, the servant of God, for all the blessings and privileges listed in the quotation above, were at that moment of history paralyzed and useless as far as the fulfilment of their mission was concerned. And so we find that in the same chapter as we are introduced to the anointed Servant with his worldwide mission (42:1–9), we also hear these withering words to the actual people of God.

'Hear, you deaf; look, you blind, and see!
Who is blind but my servant,
    and deaf like the messenger I send?
Who is blind like the one committed to me,
    blind like the servant of the LORD?
You have seen many things, but you have paid no attention;
    your ears are open, but you hear nothing.'

It pleased the LORD, for the sake of his righteousness
    to make his law great and glorious.
But this is a people plundered and looted,
    all of them trapped in pits
    or hidden away in prisons.

Who handed Jacob over to become loot,
    and Israel to the plunderers?
Was it not the LORD, against whom we have sinned?
For they would not follow his ways;
    they did not obey his law.

(Isa. 42:18–22, 24)

Familiar enough sounding words to anyone who has read the prophets (and reinforced in 43:22–8). But very significant here, because this prophet calls Israel God's servant and puts this word of rebuke almost immediately after his ringing description of the character and mission of the servant in

42:1–9. So although there is clearly a measure of continuity and identity between the Servant individual and Israel, we find here that there is a definite discontinuity and distinction between them as well. The nation of Israel, far from fulfilling its mission as the servant of God to bring him glory among the nations as his witness, actually stands under his judgement. Far from him spiritually (as well as, in a sense, geographically), they are blind, deaf and incapacitated. They need to be brought back to God, not just back to Jerusalem. Cyrus will serve God's external purpose of providing the political liberation that will bring them back to Jerusalem. Who then will restore them spiritually? Who else but the Servant figure. That is probably what is implied by 42:3 and 7. The bruised reed and smouldering wick, the blind captives sitting in darkness, probably meant Israel. The Servant would have a mission of compassionate restoration. Listen to his own testimony in the second 'Servant Song':

> And now the LORD says –
>   he who formed me in the womb to be his servant,
> to bring Jacob back to him
>   and gather Israel to himself . . .
>
> (Isa. 49:5)

The Servant, then, has a mission *to* Israel. It is the Servant of God who will accomplish the restoration of the servant Israel. But for what purpose? Another twist in the developing picture of the Servant reveals the answer. In Isaiah 49, the Servant faces apparent failure.

> But I said, 'I have laboured to no purpose;
>   I have spent my strength in vain and for nothing'.
>
> (Isa. 49:4)

This is amplified in 50:5ff., where the Servant experiences rejection and physical abuse. God's answer to the Servant's

depression is startling. It is to entrust him with an even wider
mission – not just Israel but the world!

And now the LORD says (vv. 5–6 are God's answer to v.
4) . . .

> It is too small a thing for you to be my servant
>   to restore the tribes of Jacob,
>   and bring back those of Israel I have kept.
> *I will also make you a light to the Gentiles,*
>   *that you may bring my salvation to the ends of the*
> *earth.*

The Servant, then, also has a mission to the world. But we
should be careful to note that this is indeed 'also'. That is,
the universal mission expands but does not replace or cancel
the mission of restoring Israel. In fact, this particular 'Servant
Song' is actually addressed to the nations in 49:1. It is as if
the Servant wishes to explain to the nations how it has come
about that he, who had been commissioned to restore Israel,
has become the means of bringing salvation to *them* (v. 6).
The explanation lies in God's redirection and expansion of his
mission.

To sum up what we have found so far, then: Israel was the
servant of God, chosen and upheld by him, with the purpose
of being a light to the nations, as was the original intention
of the election of Abraham. But historically, Israel was failing
in that role and mission. Israel as the servant of God was
'blind and deaf' and under God's judgement. The individual
Servant is thus at one level *distinct* from Israel because he
has a mission *to* Israel, to challenge them and call them back
to God. The restoration of Israel, God's servant, is the task
of the Servant himself. Yet at another level, the Servant is
identified with Israel and similar language is used of both.
This is because, in the surprising purposes of God, the Servant
enables the original mission of Israel to be fulfilled. That is,
through him God's justice, liberation and salvation will be

extended to the nations. The universal purpose of the election of Israel is to be achieved through the mission of the Servant.

The Servant and the mission to the Gentiles

Returning now to the New Testament, we can begin to see not only how Jesus understood his own mission, but also how *his* mission to Israel is related to the later *apostolic* mission to the Gentiles (the nations).

We saw in the opening sections of this chapter that Jesus saw his own mission in terms of the hopes of the restoration and redemption of Israel. This was clear from the way he endorsed the ministry of John the Baptist and launched his own ministry from John's.

Several other actions of Jesus have to be interpreted in this light, that is, as pointing to his mission as the restoration of Israel. His choice of twelve disciples, for example, was intentionally symbolic of an embryonic restored Israel. He called them a 'little flock' (Luke 12:32), which was a term for the remnant of Israel, and envisages them judging the twelve tribes of Israel (Matt. 19:28). There was his entry into Jerusalem, which without a word of explanation from him, was for all to see a claim to fulfil the promised royal restoration of Zechariah 9:9ff. There was his action in the temple shortly afterwards. This was more than just a 'cleansing' of the temple from traders. It was almost certainly a prophetic sign, pointing to the destruction of the temple which he also explicitly predicted. But the only reason why the temple would be destroyed, in current Jewish expectation, was if and when the new age of Israel's restoration dawned, at which point a new temple was expected. The disciples later realized that Jesus meant exactly that. Only the new temple was himself. A few nights later, as we saw above, he was claiming to inaugurate the new covenant, in the context of a passover meal which pointed to his own death as the sacrificial lamb. And three days after that, he was explaining to two disciples on the road to Emmaus that the redemption of Israel which they were hoping for had indeed been accomplished through his resurrection on the third day. A messianic king, a new temple, a new covenant, a new passover, a redeemed Israel; and all in the space of a week between Palm Sunday and Easter Day!

There can be no doubt, then, that Jesus saw himself and his mission as directed primarily to Israel. Thus far we can see him fitting the role of the Servant. But what then of the mission of the Servant to the nations?

There are some signs even during his earthly ministry that Jesus did have a universal vision of the ultimately worldwide effect of the Gospel. Indeed, sometimes his insistence on it gave great offence. His own townspeople in Nazareth were not at all pleased when he picked out two foreigners, Naaman the Syrian and the widow of Zarephath, as models of response to God in his synagogue address (Luke 4:24–30). Only rarely did Jesus himself deal directly with Gentiles, but his reaction to their faith was very significant. Marvelling at the faith of the Roman centurion in Matthew 8:5–13, Jesus used it as a springboard for a remarkable vision of a great ingathering of the Gentile nations. But what is most interesting is that he used language drawn from Old Testament texts which had referred to the ingathering of the exiles of Israel.

> I say to you that many will come from the east and the west, and will take their places at the feast with Abraham, Isaac and Jacob in the kingdom of heaven. But the subjects of the kingdom will be thrown outside ...
>
> (Matt. 8:11–12)

The background to this ingathering from different points of the compass is passages like Isaiah 43:5, 49:12 and Psalm 107:3. Like Paul, when he used Hosea 1:10 and 2:23 (which referred to Israel) to refer to the ingrafted Gentiles (Rom.

9:24ff.), Jesus was redefining and extending the meaning of the restoration of Israel to include Gentiles.

However, it is clear that the dominant burden of Jesus's mission in his lifetime was to Israel. 'I was sent only to the lost sheep of Israel', he said (Matt. 15:24). And he confined his disciples to the borders of Israel also: 'Do not go among the Gentiles or enter any town of the Samaritans. Go rather to the lost sheep of Israel'. (Matt. 10:5f.)

After his resurrection, however, we hear the familiar words, releasing the disciples from any such limits and commissioning them instead to 'go and make disciples of all nations' (Matt. 28:19). Luke's record of the 'great commission' emphasizes the idea of *witness*, which has interesting roots in the servant passages of the Old Testament. He ends his Gospel with these words of Jesus,

> This is what is written: The Christ will suffer and rise from the dead on the third day, and repentance and forgiveness of sins will be preached in his name to all nations, beginning at Jerusalem. *You are witnesses* of these things.
>
> (Luke 24:46–8)

And he begins the book of Acts in the same way. The disciples, still puzzled by events, enquire of the risen Jesus if the time has now come for the restoration of Israel. Jesus in a sense deflects their question by redirecting their mission in exactly the way God had done for the servant in Isaiah 49.

> You will receive power when the Holy Spirit comes on you; and *you will be my witnesses* in Jerusalm, and in all Judea and Samaria, and to the ends of the earth.
>
> (Acts 1:8)

'You will be my witnesses', is a deliberate echo of Isaiah 43. In that chapter God promised that he would redeem, gather and restore Israel (vv. 1–7) and then immediately declares twice 'you are my witnesses' (vv. 10, 12). As we have seen, this 'witness' in the servant passages of Isaiah is to go 'to the ends of the earth' – one of the favourite phrases of the prophet. So the shape of the mission of the Servant in Isaiah not only explains the primary mission of Jesus to Israel, but also provides the key to the launching of the Gentile mission after his resurrection.

The Gentile mission of the early church is another important clue to an understanding of the aims of Jesus. Scholars who have researched the question we started with in this chapter, 'What were Jesus's aims and intentions?', point out that at least part of the answer is found by noticing what immediately *preceded* and what very quickly *followed* his ministry. John the Baptist came first. And all the New Testament traditions stress that Jesus began his ministry from John. We have already seen how that indicates that Jesus shared John's vision that the expected restoration of Israel was being accomplished. And very soon after his death, we find that the little group Jesus left behind had become a dynamic movement committed to taking the good news to the Gentile nations, willing to face all the problems that it caused – practical, geographical, cultural and theological.

Jesus was launched by a revival movement for the restoration of *Israel*. He launched a movement for the blessing of the *nations*. He himself, therefore, was the hinge, the vital link between the two great movements. He was the climax and fulfilment of the hope of Israel and the beginning of the hope of the nations. Precisely the role of the Servant of God. How perceptive indeed was the prophetic word of old Simeon, when he held the infant Jesus in his arms and saw in him not only the fulfilment of all his hopes for Israel but also of God's promise for the nations.

> Sovereign Lord, as you have promised,
>   you now dismiss your servant in peace.

For my eyes have seen your salvation,
  which you have prepared in the sight of all people,
a light for revelation to *the Gentiles*
  and for glory to *your people Israel.* (Luke 2:29–32).

If all this is now clear to us, as it became clear to New Testament writers like Luke, we may be puzzled as to why it was that the Gentile mission of the early church actually got off to a rather slow and shaky start. Remember that Luke wrote his Gospel and the Acts long after those early days, and in the light of his theological and scriptural reflection. Why did it take angels and rooftop visions, persecution and scattering, not to mention blinding lights on the Damascus road, to drag the early Jewish Christian church into a mission to the Gentiles and even then not without some theological kicking and screaming?

Well, we are not told, explicitly. But my own feeling is that it had something to do with the remaining ambivalence and misunderstanding about the restoration of Israel that we hear in Acts 1:6. I think there is a comparison with Jesus's teaching about the Kingdom of God, which he declared had already come and was present in reality through himself, and yet was still to come in its fulness in the future. Already but not yet. Likewise, the restoration of Israel had indeed happened through his resurrection. And yet it still lay ahead in some sense. At least, it was not very obvious to the naked eye on the streets of Jerusalem even after Pentecost.

Imagine the reasoning of the disciples. According to their Jewish expectation, if the ingathering of the Gentiles were to take place, Israel had to be restored first. Both were part of the great eschatological scenario. They couldn't happen separately. Yet even after the resurrection and in spite of their eager and enthusiastic witnessing to it, Israel had not yet responded. Or rather, those who had responded were still a tiny minority, even if they began to number thousands instead of dozens. Peter's preaching in Acts 3 passionately appeals to his fellow Jews to turn and believe his witness to Jesus, so that 'the times of refreshing may come' – i.e. the redemption of Israel. The events have reached that point. The Servant has been sent first to Israel, so that God can fulfil his promise to Abraham and bless the nations. If only Israel would respond to him even now. Notice how his sermon follows exactly the pattern we have seen so far: Israel first, then the nations.

> You are heirs of the prophets and of the covenant God made with your fathers. He said to Abraham, 'Through your offspring all peoples on earth will be blessed.' When God raised up his servant, he sent him first to you to bless you by turning each of you from your wicked ways.
>
> (Acts 3:25f.)

But they wouldn't turn. So, the apostles may have thought, if Israel had not yet been visibly restored, the ingathering of the Gentiles could hardly begin yet, could it?

But then God surprised them. Here was Cornelius, a Roman Centurion who respected the Jewish God but knew nothing about Jesus. Here was Peter who knew Jesus but wanted nothing to do with unclean Gentiles. An angel. A strange vision on an empty stomach. A knock on the door. And God brings them together in an encounter so important that Luke spares two precious chapters of parchment to tell it twice (Acts 10 and 11). The conversion of Cornelius astonished Peter and his friends and then the rest of the church. They had to recognize it as nothing less than an act of God (Acts 10:44–8, 11:15–18): 'So then, God has even granted the Gentiles repentance unto life!'

Then at Antioch the Gospel showed its remarkable cross-cultural power as large numbers of Greek-speaking Gentiles 'believed and turned to the Lord' (Acts 11:21). Once again the church was compelled to recognize the hand of God (21) and the grace of God (23). The Gentile mission was an act of God before it ever became a strategy of the church. So what could have happened? Nothing less than that in some sense the promised restoration of Israel must already have happened, or be happening, and was being demonstrated precisely in the ingathering of the Gentiles. If God was doing the one, he must be doing the other. And this was exactly how James interpreted events, in the wake of the even more remarkable results of the first missionary journey of Paul and Barnabas. Listen to what he said at the council of Jerusalem.

> The whole assembly became silent as they listened to Barnabas and Paul telling about the miraculous signs and wonders that God had done among the Gentiles through them. When they finished, James spoke up: 'Brothers, listen to me. Simon has described to us how God at first showed his concern by taking from the Gentiles a people for himself. The words of the prophets are in agreement with this, as it is written:
> After this I will return and rebuild David's fallen tent.
> Its ruins I will rebuild, and I will restore it,
> that the remnant of men may seek the Lord
> and all the Gentiles who bear my name,
> says the Lord, who does these things
> that have been known for ages.'
> (Acts 15:12–18. The quotation is from Amos 9:11f.)

We should not miss the tremendous significance of this judgement. At a council of the church, convened specifically to resolve this issue, the considered apostolic interpretation of events was that the inclusion of the Gentiles into the new messianic community was an eschatological act of God. And the important point is that this turn of events not only fulfilled prophecy concerning the nations *but also* demonstrated that the prophesied restoration of Israel and its Davidic kingdom was being fulfilled. If God was gathering the nations, then Israel too was being restored.

Now, Paul was at that council. Doubtless he agreed with its theological interpretation. But he was faced with reality on the ground in his missionary work. And that reality, which broke his heart, was that while some Jews did accept the message of Jesus the Messiah, most did not. He met with rejection and resistance at every turn, even though he deliberately went to Jewish synagogues first in all his travels. How could this be squared with the idea that Israel was restored? Did it not rather show that God had simply abandoned Israel, forgotten his promises, and turned instead to the Gentiles? Such an alternative was faced by Paul in Romans 9–11 and decisively rejected.

Unfortunately many modern Christians find Romans 9–11 difficult and obscure and treat that section as a mere parenthesis or afterthought. Romans 1–8 seems to say all we think we need to know about the riches of the Gospel. But in fact these later chapters are critical in understanding Paul's whole theology of history and mission.

In Romans 1–8 Paul demonstrates that our salvation depends entirely on God and not ourselves. Specifically, it depends on God's grace and God's promise, as the Hebrew scriptures so clearly proved. But then the question arises, How can we trust God's promise to ourselves if God has failed to fulfil his promise to Israel? If it were true, as appearances suggested, that God had just abandoned Israel in spite of all his covenants and promises, then why on earth should the Gentiles have any confidence in the promises of such a God? Unless Paul can show that God had *not* failed Israel, all his talk about salvation for the Gentiles would be hollow and baseless.

So Paul sets out to prove two affirmations: that God's promise had *not* failed (Rom. 9:6), and that God had *not* rejected Israel (11:1–2). He does so by pointing out that even in the

Old Testament not all Israelites were among those who truly responded to God. The prophets spoke of a remnant, through and to whom God would fulfil his promises. That remnant, to whom Paul himself belonged, now included both Gentiles and Jews who believed in the Messiah Jesus and received God's righteousness by faith. Gentile believers, therefore, were not some new people to whom God had transferred his favours. Rather they were like wild olive shoots that had been grafted on to the original stock. They had in fact become part of Israel. And that grafting in of the Gentile nations was nothing less than the original purpose of God in calling Israel in the first place. It was by *that* means, in *that* way, that 'all Israel will be saved'.

So, Paul argued, the salvation of the Gentiles, far from proving that God had rejected Israel, in fact proved the opposite. God was still in the business of saving and restoring Israel. The restoration of Israel had already taken place (in the resurrection) and yet still lay ahead in its fulness. The mission to accomplish the ingathering of the nations fills the gap and tension between the two poles of Paul's thinking.

All this was Paul's mature reflection. But it is evident that even in the earliest days of his missionary work he had a rationale for his strategy of going first to the Jews and then to the Gentiles. And it was based explicitly on the Servant pattern which shaped the ministry of Jesus. In Pisidian Antioch Paul and Barnabas were invited to bring a message to the Jewish synagogue, after the reading of the Law and the Prophets. After briefly reviewing the biblical story, Paul affirms his fundamental conviction that the resurrection of Christ was God's means of achieving the restoration of Israel.

> We tell you the good news: What God promised our fathers he has fulfilled for us, their children, by raising up Jesus.
>
> (Acts 13:32)

Many Jews believed on that occasion. But when opposition was aroused the following week, Paul solemnly redirected his mission to the Gentiles, using a very significant biblical text as his warrant for doing so.

> Then Paul and Barnabas answered them boldly: 'We had to speak the word of God to you first. Since you reject it and do not consider yourselves worthy of eternal life, we now turn to the Gentiles. *For this is what the Lord has commanded us,*
>   'I have made you a light for the Gentiles,
>   that you may bring my salvation
>   to the ends of the earth.'
>
> (Acts 13:46-7)

This is a direct quotation from Isaiah 49:6, where it was the word of God to the Servant in response to his struggles and depression in v. 4. We have already seen how deeply the pattern of the Servant influenced Jesus. Here we see that Paul also found in it the pattern of his own mission. He takes words originally addressed to the Servant of the Lord and affirms that they were God's command to himself and his missionary team. The twofold mission of the single Servant in the prophetic vision has actually been divided between two persons in its historical outworking – Jesus, the restorer of Israel, and Paul, the apostle to the nations.

Paul has sometimes been accused of distorting the simple teachings of Jesus. It seems to me, on the contrary, that there is a fundamental oneness of understanding between them at this point, which derives from the profound reflection on their Hebrew scriptures that both of them engaged in. Both saw the prime importance of God's people Israel. Both saw God's purpose for Israel being fulfilled in and through the Messiah. Both saw the mission of the Servant as the hinge between God's promise to Israel and God's promise, through Israel, for the nations. Jesus wept over Jerusalem. Paul sorrowed and agonized over the hardness of heart of his own people. Jesus envisaged a great ingathering of the nations to the Lord's banquet. Paul gave his life to distributing the invitations.

It is perhaps to Luke that we owe the observation of such a degree of agreement between Paul and Jesus. After all, he had the unique opportunity of living with the one for much of his mission to the nations and of researching the other in his mission to Israel. Luke has provided us with more of the New Testament than any other single writer in it. So in some ways we owe the very shape of the New Testament to him, not just externally, in the ordering of the books, with Acts standing between the Gospels and the Epistles, but also theologically.

For Luke begins his Gospel with the most extended emphasis on the fulfilment of all Israel's hopes for redemption and restoration. The songs and prayers and scriptures which are festooned around the births of John the Baptist and Jesus in Luke 1 and 2 are saturated with the motif of fulfilment of Old Testament prophecies about Israel: John's mission is to bring Israel back to God (1:16f.); Jesus would possess the throne of David forever (1:32); God has been faithful to Israel as against the powerful of the earth (1:52–5); their salvation is now being accomplished (1:68ff.); the arrival of Jesus fulfils the hope of Israel and the nations (2:29–32), and thus arouses thanksgiving among those 'who were looking for the redemption of Jerusalem' (2:36–8).

Luke then ends his Gospel and begins Acts with the note of fulfilment overflowing into mission to the nations (Luke 24:44–7, Acts 1:1–8). Finally, he concludes his whole work with Paul in Rome, still hard at work summarizing for Jewish visitors his whole ministry as having been 'because of the hope of Israel' and proving from the scriptures that that hope had been fulfilled by the coming of the Kingdom of God in the person of Jesus the Messiah. But at the same time we find him more confident than ever, in view of where he was, that 'God's salvation has been sent to the nations' (Acts 28:23–8).

From the temple in Jerusalem to a guesthouse in Rome; that is the span of Luke's great story. From the heart of Israel to the hub of the nations; that is the dynamic thrust of the New Testament – geographically, historically and theologically. It was a story shaped by the mission of God himself as Jesus and his apostles discerned it in their Hebrew scriptures.

Our mission in the light of Christ's

What, then, does all this say to us? It is, I hope, illuminating to reach a deeper understanding of how Jesus understood his own identity and mission through his reflection on his scriptures, as we have strolled or stumbled our way through the last two chapters. We have dug over rather a lot of the soil in which the roots of his consciousness spread and drew their nourishment. And we have finished up seeing how influential his Servant identity was on the perception and shape of the mission of the early Christian church. But I want to conclude this chapter with four points where these biblical insights must have an impact on our view of how we as modern Christians must live out our own mission.

THE UNITY AND CONTINUITY OF MISSION

First of all we should by now be impressed with the continuity and integration of the mission of God's people, from ancient Israel right through to our own day. We saw the link between the whole people of Israel as the servant of God and the individual Servant figure. And we saw how Jesus the Messiah saw himself in relation to both – embodying Israel and yet also with a ministry to Israel. And then we saw how Paul identifies the mission of the Servant with the mission of the church in reaching out to bring the Gospel to the nations, just as the Servant was commissioned to bring salvation to the ends of the earth. The continuity of mission and witness to the nations thus runs through Israel, the Servant, Jesus, the church.

So we ought to realize then that missionary commitment is not some kind of optional extra for the extra-enthusiastic. Nor was it just a new idea invented by Jesus to give his disciples something to do with the rest of their lives. Still less was it a merely modern movement of the church that coincided with colonial expansionism. Mission lies at the very heart of all God's historical action in the Bible. Mission to his fallen, suffering, sinful human creation, and indeed ultimately to his whole creation as well. That is why he called Abraham, sent Jesus, and commissioned his apostles. For there is one servant people, one Servant King, one servant mission.

'TO THE JEW FIRST'

Secondly, we must take seriously the order of the servant mission as expressed both in Jesus's ministry and in Paul's repeated aphorism, 'To the Jew first'. Paul insisted that even though many Jews rejected Jesus as their Messiah, God had not rejected Israel. Israel would be saved. They would be saved along with Gentiles, both through Jesus Christ. And since the Christ had come through Israel and been sent to Israel, he must be offered first to Jews. So Paul's expression, 'To the Jew first', was not only a matter of missionary strategy which he followed as he moved from city to city. It was also a theological conviction. The church was not a new Gentile phenomenon, even if it looked like that as its membership became increasingly Gentile. It was a new *humanity*, composed of both believing Jews and Gentiles. But it was also organically and spiritually continuous with the original people of God, as his olive tree picture in Romans 11 shows. Israel had been redefined and extended, but the Jewish roots and trunk were not replaced or uprooted just because unbelieving branches had been lopped off.

Evangelism among Jews is a matter of considerable controversy today. There are powerful voices arguing that it is historically offensive because of the atrocities of Christians against Jews, culturally inappropriate and theologically mistaken.

One particular theological viewpoint rejects the need for evangelism among Jews. Jews, it is said, are already in covenant relationship with God and have no need of 'conversion' to Christianity. Jesus, as the founder of what is now predominantly Gentile Christianity, is the Christian saviour. He is simply unneeded by Jews. This is the view of the so-called 'Two Covenant Theory'. The new covenant through Jesus is for Gentile Christians. Jews are saved through their own original covenant. Evangelism in the name of Jesus is therefore rejected.

There are three reasons why I cannot accept this view and regard it as fundamentally unbiblical. First it ignores not only the Jewishness of Jesus but also his whole conscious identity and mission that we have been exploring all through this book. Jesus came within Israel, to Israel and for Israel. To say that Jews don't need him is to undermine everything Jesus believed about himself and about God's purpose in sending him to his people.

Secondly, it fails altogether to see the integral link between Jesus's mission to Israel and God's purpose of extending salvation to the Gentiles. This, we have seen, is the essence of the Servant identity of Jesus. This was not only the historical interpretation of the earliest church, but is fully scriptural – that is, in accordance with the Hebrew Bible. Jesus is the saviour of the world *because* he is the Messiah of Israel. He cannot be one and not the other. If he is not the Messiah for the Jews, then he cannot be the saviour of the Gentiles. So if evangelism among Jews (in the sense of graciously calling them to see in Jesus the Messiah who fulfils their historic scriptural faith) is disallowed, it cuts the nerve of all other evangelism. The Gospel has to be Good News for the Jews if it is to be Good News for anyone else. And if it *is* Good News for them, then to fail to share it with them is the worst form of anti-semitism.

And thirdly, the 'Two Covenant Theory' utterly subverts Paul's claim that the very heart of the Gospel was that in it God had created *one* new people. It simply cannot be squared with Ephesians 2 and 3. Or even Romans 9–11. For Jesus was not just the Messiah of Israel. He was also the new Adam. In him God's purpose for humanity as a whole was achieved, precisely *not* through two separate covenant arrangements but by a single new people in Christ.

> His purpose was to create in himself one new humanity out of the two [Jew and Gentile], thus making peace, and in this one body to reconcile both of them to God through the cross, by which he put to death their hostility. (Eph. 2:15–16)

This mystery is that through the gospel the Gentiles are heirs *together* with Israel, members *together* of *one* body, and sharers *together* in the promise in the Messiah Jesus (Eph. 3:6).

MISSION IN SERVANTHOOD

My third reflection on the depth of the influence of the Servant figure on Jesus and the church is that it ought to be the model and pattern for all Christian mission in the name of Jesus. One of the most astonishing things about Jesus is that whereas his contemporaries looked for a Messiah who would come in triumphant power, he came in humility and initial obscurity, and devoted his life to compassionate service

to those whom society scorned, oppressed, excluded or overlooked. And having made the point that he himself had not
come to be served but to serve, he modelled it unforgettably
in washing the disciples' feet *and then explicitly setting that
as the example of how we should act.*

The spirit of servanthood, written into the prophetic vision
of the Servant, lived out in the ministry of Jesus, should be
the motive and the method of all Christian mission. First of
all, of course, it ought to be characteristic of relationships
within the church. Paul never strayed far from its influence.
After a lengthy exhortation to Gentile and Jewish Christians
at Rome to be tolerant of each others' conscientious scruples
he points to the example of Christ – as the Servant!

> Accept one another, then, just as Christ accepted you,
> in order to bring praise to God. For I tell you that
> Christ has become a servant of the Jews on behalf
> of God's truth, to confirm the promises made to the
> patriarchs, so that the Gentiles may glorify God for his
> mercy.
>
> (Rom. 15:7–9)

For Paul the Gospel is as ethical as it is missionary!

With such an example before us in both Old and New
Testaments, and with the explicit command of Jesus, it is one
of the great tragedies of history that the Christian church has
so often fallen back into the triumphalistic and domination
patterns of the world and then baptized them and called them
'mission'. We have imagined that the best way to save the
world was to run the world. With the tragically ironic result
that Christian mission in the name of the Servant has been
indelibly associated in the minds of many with power – military, cultural, economic and political. It is an image that is
hard to live down. But the historical abuse of mission is no
reason to abandon it altogether. For the mandate of the Ser-

vant King still stands. He still calls for servants, for those who will serve him by serving the world.

MISSION IN ITS WHOLENESS

My fourth and final point, which draws this chapter to an overdue conclusion and also prepares the way for the next chapter, takes us back once more to those Servant Songs in the book of Isaiah. The 'career' of the Servant is described with a tantalizing mixture of explicit detail and reserve. The climax, of course, comes with his violent suffering and death and triumphant vindication in chapter 53.

But it is in Isaiah 42 that we find the greatest detail regarding the actual purpose, character and goal of the Servant's mission. The strongest emphasis in the opening verses is on his mission of bringing justice to the nations. In fact the nations are described as waiting for him to bring the law (*torah*) and justice (*mishpat*) of God to them. In other words, the Servant has the task of making real to the rest of humanity the whole package of ethical values and social priorities that God had entrusted to Israel. Being a 'light to the nations' includes this moral teaching dimension as well as the extending of the saving light of the covenant. The same picture, though with a different movement (the nations come to Zion, rather than the Servant going to the nations) is found in Isaiah 2:2–5. As the song in Isaiah 42:1–9 continues, this fundamental mission of justice is augmented by compassion, enlightenment and liberation. Justice and gentleness. Healing and wholeness. The picture is very rich indeed.

Now if we accept the unity and continuity of the servant mission, from Israel, through the prophetic Servant, in the life and death of Jesus and then on to the mission of the church, then we have to see these as important dimensions of our mission as a whole. Christian mission, if it is true to the whole biblical pattern, cannot be confined to verbal proclamation alone. The mission of the Servant included justice, compassion, enlightenment, liberation. Jesus included these objectives in his self-definition in Luke 4:18ff. Yet it is clear that in his own lifetime he did not complete the task entrusted to the Servant of bringing the law and justice of God to the nations. Is it not then surely the case that these are aspects of the mission which he has entrusted to his servant church, those who, being 'in Christ' are commanded to carry forward 'all that he began to do and to teach'?

But what did Jesus himself understand by these words? What were his own moral values and priorities? That is what we shall turn to in the final chapter. What we have seen in this one is that the Old Testament set forth a mission. A mission which Jesus accepted as the driving aim of his own life and then entrusted to his followers.

CHAPTER FIVE

Jesus and his Old Testament Values

Matthew 3 ends with Jesus, still dripping from his baptism in the Jordan, basking under an open heaven in the loving approval of his Father, sealed by the visible sign of the Holy Spirit.

Matthew 4 is an abrupt contrast. The chapter divisions in our Bible were not originally part of Matthew's writing, so he just went straight on from the words,

> 'This is my Son, whom I love; with him I am well pleased',

to say,

> Then Jesus was led by the Spirit into the desert to be tempted by the devil. After fasting for forty days and forty nights, he was hungry. The tempter came to him and said, 'If you are the Son of God, tell these stones to become bread.'

Jesus tested in the wilderness

'If you are the Son of God ... !' The very words show the force of the struggle Jesus went through in the wilderness. Was he certain of his identity? Shouldn't he just prove it to himself before testing it out on others? And if he really was what the words meant, then the mission and responsibility that now lay on his shoulders were immense.

What had he taken on? He had, in a sense, taken on the identity of Israel, as the Davidic messianic king. And he had, in another sense, taken on the mission of Israel, as the Servant of God. And therefore he had also taken on the *moral responsibility* of Israel – the obligations and commitment of covenant loyalty to God himself. He must live as God had wanted Israel to live. He must obey where they had rebelled. He must succeed where they had failed. His identity was not to be just a matter of labels or titles or honours. It was to be lived out in the total orientation of his life towards God, through his values, priorities, convictions, teaching, actions and relationships.

Where did he turn for the resources to face such a challenge? Where else but to his Bible. He met and deflected each of Satan's temptations with a word of Scripture. However, this was far from any superficial 'rent-a-reference' technique, as if the intense struggles with the meaning of his personal identity and future mission could be bought off by a spot proof-text. It is clear that Jesus was meditating deeply on his Bible and the struggle was partly created, partly solved, by what he found there. In this chapter we shall be looking at how Jesus was moulded and formed in his values and in the priorities and principles of his life and teaching by the Hebrew scriptures.

One particular section of the Old Testament seems to have been the focus of Jesus's attention during those forty days of solitude. All three of his replies to the devil are drawn from two chapters in the first part of Deuteronomy (8:3, 6:16 and 6:13). What special significance did he find there?

The book of Deuteronomy records what are presented as sermons of Moses to Israel at the point when they were just on the other side of the Jordan, after the forty years of wandering in the wilderness and immediately before crossing to conquer the land. It was a critical moment for them – the end of one period and the beginning of the next. For Jesus, too, the obscure safety of life as a village carpenter had come to an end. He had crossed his Jordan into a public and costly mission. The very crowds with whom he had mingled anonymously around John the Baptist would soon be surging around him, hungry for his bread – and then for his blood. The Israelites had heard from Moses a rallying call to uncompromising loyalty to God. Forty years of testing in the wilderness were brought to an end with a rousing word of encouragement to face the challenge ahead. No wonder Jesus turned to those words of Moses as he wrestled with the cost of obedience. Imagine him, the Son of God, hungry and exhausted after forty days of struggle in the desert, reading or recalling these words:

> Remember how the LORD your God led you all the way in the desert these forty years, to humble you and to test you in order to know what was in your heart, whether or not you would keep his commands. He humbled you, causing you to hunger and then feeding you with manna, which neither you nor your fathers had known, to teach you that man does not live on bread alone but on every word that comes from the mouth of the LORD. Your clothes did not wear out and your feet did not swell during these forty years. Know then in your heart that as a man disciplines his son, so the LORD your God disciplines you.

> (Deut. 8:2–5)

'This is my beloved Son . . .';
'As a son, the Lord your God disciplines you . . .';
'If you are the Son of God . . .', then why be hungry?
' . . . feeding you with manna . . .' If he fed Israel,
why not ask him to feed you . . . *if* you're his Son?

Was this the whirling confusion of thought in the mind of Jesus, within which he recognised the testing, seductive voice of the enemy who would dog his steps all the way to Gethsemene? But the thrust of the ancient word cleared the fog. *Why* had God let Israel be hungry and then fed them? To teach them dependence, not on bread, but on God himself and his promise. God gave Israel food to show them there was something more important than food. Later Jesus would do the same for the crowds, though even his disciples would be slow to grasp the point (John 6). But for the present, he had the word that came from the mouth of his Father; bread could wait.

A Father God can be trusted to know and to meet the needs of his people. Jesus found this truth in his scriptures, proved it in the testing of his own experience, and was very soon teaching it to his followers. A life orientated towards God is free from anxiety and faithless worry, not because food and clothes don't matter, but because a) there are things which matter more, and because b) God knows we need them. The radical earthiness of Jesus's teaching in Matthew 6:25–34 shifts the whole life-perspective of the children of God. It comes as a shaft of light out of Deuteronomy, refracted through the personal testimony of Jesus himself.

The devil learns fast. He is not very original, but he picks up the game. If Scripture is to be quoted, he can join in. And if the identity and mission of Christ is the issue, he can even show his hermeneutical skills by applying Scripture in a Christ-centred way. If Jesus believes he is called to a mission to Israel, (and *if*, of course, he is the Son of God), then let him try the miracle option. Jump from the temple, the place where God is and the crowds are. Better even than the charity option of bread for the masses, a spectacular demonstration of his power and of God's special protection of his person from harm would surely convince the crowds of his credentials. You need a verse? Try Psalm 91:11–12. Soft landings guaranteed.

Again, Jesus replies with a scripture which goes to the heart of proper response to God and exposes the superficiality of Satan's suggestions. Psalm 91's promise of God's protection was for the humble and obedient worshipper, not for the stunt man. The right attitude to God was to trust in that protection when it would be needed, not to test it out beforehand, to see if God really meant it. There are circumstances when desire for the spectacular or the miraculous is a sign of unbelief, not faith, and Jesus spotted such a trap here. So he parries Satan's misapplication of a scripture with a direct command given by Moses in the light of Israel's complaints: 'Do not test the LORD your God' (Deut. 6:16). And in any case, as we saw so clearly in the last chapter, Jesus saw that the path ahead of him led through rejection, suffering, physical crushing and finally death. He held no certificate of immunity, from the laws of God or of gravity. And he certainly would not buy Satan's spurious promise, even signed with a Psalm.

Finally (for the moment), Satan tries the political option. No record of a proof-text this time, but maybe he was using the thought implanted from the Father's voice with its echo of Psalm 2.

'You are my Son, today I have begotten you'.

And how does the Psalm go on?

'Ask of me, and I will make the nations your inheritance,
the ends of the earth your possession.'

'Ask of who, Jesus?' whispered Satan. 'If the world is your mission, why take the slow road, the hard road, the Servant's road, the Father's road? There is a quicker route to the messianic kingdom, surely, and the crowds back there will help you take it – make you take it, even. Why disappoint them and destroy yourself? Do as I say and the world will be at your feet.'

This time Jesus's reply went right to the roots of the faith of Israel: 'Worship the LORD your God and serve him alone.' The text (Deut. 6:13ff.) went on, 'Do not follow other gods, the gods of the peoples around you, for the LORD your God is a jealous God.' Popularity is no proof of deity. Since there is only one living God, he is to be loved and obeyed exclusively, no matter how many or how attractive the apparent alternatives. Jesus's Jewish 'creed' would have been echoing in his heart, since it comes just a few verses before the one he used to dismiss Satan.

> Hear, O Israel: The LORD our God, the LORD is one.
> Love the LORD your God with all your heart and with
> all your soul and with all your strength.
>
> (6:4–5)

Monotheism is a fighting faith. One Lord, one love, one loyalty. That was supposed to have been the defining characteristic of his people Israel, but for centuries the virus of endemic human idolatry had lain in their bloodstream and erupted with a regularity that astonished prophets and historians. Jesus took up the fight again, with an uncompromising affirmation of the faith of Moses as his own. Tested, like Israel, God's firstborn son in the wilderness, he the Son of God committed his human life to the full personal and moral consequences of Israel's monotheism.

So, in the temptation narrative we see Jesus using his Hebrew Bible to define and affirm the whole orientation of his life towards God. He was meditating on the section of Deuteronomy which 'preaches' the fundamental attitudes and commitments that God expects from his people as their side of the covenant relationship. These chapters of basic orientation come before the details of the laws themselves. God was concerned not about mere conformity to laws, but about the whole shape of a person and society, the inner drives of the heart, the direction of the walk of life. And in wrestling with the future direction of his own calling, Jesus accepts that the values, priorities and convictions of his own life must be shaped by the words of Moses to Israel. Words in which he heard the voice of his Father God as surely as he did when he stepped out of the Jordan.

THE BASIC ORIENTATION OF LIFE BEFORE GOD: DEUTERONOMY 4–11

It would be well worth taking a pause to read Deuteronomy 4–11, trying to imagine their impact on Jesus as he meditated on them in the wilderness. Notice some of the key themes that occur again and again as Moses preaches from the heart to the heart. The repeated command is to obey God's laws wholeheartedly, since that is the way to life and blessing for a people who have already experienced God's redemption.

Notice the stress on the uniqueness of Israel's historical experience, and how it was designed to impress on them the uniqueness of their God, Yahweh, and so lead them to healthy living before him (4:32–40). Notice the scale of values and priorities embedded in the ten commandments (5:1–22), a sense of what matters most which influenced the teaching of Jesus greatly. We shall look at this later.

There are warnings about the dangers of forgetting God in the midst of the enjoyment of the very blessings of God, especially material abundance (6:10–12, 8:6–18). One of the sharpest edges of the teaching of Jesus was precisely on the dangers of wealth. The parable of the rich fool immortalizes the equally challenging but less well known teaching of Deuteronomy 8:17–18. But then these warnings are balanced with others about the danger of forgetting or doubting God in times of need and hardship (6:16, 8:1–5), which likewise find an echo in Jesus's teaching about positive faith in God's providence.

Flattery is the mark of a false prophet. Neither Moses nor

Jesus had any time for it. On the contrary, both made a point
of popping the balloons of arrogance that Israel blew up out
of their consciousness of divine election and their historical
experience of God's actions on their behalf. Three times in
three chapters Moses disillusioned Israel of any idea that they
could claim some credit for their remarkable history. It was
not because of *numerical* superiority, as if they were some
great nation. Far from it.

> The LORD did not set his affection on you and choose
> you because you were more numerous than other peo-
> ples, for you were the fewest of all peoples. But it was
> because the LORD loved you and kept the oath he
> swore to your forefathers that he brought you out with
> a mighty hand and redeemed you ... (7:7–8)

It was not because of *economic* superiority, as if they could
boast of their own productive abilities. Any such ability came
from God in the first place.

> You may say to yourself, 'My power and the strength
> of my hands have produced this wealth for me.' But
> remember the LORD your God, for it is he who gives
> you the ability to produce wealth ... (8:17–18)

And it was not because of any *moral* superiority, as if they
could boast of their own righteousness over against the wickedness of their enemies.

> Do not say to yourself, 'The LORD has brought me
> here to take possession of this land because of my
> righteousness.' No, it is on account of the wickedness
> of these nations that the LORD is going to drive them
> out before you. It is not because of your righteousness
> or integrity ... for you are a stiff-necked people.
>
> (9:4–6)

The fact was that if any nation had deserved to be destroyed

it was Israel, and on at least two occasions only the intercession of Moses had stood between them and such a fate
(9:7–29). No, the historical report-card of Israel was nothing
to take home with pride. The devastating use that Jesus made
of Israel's history in some of his parables (e.g. the tenants of
the vineyard), along with the threat of impending destruction,
was one of the most controversial elements in his teaching
which led directly to the official plot on his life.

Many of the parables of Jesus are about the sharpness of
choice and decision. Wheat or weeds; sheep or goats; wise or
foolish; rock or sand; God or mammon. They are full of con-
trasts between one kind of behaviour or attitude and another.
Jesus leaves no middle ground for the apathetic. Shoulder-
shrugging was not an option. You followed or you walked
away. The same kind of moral and spiritual starkness charac-
terizes Deuteronomy. You either love God or you hate him
(7:9–10). You prove any profession of love in practical obedience. Any other way of life is to hate him. Indifference is
practical hatred. And so too the consequences of our choices
are simple: blessing or curse. Moses lays it out before the
people with literally monumental clarity. He identifies whole
mountains with one or the other (11:26–32, 27:1–26)! The
closing chapters of Deuteronomy portray this choice with
evangelistic zeal:

> See, I set before you today life and prosperity, death
> and destruction. For I command you today to love the
> LORD your God, to walk in his ways, and to keep his
> commands, decrees and laws; then you will live . . .
> This day I call heaven and earth as witnesses against
> you that I have set before you life and death, blessings
> and curses. Now choose life so that you and your
> children may live and that you may love the LORD
> your God, listen to his voice, and hold fast to him. For
> the LORD is your life . . .   (Deut. 30:15–20)

SIMPLE OBEDIENCE

There is, then, a basic simplicity about the moral teaching of Jesus which reflects the same characteristic of the Old Testament. This is not, of course, to say that obedience is *easy*. There is a commitment, a cost, a challenge. There is precisely the struggle against tempting alternatives that Jesus himself faced and recognized as idolatrous and satanic. What it *is* saying is that obedience ought not to be *complicated*, either by the competing claims of other gods (the moral maze of polytheism), or by the confusing rules of human experts (the moral bondage of legalism). You get the feeling in reading the Gospels that the common people heard Jesus gladly and responded to his invitation to enter the kingdom of God, not because he made things easy (quite the opposite), but because he made them simple.

Matthew found that he could summarize the preaching of Jesus in four terse phrases: 'The time is fulfilled; the kingdom of God is at hand; repent; and believe the good news.' Each of them, of course, like the label on a filing cabinet drawer, points to a whole array of content inside. But there is a memorable simplicity. Jesus himself could summarize the whole law in two fundamental commandments – to love God and to love one's neighbour. His so-called Golden Rule: 'In everything, do to others what you would have them do to you', was not a revolutionary bright idea of his own. He clearly says that it sums up the law and the prophets. It expresses the essence of the Old Testament.

Jesus treated his scriptures, not as a maze in which every alley has to be explored whether it leads anywhere or not, but as a map on which every feature is there to help you plan a journey with a clear sense of direction and a single destination.

It is important that we hold on to that essential simplicity, because one of the complaints many folk have about the Old Testament law is that it appears so complicated and detailed that any serious attention to it seems bound to land you up in legalism. However, once you get your orientation right, as Jesus did through his testing in the wilderness and his meditation on the challenge of Deuteronomy, it is possible to have a clarity and simplicity in the fundamental values and priorities of the law. That is what we find in the teaching of Jesus. It was not just a repetition of all the laws, like a shopping list. Nor was it a new law that disregarded the original. Rather, he restored the true perspective and essential *point* of the law. He brought back the urgent appeal of Moses for a single-minded, uncomplicated loyalty to God himself.

> And now, O Israel, what does the LORD your God ask of you but to fear the LORD your God, to walk in all his ways, to love him, to serve the LORD your God with all your heart and with all your soul, and to observe the LORD's commands and decrees that I am giving you today for your own good?
>
> (Deut. 10:12–13)

Jesus and the law

Jesus said very emphatically that he had not come to abolish the law, but to fulfil it (Matt. 5:17–20). So we shall survey some of the major features of the law and see how Jesus builds his own system of values and priorities on them.

THE LAW AS RESPONSE TO REDEMPTION

The very first thing we must do in looking for an understanding of the law in the Hebrew Bible is to observe where it comes. As we saw in chapter one, it comes in the context of a story. Before we face the ten commandments in Exodus 20

we have had a book and a half of narrative. And we have also
seen in chapter one how that is a story of God's relationship
with his people, through the family of Abraham and then
with the nation in Egypt. It is a story of constant blessing,
protection, promise and fulfilment, reaching its climax in the
great act of liberation – the exodus. It is the story, in other
words, of God's grace in action.

Before God gave Israel his law he gave them himself, as
their redeemer. So when he finally gets them to the foot of
Mount Sinai, he opens the whole proceedings of law and
covenant with the words,

> You have seen *what I have done,* ... and how I
> carried you on eagles' wings and brought you to
> myself. Now, if you obey me fully and keep my coven-
> ant ...
>
> (Ex. 19:4)

It was true enough. Only three months before, they had been
making bricks as slaves in Egypt. Now they were free. The
long trudge through the wilderness might have raised some
quibbles over the 'eagles' wings', but they were certainly out
of Egypt, 'the house of bondage'. And it was God who had
taken the initiative in getting them out. In his grace and in
faithfulness to his covenant promise, he had acted first and
redeemed them. He had not sent Moses with the ten commandments under his cloak to tell Israel that if they would
keep the law, God would save them. Precisely the other way
around. He saved them and then asked them to keep his law
in response.

So the law, then, was given to Israel in the context of a
relationship that had already been established by God. It was
never intended as a means of achieving salvation, but rather
as guidance for living in a way that pleased the God who had
saved you. That is why the ten commandments begin with a
statement, not a command.

I am the LORD your God, who brought you up out of
Egypt, out of the land of slavery.

(Ex. 20:2)

That is why, when an Israelite son asked his father what all
the law *meant*, the answer was a story – the old, old story of
God's saving love and deliverance. The very meaning of the
law was to be found in the Gospel.

> In the future, when your son asks you, 'What is the
> meaning of the stipulations, decrees and laws the
> LORD our God has commanded you?' tell him: 'We
> were slaves of Pharaoh in Egypt, but the LORD
> brought us out of Egypt with a mighty hand. ... He
> brought us out from there to bring us in and give us
> the land that he promised on oath to our forefathers.
> The LORD commanded us to obey all these decrees
> and to fear the LORD our God, so that we might always
> prosper and be kept alive, as is the case today. And if
> we are careful to obey all this law before the LORD
> our God, as he has commanded us, that will be our
> righteousness.'

(Deut. 6:20–25)

'*Our* righteousness', indeed – but only in response to *his*
righteousness, which was his saving grace in liberation from
Egypt. Obedience flows from grace; it does not buy it. Obedience is the fruit and proof and sustenance of a relationship
with the God you already know.

The same priority of relationship with God over the details
of behaviour is found in the teaching of Jesus. When Matthew
introduces us to Jesus as teacher, in his great Sermon on the
Mount in chapters 5–7, he shows how before Jesus got down
to detailed questions about actual behaviour, he sketched in
a portrait of the happiness that comes from a character orientated to God. The beatitudes (Matt. 5:3–12) are not laws; they

are descriptions of a quality of life in relation to God, the kingdom of God, and Jesus himself. The beatitudes deal with a person's attitudes, stance, commitments, relationships, priorities and loyalties. Blessedness flows from having all these dimensions of life centred on God. The good deeds which will then follow will result in praise, not for oneself, but for God the Father from whom such 'light' comes (5:16).

Jesus's urgent announcement of the arrival of the kingdom of God (which we shall look at later) and his call to people to 'enter' it also point to this priority of getting one's life into a right relationship with God in order to be able to please him. His portrayals of God as the generous father, the waiting and forgiving father, the generous vineyard owner, the creditor who releases an enormous debt, all speak of the priority of grace. He taught that obedience flows from love, in his own case (Jn 14:31) and for his followers (John 14:15, 15:9–17), and that love flows from forgiveness (Luke 7:36–50). With characteristic simplicity he stated the fundamental priority:

> Seek first the kingdom of God and his righteousness and all these other things will follow.
>
> (Matt. 6:33)

His attitude to the law, then, was explicitly not to reject it, but to see its function as relative to the priority of knowing God himself. There is much in the life and teaching of Jesus which reflects the ethos of Psalm 119 – a Psalm which rejoices in the law, but rejoices more in the richness of relationship with God himself which is then *expressed* through diligent obedience. In fact, the Psalmist interweaves his wonder at the promise, the grace, the goodness, love and salvation of God with his determination to live according to God's law. He delights in the law because it enables him to please the God he loves.

You are my portion, O LORD;
   I have promised to obey *your words*.
I have sought *your face* with all my heart;
   be gracious to me according to *your promise*.
I have considered my ways
   and have turned my steps to *your statutes*.
I will hasten and not delay
   to obey *your commands*.
The earth is filled with *your love*, O LORD;
   teach me *your decrees*.

(Ps. 119:57–64)

MOTIVATIONS FOR OBEDIENCE

A feature of Old Testament law which is rather distinctive in comparison with other ancient collections of law is the common 'motive clause'. That is, phrases which are added to particular laws giving reasons or motives why people should keep them. They are particularly common in Deuteronomy, because that is presented in a preaching style where encouragement and motivation are natural. But they are not confined to that book and can be found in Exodus and Leviticus also. The effect of them is to show that God was not merely concerned with external or mechanical obedience to rules for their own sake, but wanted to inculcate an ethos of intelligent and willing moral behaviour in Israel.

Some of the characteristic motivations and incentives are reflected in the teaching of Jesus, showing how authentically he recaptured the ethos and point of the Torah. The following four points of motivation in Old Testament law should ring familiar bells from the sayings of Jesus.

i) Gratitude for what God has done.
This follows naturally from the law being set in the context of the story of God's redemption of his people, as we saw

above. In the light of all that God had done for his people,
how should they respond? Sheer gratitude should trigger
obedience out of a desire to please the God of such faithfulness and salvation. The God who loved Israel's forefathers
enough to rescue their descendants from slavery is a God to
be loved in return, with a covenant love expressed in obedience. 'We love because he first loved us,' is not an Old
Testament text, but it echoes the heartbeat of Old Testament
ethics – as does its sequel that if we love God we must love
our brother (1 John. 4:17–21).

This motive of gratitude for what God had actually done in
liberating his people from oppression surfaces most often, as
might be expected, when the law is dealing with how Israelites were to treat vulnerable people in their own society – the
poor, the stranger, the debtor, the slave. These were the
very conditions from which God had rescued Israel, so their
behaviour should, in gratitude, be correspondingly generous.
Notice in each of the following examples how the command
to compassionate and generous behaviour is based on Israel's
own past experience.

> Do not ill-treat an alien or oppress him, for you were
> aliens in Egypt.
>
> (Ex. 22:21)

> Do not oppress an alien; you yourselves know how it feels
> to be aliens, because you were aliens in Egypt.
>
> (Ex. 23:9)

> When an alien lives with you in your land, do not ill-treat
> him. The alien living with you must be treated as one of
> your native-born. Love him as yourself, for you were
> aliens in Egypt. I am the LORD your God . . . who brought
> you out of Egypt.
>
> (Lev. 19:33–6)

> If one of your countrymen becomes poor and is unable to

196

support himself among you, help him as you would an
alien or a temporary resident, so that he can continue to
live among you. . . . You must not lend him money at
interest or sell him food at a profit. I am the LORD your
God, who brought you out of Egypt to give you the land
of Canaan and to be your God

(Lev. 25:38)

Because the Israelites are my servants, whom I brought
out of Egypt, they must not be sold as slaves.

(Lev. 25:42)

If there is a poor man among your brothers, . . . do not
be hard-hearted or tight-fisted towards your poor brother.
Rather be open-handed and freely lend him whatever he
needs. . . . When you release him [the debtor-slave after
six years], do not send him away empty-handed. Supply
him liberally from your flock, your threshing-floor and
your winepress. Give to him as the LORD your God has
blessed you. Remember that you were slaves in Egypt
and the LORD your God redeemed you. that is why I give
you this command today.

(Deut. 15:7–16)

The clearest example of this motivation in the teaching of
Jesus comes in the parable of the ungrateful debtor (Matt.
18:21–35). The mercy displayed by the king in forgiving an
enormous debt ought to have generated a grateful response
in the forgiven servant, shown in a corresponding forgiveness
of the trivial debt owed to himself. Mercy received should
lead to mercy offered. Israel, of all people, should have known
this. As can be seen from the laws above, a people whose
very historical existence and survival proved the merciful
grace and favour of God should know how to act towards the
needy out of gratitude for what God had done for them.

The parable of Jesus ends on a sober note of warning, which

also reflects the influence of the law. For the passages about generosity and behaviour based on gratitude were not just cheerful recommendations – 'It would be really rather nice if you could all be kind to each other'. They were an integral part of a whole covenant law that was sanctioned by God's threatened judgement on disobedience. It is a feature of the Torah that love is commanded. In other words, while it certainly has an emotional dimension, it is not left at that level. Love is an act of the will which is demonstrated in obedience, which is commanded. Similarly with gratitude. Of course it has an emotional dimension – which the book of Psalms overflows with. But the behaviour it motivates is commanded, not just an optional preference for the more sensitive souls.

So Jesus portrays the sticky end of the unmerciful debtor to make the point that mutual forgiveness is not a nice thing for the soft-hearted, but an essential mandate of the King on those who submit to the reign of God. Their behaviour to one another must prove the genuineness of their gratitude to the God of incredible, unbounded forgiveness.

There is an interesting reflection of this feature of the law in the teaching of the Wisdom literature. In the book of Proverbs there is a lot about compassionate attitudes and actions towards the poor which are linked to our response to God. In this case, it is not so much God as redeemer to whom we should prove our gratitude by generosity to others, but rather God as creator, to whom we are accountable for our treatment of any human being made in his image. Some characteristic texts include:

He who oppresses the poor shows contempt for their Maker,
    but whoever is kind to the needy honours God.

(Prov. 14:31)

He who mocks the poor shows contempt for their Maker.

(Prov. 17:5)

He who is kind to the poor lends to the LORD,
and he will reward him for what he has done.

(Prov. 19:17)

If a man shuts his ears to the cry of the poor,
he too will cry out and not be answered.

(Prov. 21:13)

The righteous care about justice for the poor,
but the wicked have no such concern.

(Prov. 29:7)

It seems that Jesus had imbibed this flavour of the Wisdom tradition in some of his teaching specifically about the poor: 'Whatever you did for one of the least of these brothers of mine, you did for me'.

(Matt. 25:31–46)

ii) Imitation of what God is like

The way God had acted on behalf of Israel was to provide not merely the motive for ethical obedience but also the model for it. The law was meant to enable Israel to be like Yahweh, their God. His character and behaviour were to be their moral target.

A favourite expression in the Hebrew Bible for how one ought to live is 'walking in the way of the LORD' – that is, *God's way*, as distinct from the ways of other gods, or of other nations (2 Kgs 17:15), or one's own way (Isa. 53:6), or the way of sinners (Ps. 1:1). Right at the start, God had chosen Abraham for the explicit purpose that he and his descendants should 'walk in the way of the LORD by doing righteousness and justice' (Gen. 18:19). The idea of imitation is strong. You observe what God characteristically does and then follow suit.

O let me see thy footsteps and in them plant my own.

We saw above how Moses includes among his fundamental

requirements of God that Israel should 'walk in all his ways' (Deut. 10:12). Almost as if someone had asked him what that means, he goes on to explain:

> The LORD your God is God of gods and Lord of lords, the great God, mighty and awesome, who shows no partiality and accepts no bribes. He defends the cause of the fatherless and the widow, and loves the alien, giving him food and clothing. *And you are to love those who are aliens*, for you yourselves were aliens in Egypt.
>
> (Deut. 10:17–19)

Israel's social behaviour was to be modelled on the character of God in all its richness.

We spoke earlier about the essential simplicity of the law. Perhaps nowhere is this principle put more simply, or more bluntly, than at the beginning of Leviticus 19.

> You shall be holy, because I, the LORD your God, am holy.
>
> (Lev. 19:2)

We might think that 'holiness' in the Old Testament was only a matter of ritual practices, food laws, and all the symbolic details of Israel's religion. But read the rest of Leviticus 19. It is quite clear that being holy did not mean what we might call being extra specially religious. In fact only very few of the laws in the chapter are about religious rituals. Rather, it shows that the kind of holiness God has in mind, the kind that reflects his own, is thoroughly practical and down to earth. Look at the details of Leviticus 19. Holiness means:

* generosity to the poor when you get returns on your agricultural investments (9f., cf. Deut. 24:19);

* fair treatment and payment of employees (13, cf. Deut. 24:14);

* practical compassion for the disabled and respect for the elderly (14, 32, cf. Deut. 27:18);
* the integrity of the judicial process (15, cf. Deut. 16:18–20);
* safety precautions to prevent endangering life (16b, cf. Deut. 22:8);
* ecological sensitivity (23ff., cf Deut. 20:19f.);
* equality before the law for ethnic minorities (33f., cf. Deut. 24:17);
* honesty in trade and business (35f., cf. Deut. 25:13ff.).

We call such matters 'questions of social ethics', or 'human rights' and think we are very modern and civilized for doing so. We go to great lengths to get them written pompously into Declarations for this and Charters for that and Codes for something else. God just calls them 'holiness'. All through this chapter runs the refrain, 'I am the LORD', as if to say, 'You must behave this way because this is what I would do. Imitate me.'

In short, to love your neighbour as yourself (18, 34), is not a revolutionary new love ethic invented by Jesus. It was the fundamental ethical demand of Old Testament holiness which Jesus reaffirmed and sharpened in some cases.

Leviticus 19, in fact, appears to have had a major influence on the teaching of Jesus (and is incidentally also strongly formative in the ethics of the letter of James). But whereas his contemporaries perceived in it a command to a quality of holiness that required strict religious purity and a protective separateness in national life, Jesus chose to emphasize its ethical thrust, particularly as regards compassionate and caring relationships.

Scholars who have studied most closely the conflicts between Jesus and the Pharisees in particular point out that the clash was not merely about sincerity and hypocrisy, or about internal and external obedience, or anything so simple. Jesus utterly shared with the Pharisees the consuming desire that God's people should be holy. He shared with them too a deep love for the Torah and the assumption that the way to holiness was to be found there in God's revelation. He also shared the dominant motivation of imitation of God as the energizing force for moral behaviour.

But whereas they pursued a programme of holiness which demanded performance of the ritual requirements of the law to near perfection, a holiness which was characterized by exclusion – whether of Jews who failed or refused to live that way, or of the Gentile nations in general and the Romans in particular, Jesus introduced a complete paradigm shift in the meaning of holiness itself. Imitation of God for him pointed primarily to the other characteristics of God he found in the Torah: the God of indiscriminate Creator-benevolence to all humanity and even to the creatures; the God of merciful deliverance and incredible grace in forgiveness; the God whose love embraced especially the outcasts and whose covenant with Abraham was specifically for the blessing of the nations. In other words, he defined holiness more in terms of God's *mercy*, and called for an imitative mercy on the part of all who would submit to his reign.

The transforming power and radical shift of behaviour patterns that Jesus brought with this teaching is clearly seen in his famous 'love your enemies' challenge. Notice how the motivation is strongly a matter of imitation of God – the God of grace and mercy, and how Jesus echoes Leviticus 19:2, but understands holiness as the perfection of loving mercy in the most earthy and practical ways.

> But I tell you who hear me; Love your enemies, do good to those who hate you, bless those who curse you, pray for those who mistreat you [that you may be sons of your Father in heaven. He causes his sun to

rise on the evil and the good and sends rain on the righteous and the unrighteous, Matt. 5:45]. If someone strikes you on one cheek, turn to him the other also. If someone takes your cloak, do not stop him from taking your tunic. Give to everyone who asks you, and if anyone takes what belongs to you, do not demand it back. Do to others as you would have them do to you.

If you love those who love you, what credit is that to you? Even 'sinners' do that. And if you lend to those from whom you expect repayment, what credit is that to you? Even 'sinners' lend to 'sinners', expecting to be repaid in full. But love your enemies, do good to them, and lend to them without expecting to get anything back. Then your reward will be great and you will be sons of the Most High, because he is kind to the ungrateful and wicked. [Be perfect, therefore, as your heavenly Father is perfect, Matt. 5:48.] *Be merciful, just as your Father is merciful.*

(Luke 6:27–36)

iii) *Being different*

The word holy, then, does not mean particularly religious. What it actually does mean, essentially, is 'different'. It speaks of something or someone being distinctive, set apart and separate. It is the fundamental description of God himself precisely because he *is* different – utterly 'other' than anything or anyone in the created world. In many contexts in the Old Testament, the holiness of Yahweh is contrasted with the idols of the nations. Yahweh is the living God, the *Holy One* of Israel, the God who is utterly different. For Israel, then, being the people of Yahweh meant being different too. When God said 'You shall be holy because I, the LORD your God am holy', what it meant, colloquially, was 'You must be a different kind of people because I am a different kind of God.'

When God got Israel to Mount Sinai, the first thing he impressed upon them, as we saw above, was *his own* initiative in delivering them from Egypt. The second thing he stressed was what he had in mind for *them.*

> Although the whole earth is mine, you will be for me
> a kingdom of priests and a holy nation. (Ex. 19:6)

Israel would be a nation among other nations, but they were to be holy – i.e. *different* from the rest of the nations. This had very practical implications, whether they looked back to where they had left, or looked forward to where they were going.

> You must not do as they do in Egypt, where you used
> to live, and you must not do as they do in the land of
> Canaan, where I am bringing you. (Lev. 18:3)

> You shall be holy to me; for I Yahweh am holy, and
> have separated you from the peoples that you should
> be mine. (Lev. 20:26)

Even the foreigner Balaam recognized this conscious sense of distinctiveness about Israel,

> I see people who live apart and do not consider them-
> selves one of the nations. (Num. 23:9)

This could sound like the most awful snobbishness. But that would be to misunderstand it entirely. Israel was not to regard themselves as better than the nations out of self-righteous pride (as we saw above). Rather, by reflecting the character of their God, they were to be a light to the nations - a light witnessing to the moral values of God himself. Switching on the light in a dark place is not snobbish. It's common sense. God created Israel to be a light in a dark world. But a light is only seen if it shines, and in the same way, Israel would only be seen through their practical obedience to God's law. Then their visibility would raise questions about the God they worshipped and about the social quality of life they exhibited. This is exactly what is in mind in the motivational words of Deuteronomy 4:5–8.

> Observe these laws carefully, for this will show your wisdom and understanding *to the nations,* who will hear about all these decrees and say, 'Surely this great nation is a wise and understanding people.' What other nation is so great as to have their gods near them the way the LORD our God is near us whenever we pray to him? And what other nation is so great as to have such righteous decrees and laws as this body of laws I am setting before you today?

It is a short step to the familiar words of Jesus to his disciples about the exemplary quality of their lives and its effect on the observers around us:

> You are the light of the world. ... Let your light shine before men, that they may see your good deeds and praise your Father in heaven.
>
> (Matt. 5:14–16, cf. 1 Pet. 2:12)

And there is also a clear call from Jesus to be different. He pointed to the familiar patterns of relationship and ambition in pagan society and said, 'It shall not be so among you' (Luke 22:25ff., Matt. 5: 46f. 6:31ff.). He also pointed to the very best of religious uprightness among their fellow Jews and told his disciples they must be and do differently even from that (Matt. 5:20, 6:1–8).

iv) For our own good

In the Old Testament, obedience to the law was not just an arbitrary duty, 'because rules is rules'. A frequent motivation

is the encouraging assurance that it is for our own good. This
is the thrust of the exhortations in Deuteronomy.

> The LORD commanded us to obey all these decrees
> and to fear the LORD our God *so that we might always*
> *prosper and be kept alive.* (6:24, and see also 4:40, 5:33,
> 30:15–20, etc.)

The assumption behind this kind of motivation is that God,
as the creator of human beings, knows best what kind of social
patterns will contribute to human wellbeing. His laws were
not meant to be negatively restricting, but to provide the
conditions in which life can be most truly humane and bene-
ficial. Obedience therefore brings blessing, not as a reward,
but as a natural result. Just as physical health is not some
kind of bonus or Brownie badge for good behaviour. It is
simply the natural product of sensible living in the way our
bodies were designed to.

Another way of looking at this, and in any case an illuminating exercise, is to apply the question 'Who benefits?' to the
range of social legislation in the Torah. Whose interests are
being protected? What kind of vulnerability is being cared
for? The answer so often will be found to be that the law is
benefiting the weaker, poorer, defenceless categories of
people in Israel's community: the debtor, the slave, the home-
less widow or orphan, the landless worker, prisoners of war,
women and children, refugees.

It is very important to see that the law was given for
people's sake, not for God's sake. Of course it is true that our
obedience makes God happy. But the purpose of the law was
not to make *him* happy, but *us*. That is what the Psalmists
recognized when they exclaim things like 'O how I love your
law', or say they prefer it to gold or honey. They could see
that obedience to God's law, far from being the dry crust of
stale legalism we might imagine, was actually the surest route
to personal fulfilment and satisfaction, genuine freedom, and

social harmony and prosperity. The law was a gift of grace, a blessing, a treasure, one of the many great privileges God had entrusted to Israel – for their own good and then for the blessing of the rest of humanity.

Jesus, in tune with this whole ethos of the Torah, was enraged by the way the legal experts of his day had turned the law from its prime purpose of being a blessing and a benefit into being a burden on ordinary people. We must note carefully that Jesus did not condemn or reject the law itself. Nor did he condemn the scribes and Pharisees for their love and passion for the law. In fact he said that insofar as they taught what Moses taught, they were to be obeyed, but not imitated (Matt. 23:2–3). What his penetrating observations exposed, however, was the way that detailed passion had robbed the law of its whole point.

What was the point of having a law for the benefit of parents, if the regulations built on top of it worked in the opposite direction (Mark 7:9–13)? What was the point of having laws about tithing, whose prime purpose was to provide justice and compassionate welfare for the poor (Deut. 14:28–9), if they became so meticulous in detail that the major issues of justice and mercy were neglected (Matt. 23:23)? Above all, what was the point of having a sabbath law explicitly for human need, if it was turned into a reason for neglecting or postponing human need?

The sabbath controversy is most interesting, partly because it was clearly a major and long-running issue between Jesus and those who opposed him, but mainly, for our purpose here, because it illustrates beautifully how Jesus 'saw the point' of the law in a way which his opponents so often seemed to miss.

The sabbath law in the ten commandments is given in two different forms. In Exodus 20:8–11, its theological basis is the creation account in Genesis 1 and God's own sabbath rest after creation. In Deuteronomy 5:12–15 it is based on the fact of God's redemption of Israel from Egypt. But in both cases the *beneficiaries* of the law are listed carefully and include all domestic workers, male and female slaves, foreign workers in the community and even working domestic animals. Yes, the sabbath was a holy day for the Lord. But it was also social legislation for the benefit of the whole of society, with particular emphasis on those most easily exploited. Indeed, Deuteronomy adds the revealing touch 'so that they may rest as you do'. The sabbath was not to be a day for the leisure of a few supported by the continuing toil of the many. I believe it was Harold Macmillan, former British Prime Minister, who described the Old Testament sabbath law as 'the greatest piece of workers' protection legislation in history'. Exodus, likewise, apart from the ten commandments, puts the sabbath law as the climax of a series of laws for the benefit of the poor – in the law courts, in social life generally, and in agricultural practice (Ex. 23:1–12).

Jesus, then, confronted with disapproval of the action of his disciples in satisfying their hunger on the sabbath, or of his own deliberate acts of healing on the sabbath, very pointedly makes it clear that the sabbath, far from being the day for avoiding such things, was precisely the best day for them (Matt. 12:1–14, Mark 2:23–8). It was the day above all days for bringing blessing and healing. Yes it was God's day - but for human benefit.

So when he summed it all up, in another of those sayings full of potent, memorable simplicity, 'Man was not made for the sabbath, but the sabbath for man', he was not propounding some new idea – even though it was radical and shocking in the context of disapproval and misunderstanding into which he spoke it. Rather, as in so much of what he said and did, he was recapturing the original, authentic point and thrust of the law. The priorities and values he taught were the true heart of the law. The irony and tragedy of his conflict with the scribes and Pharisees was that it was precisely they who thought themselves the true guardians and teachers of the law in all its glory. So they thought. But in Jesus's estimation they had not only perverted the true purpose of the law, but were also preventing it from benefiting the very people it was given for (Matt. 23:4, 13f.).

THE LAW'S SCALE OF VALUES

When one of the teachers of the law asked Jesus what was the greatest commandment in the law, it was a significant question. The rabbis of his day debated it. For them, it was a somewhat academic question. The whole law in every detail was binding, so it didn't ultimately matter which detail was given pride of place. When Jesus answered it, however, with his famous double commandment, to love God with all one's heart and to love one's neighbour as oneself, he gave his answer a new twist at the end. 'On these two commandments,' he said, '*hang* all the law and the prophets' (Matt. 22:34–40). In other words, they are like the hook from which the rest of the scriptures are suspended. They have a fundamental priority. They are the scale or criteria by which the rest should be ordered. They show you what really matters.

In Mark's account, the man responded to Jesus's answer with considerable insight about the scale of values in the law.

> You are right in saying that God is one and there is no other but him. To love him with all your heart, with all your understanding and with all your strength, and to love your neighbour as yourself *is more important than* all burnt offerings and sacrifices.
>
> (Mark 12:32–33)

Jesus commended him by saying he was 'not far from the kingdom of God'. In other words, this enquirer's appreciation of priorities coincided with the way God himself operates. He shared the same value-system as Jesus himself had discerned in the Hebrew Bible. For once again we have to be clear that this perception, expressed by both Jesus and this thoughtful teacher of the law, was not a clever new theory about Israel's law. It was only drawing out with clarity something which the Old Testament itself had declared. So let us examine the priority scale we find there.

i) *God comes first*

It would be hard to miss this! The ten commandments make it very obvious by putting the three commandments related directly to God at the head of the list. In fact the order of the commandments in the decalogue is revealing in itself as a clue to the priorities of God's law. They begin with God and end with the inner thoughts of the heart. And yet in a sense, the first and the tenth correspond with each other, since covetousness puts other things or people in the place that God should occupy: 'covetousness which is idolatry', as Paul said more than once (Eph. 5:5, Col. 3:5, cf. Luke 12:15–21).

After God and his name, comes the sabbath, which, as we have seen, was for the benefit of the whole community, especially for workers. Then comes the family (respect for parents), then individual life (no murder), marriage (no adultery), property (no theft), and the integrity of the judicial process (no perjury). God, society, family, individuals, sex, property. It is an order of values that western culture has more or less completely reversed.

The demand of putting God before all else could be costly. There is a sharp edge to biblical faith. Deuteronomy 13 is an interesting example of this. The chapter warns Israel against the insidious temptations to be drawn away from total loyalty to God into other forms of idolatry. Among the sources of such temptation it cites miracle-working religious leaders (vv. 1–5) – a modern enough phenomenon.

Then it goes on to an area that can produce the greatest

tension of all – one's own family (vv. 6–11). The tension in these verses is all the more sharp when you remember how central the family was in Israel's life. The whole social structure of the nation was organized around kinship, and the extended family unit was the basis of economic life as well as fundamental in the covenant relationship with God. In the law, every effort was made to protect it and to preserve its economic well-being. Individuals got their primary sense of identity from the wider family, owed it loyalty, and could face serious sanctions for spurning its authority.

But what do you do if your loyalty to God conflicts with your loyalty and love for your own closest family circle? What if the family itself becomes the source of idolatry – i.e. becomes a stumbling block in the way of complete loyalty to God? The dilemma is one that believers have faced all through the ages and is still very real for some people today. Deuteronomy's answer was uncompromising.

So was Jesus. We can feel something of the starkness of this Old Testament text in the words of Jesus, warning his disciples that the claims of the reign of God must come before the family – and even one's own life.

> If anyone comes to me and does not hate his father and mother, his wife and children, his brothers and sisters – yes, even his own life – he cannot be my disciple.   (Luke 14:26)

He himself had to resist the apparent attempts of his own family to deflect him from his course of obedience to his calling (Matt. 12:46–50), and gave his famously abrupt answer to the one who wanted to fulfil family commitments before following Jesus (Matt. 8:21–2).

Remember, all this comes from the same Jesus who berated the Pharisees for the way they nullified the law about honouring parents. The same Jesus who made arrangements for the care of his mother in the midst of his own death agonies.

Jesus was not (as has sometimes been alleged) anti-family. He was anti-idolatry. And the family, when it takes the place of ultimate value in a person's life, when it stands in the way of his submission to the reign of God, when it hinders his mission, is as much an idol as any stone statue. If it ever threatens to take that role, it is to be 'hated' in comparison to God. God first.

ii) Persons matter more than things

One of the most fundamental principles of the law in the Hebrew Bible is the sanctity of human life. Nothing (in the literal sense of *no thing*) is worth more than a person. This is not contradicted by the fact that a number of offences were sanctioned by the death penalty. The reasons behind the death penalty in the Old Testament are complex, but understandable. It was not just an indication of a vengeful, primitive society where life was cheap.

Broadly speaking the death penalty applied to two kinds of offence: those which directly offended God himself and those which threatened the stability of Israel as a covenant society. The first were 'vertical' – issues like idolatry, blasphemy, etc. The second were 'horizontal' – affecting other persons, such as sabbath-breaking, intentional murder and acts which threatened the family (rejection of parental authority, fracture of the sexual integrity of marriage, etc.). Most of the ten commandments, through the details of other laws based on them, were sanctioned by the death penalty. This shows how seriously Israel took them, even though there is relatively sparse evidence that execution ever happened for many of the offences listed as capital. It is possible that in many cases, execution was the 'maximum penalty', frequently reduced to other penalties in practice.

However, what is more interesting, but not often noticed, is what the death penalty did *not* apply to. In Israelite law no offence involving *property* carried a death penalty. This is referring to ordinary judicial procedure. Exceptional cases like Achan had to do with fundamental violations of the covenant in the context of war. Theft *was* treated seriously – as is clear from it being included in the ten commandments. But you could not be put to death for stealing in ancient Israel – which makes it a lot more 'civilized' than most western countries until fairly recently. The reason? No amount of material property was worth a human life. Life and property could not be measured against each other. Interestingly, *kidnapping*, the theft of a *person* (usually then sold into slavery) *was* a capital offence (Ex. 21:16). The other side of this coin is that deliberate murder was not to be punished by a mere fine. If someone took a life, he could not 'get off' by paying any amount of money. Life and money could not be matched. The fact that the law specifies this point (in Numbers 35:31–4) in relation to the one issue of intentional murder, makes it possible that the death penalty may have been commuted in other capital cases sometimes where life was not directly involved.

iii) Needs matter more than rights

The law of Israel, however, went further than showing the absolute value of human life in comparison with material things. It also puts human needs before claims and rights. There is an ethos in the Torah that calls for an attitude of consideration for the needs and sensitivities of others, even in situations where you may have a legally legitimate claim or right. Here are a few examples. We might feel that slaves, captives, debtors and poor people ought not to exist at all in an ideal society, and we'd be right. But given that human society is fallen and sinful, and that even in Israel such social conditions and results of evil did in fact exist, it is very noticeable how the Hebrew law tries to restrain the 'rights' of the stronger party and attend to the needs of the weaker party in each case.

The runaway slave

> If a slave has taken refuge with you, do not hand him
> over to his master. Let him live among you wherever
> he likes and in whatever town he chooses. Do not
> oppress him.
>
> (Deut. 23:15–16)

This is an astonishing law. It cuts right across the whole
grain of slave legislation in the ancient world (and indeed in
modern times). The almost universal rule was that runaway
slaves were to be returned, under stiff penalties for them or
anyone who sheltered them. Hebrew law swims against the
stream and puts the needs of the slave above any legal 'property' rights of his owner. In fact this law undermines the
whole institution of slavery. It is one of several places in the
Old Testament where slaves are given human rights and
dignity beyond anything in the world of that age.

(e.g. Ex. 21:26–27, Deut. 15:12–18, Job 31:13–15).

The female captive

There was no Geneva Convention in the ancient world gover-
ning the treatment of prisoners of war. Little mercy was
given or expected. Women and girls were especially prized by
victorious armies. Once again we find that Hebrew law, on
the one hand starts where real life actually is and acknowl-
edges the harsh reality that prisoners are taken in wartime,
but on the other hand tries to mitigate that harshness for its
most vulnerable victims – the women.

> When you go to war against your enemies and the
> LORD your God delivers them into your hands and
> you take captives, if you notice among the captives a
> beautiful woman and are attracted to her, you may
> take her *as your wife*. Bring her into your home and
> have her shave her head, trim her nails and put aside
> the clothes she was wearing when captured. After she

has lived in your house and *mourned* her father and mother *for a full month*, then you may go to her and be her husband and she shall be your wife. If you are not pleased with her, let her go wherever she wishes. *You must not sell her* or treat her as a slave, since you have dishonoured her.

(Deut. 21:10–14)

Notice how the law carefully restricts the 'rights' of the victorious soldier. Rape is not an option at all. Nor can he just take the woman for temporary sexual pleasure. If he wants her, he is to take the full responsibility and commitment of giving her the status of wife, with all the legal and social benefits that went with that. And even then he is not to invade her privacy immediately, as the right of a bridegroom might dictate. She is to have a full month to adjust to the grief and loss she has already suffered. And if in the end the man regrets his action, the woman is not to be further debased as if she were slave property, but given the normal, though tragic, freedom of a divorced wife.

The last line of the law is an implicit criticism of the whole practice. As we know from Jesus's comments on the divorce law, the law of Moses *permitted* some things which it did not wholly *approve* of. God took account of human 'hardness of heart'. The same thing goes for slavery, polygamy, and even, we might add, monarchy. The important thing, it seems to me, is not to criticize the Hebrew law for failing to eradicate all social evils (especially the ones we struggle most with ourselves, such as the oppression of women), but rather to observe the ways it tried to mitigate their worst effects by attending to the needs of the most vulnerable party in any situation. The basic human needs of the victim take priority over the rights or claims of the victor.

The debtor's pledge

Do not take a pair of millstones – not even the upper one – as security for a debt, because that would be taking a man's livelihood as security.

When you make a loan of any kind to your neighbour, do not go into his house to get what he is offering as a pledge. Stay outside and let the man to whom you are making the loan bring the pledge out to you. If the man is poor, do not go to sleep with his pledge in your possession. Return his cloak to him by sunset, so that he may sleep in it.

(Deut. 24:6, 10–13)

Debt is degrading. It can even become dehumanizing. Debtors become the victims of practices so brutal that it is not surprising the word 'shark' is often applied to those who exploit human poverty by sucking the needy into bondage and fear through unscrupulous loaning tactics.

Old Testament law recognises reality by permitting, indeed commanding, loans to those who need them. It prohibited the taking of interest, which was one of the most radical dimensions of biblical economics. But it permitted the taking of pledges as security for a loan. However even this creditor's right to take a pledge is limited in the interests of the debtor. The law protected the debtor's means of subsistence on the one hand and his privacy and dignity on the other. The millstones ground the flour for daily bread. The cloak gave warmth for nightly sleep. To take those things was to rob someone of basic human needs. No legal right justified such behaviour. Needs come before claims.

The gleanings of the harvest

When you reap the harvest of your land, do not reap to the very edges of your field or gather the gleanings of the harvest. Do not go over your vineyard a second

time or pick up the grapes that have fallen. Leave
them for the poor and the alien.

(Lev. 19:9–10, cf. Deut. 24:19–22)

Surely a landowner has the right to enjoy the full return on
his investment of effort and seed on his own property? Not
so, says the law. The needs of the poor come before the claims
of ownership. He must deliberately *not* take all the produce
for himself. This law of gleanings was in addition to the trien-
nial tithe which was also available for the sustenance of the
landless poor (Deut. 14:28–9). Property rights are never the
bottom line of a moral argument. In any case, as God rather
bluntly pointed out, 'The land is mine and you are *my* tenants'
(Lev. 25:23). Tenants have no absolute right of disposal of
what is the landowner's property. He dictates how it is used.
Here the divine landlord instructs the tenants to make sure
that adequate provision is made for the needs of the poor.

When we survey the life and teaching of Jesus, there is a
strong reiteration of this dimension of the Torah. Human life
and human needs take precedence over all other personal
claims or rights, as well as over rules and regulations. His
parables evoke situations where a person could have felt justified in acting in one way, but chooses to act in mercy or
generosity. The Samaritan had good cause to ignore the
Jewish casualty, but didn't. In fact, by loving the neighbour
in him, he obeyed the Torah in a way which its very custod-
ians (the priest and Levite) failed to. The Prodigal's father
could have written him off but chose a different way. The
owner of the vineyard could have paid the latest workers just
a fraction of the daily wage, but chose to meet their needs
rather than satisfy the jealous justice claims of the earlier
hired hands.

Or, conversely, the rich fool could have responded to his
embarrassment of produce by following the Torah and sharing
the excess with the needy. His self-centred greed costs him

his life. More explicitly, at the end of the parable about the rich man and Lazarus, 'Abraham' condemns the rich man because his utter failure to meet the obvious need of Lazarus was a failure precisely to heed the law and the prophets (Luke 16:29–31).

Again, the sabbath controversy illustrates this most clearly. Human hunger comes before human regulations. Jesus backs that up with an interesting quotation from the prophet Hosea, showing that in the Old Testament itself there was a strong awareness that the moral values of mercy and justice have priority in God's mind over the ritual laws:

> If you had known what these words mean, 'I desire mercy, not sacrifice,' you would not have condemned the innocent.
>
> (Matt. 12:7, Hos. 6:6)

Jesus used the same text on another occasion to answer criticism of his social intercourse with those whom society marginalized (Matt. 9:10–13). Clearly it provided a significant priority guide for his own life. Likewise the healing and saving of human life matters more than sabbath laws, with an obvious comparison with animal welfare (Matt. 12:9–14).

He taught the uncomfortable message about putting even the unreasonable demands of others above the legal limits of one's own responsibility (Matt. 5:38–48). In the parable of the sheep and the goats, response to human need is presented as the criterion of final judgement (Matt. 25:31–46). He put the need of a distraught woman for the loving assurance of forgiveness above the social etiquette of table manners (Luke 7:36–50), the need of a sick woman above the ritual defilement of menstrual uncleanness (Mark 5:25–34). He went about among those to whom official society gave no rights and met their needs – for food, friendship, forgiveness, love, healing, acceptance, dignity.

Jesus and his Old Testament Values

'Do not think,' said Jesus, 'that I have come to abolish the Law or the Prophets.' The radical and shocking nature of some of what he said and did must have given grounds in his own day for thinking that. But as we survey the whole range of his life and teaching in relation to the law we can see what he meant. 'I have not come to abolish them,' he went on, 'but to fulfil them' (Matt. 5:17). Exactly what he meant by 'fulfil' here has been much disputed among the scholars. Some have suggested that it meant that Jesus was showing the inner, hidden, meaning of the laws. But that is not quite satisfactory, since it implies that when you read the Torah, you have to say, 'What the law actually says is *this*, but what God *really* meant was something different.' No, the law meant what the law said. God was not playing 'Hunt the thimble' with Israel at Mount Sinai.

My own view, which does not deny the various technical meanings of the word given in the commentaries, is more in line with the above pages. Jesus was bringing into full clarity the inherent values and priorities of the Torah. His own teaching certainly built on and surpassed the law itself. But it was facing in the same direction. His own whole life was orientated by a deep reflection on the fundamental demands of the law, since he found in it the mind of his Father God. To a people who had lost sight of the wood for the trees, he brought back a sense of what really mattered first in God's sight. But he showed, by his quotation of the Hebrew scriptures themselves, that he was not imposing on the Torah an inappropriate selectivity. Rather, the Torah itself, carefully read and understood, declares its own scale of values and sense of priorities. As we noted earlier, Jesus brought back to light the simplicity and clarity of the *point* of the Torah from the layers of well-meant regulations that had been intended to protect it but had in effect buried it.

No wonder, then, that 'the crowds were amazed at his

teaching, because he taught as one who had authority, and not as their teachers of the law' (Matt. 7:28–9). For that was indeed the point. Jesus was actually *not* just a teacher of the law. For all that he shaped his own life and values by it and restored its great central thrust in his teaching, he himself took precedence. Response to him became determinative as the law had been. Life and security were to be found in him rather than in the law.

When Jesus replied to the rich young man's enquiry about the source of eternal life, his answer was authentically scriptural. Keep the commandments and you will live, he said. He certainly did not mean that obedience deserved life in a meritorious way, but rather that obedience proved the relationship with God from which life flowed. This was precisely the point so repeatedly underlined by Moses in Leviticus 18:5 (which Jesus and Paul both quote), Deuteronomy 30:16 etc. But when Jesus went on to invite the man to a costly discipleship, in which Jesus himself became the key to the life of the Kingdom of God and everything else had to be renounced, he turned away. The law in itself gave no life. Life came from the *source* of the law, God himself. That source confronted the man and he walked away. Another rich fool, only in real life, not in a parable.

Fool was not my choice of word for him, but Jesus's own. Not that Jesus called him a fool there and then, of course. On the contrary, we sense the sad longing in the heart of Jesus at the man's decision, when Mark tells us that 'Jesus looked at him and loved him' (Mark 10:21). But he heard the words of Jesus and would not do them. And that, said Jesus on another occasion, is the action of a foolish person. For it is upon our active response to Jesus's words that our security and destiny depend.

The immediate cause of the crowd's astonishment after the Sermon on the Mount was the way it ended, with Jesus's story of the two house-builders (Matt. 7:24–7). The critical difference between the wise man and the fool was not over their obedience to the *law* (as would have been expected from, say, the book of Psalms or Proverbs), but their response to *Jesus*. The word of Jesus now occupies the seat of judgement. To do or not to do, that is the question, once you have heard. One way lies life and safety, the other way, collapse and death.

If Jesus *had* been only a teacher of the law he might have caused a stir with his radical and challenging exposure of its priorities over against the traditional accretions. He might have carved out a name as a great and original thinker. Might even have had a school of interpretation named after him. But they would not have set out to *kill* him. The experts in the law had some fairly serious disagreements and major disputes in Jesus's day, and indeed tried to embroil Jesus in some of them. But they did not kill each other over disputed legal teaching.

Yet surely we gasp with some astonishment ourselves when we read as soon as Mark 3:6 that the Pharisees were plotting to kill him. Why? Because he not merely acted and taught in a way which contravened their understanding of the law, but actually set himself in its place. He claimed authority over the sabbath. He took it on himself to forgive sins – a prerogative only for legally constituted authorities. He invited people to take *his* yoke upon themselves, rather than the yoke of the law. He asserted that 'sinners' were entering the kingdom of God through their response to him, and conversely that those who rejected him had excluded themselves. Such claims not only appeared an intolerable arrogance, they called in question the whole constitution of Israel as a community whose claim to God was based on covenant loyalty to the law. By putting himself in that place Jesus threatened the whole system. There was ultimately only one way to deal with that, and it was not by polite rabbinical counter-argument.

So they set out to kill him and be rid of the threat. And

that was the way, as Jesus observed, in which many a prophet had been dealt with. And so we turn next to think of Jesus as a prophet and in the light of the great prophets of the Old Testament.

Jesus and the prophets

At Caesarea Philippi Jesus asked his disciples what was the word on the street about him. Who did people think he was? The answer was interesting. Some thought he was John the Baptist revived and reunited with his severed head. Others thought he was Elijah, who was supposed to be sent before the great Day of the Lord. Others thought he was Jeremiah. Or one of the prophets anyway. A prophet at the very least, that was how the crowds saw Jesus. Why? What was it about Jesus that led to these rumours and perceptions? There must have been something in the behaviour and teaching of Jesus which brought to mind the great traditions in their Scriptures about the prophets of old.

'The Prophets' make up an enormous chunk of the Hebrew canon, of course. 'The Latter Prophets', which means the books of the prophets as we know them (distinguished from 'The Former Prophets', which means what we call the history books from Joshua to 2 Kings), include the three major prophets, Isaiah, Jeremiah, Ezekiel, and the twelve minor prophets, Hosea to Malachi. They are all different and cover nearly four hundred years of Israel's history, as we saw in chapter one. Yet we can isolate a few central themes which dominate their messages over the generations. Obviously, this is to simplify things enormously, and you really have to study each prophet on his own terms and in his own context to understand them fully. Nevertheless, it is helpful to have a broad over-view of prophetic concerns, with which we can compare Jesus to see how and where he fits and why he was reckoned among the prophets.

Three major areas of life occupied the energies of the prophets a lot of the time. Firstly, there was the spiritual aspect, concerned with the people's relationship with God, the threat of idolatry, the hypocrisy of worship that was unrelated to practical moral living. Secondly, there was the social and economic aspect, concerned with the forces and processes in Israel's society that were causing poverty, exploitation, debt and corruption. Thirdly there was the political aspect, concerned with the use and abuse of power by those who wielded it – in the palace, the temple, the courts, etc. The crowd's idea that Jesus might be Elijah or Jeremiah is unwittingly helpful at this point, because those two prophets between them illustrate all three areas very well.

SPIRITUAL LOYALTY TO GOD

Elijah stood on Mount Carmel as the great champion of the faith of Yahweh against Baal (1 Kgs 18). He presented the people with the starkness of choice: 'If Yahweh is God, serve him; but if Baal is God, serve him.' In other words, you can't go on trying to serve both. We have already seen earlier in this chapter how Jesus reiterated this ultimate choice, echoing the great Old Testament prophetic challenge. 'You cannot serve God and mammon', he said. To submit to the reign of God means rejecting all competitors. And just as the prophets of old had exposed the hypocrisy of Israel in claiming to worship God while ignoring his covenant law, so Jesus displays full prophetic stature in his condemnation of the claims and postures of the religious elite of his day. His use of the expression 'Woe to you . . . was a clear echo of the prophetic word of judgement. It was no polite term of disagreement, but a solemn pronouncement of God's wrath upon someone

Isaiah 5 is a graphic illustration and background for a chapter like Matthew 23.

Like the prophets, Jesus was consumed by a spiritual jealousy for the honour of God. Like them, he attacked quite mercilessly those who imagined that God was impressed by religion divorced from the moral and social values of God himself. Like them, he suffered for doing so. We saw in chapter one that this was a significant theme in the prophetic message in the pre-exilic period. On more than one occasion Jesus quoted Hosea 6:6

I desire mercy, not sacrifice,
and knowledge of God rather than burnt offerings,

in order to stress the fundamental priority of moral obedience to God over the ritual expression of religious commitments. That verse is only one of many that he could have quoted which make the same point even more graphically. It would be worth pausing again to read the following passages, reflecting on the impact they would have had on Jesus's sense of values and priorities: Isaiah 1:11–20, 58:1–7, Jeremiah 7:1–11, Amos 5:21–24.

ECONOMIC ISSUES

The same Elijah who stood on Mount Carmel to defend the name of Yahweh from idolatry, also confronted Ahab over the illegal seizure of a vineyard. The story of Naboth in 1 Kings 21 is a graphic illustration of the second main area of prophetic concern – the economic realm.

Two things about the land of Israel stand out very clearly in the Hebrew scriptures. On the one hand, it was God's gift to Israel. He had promised it to Abraham, and then kept that promise in the great historical events of exodus and conquest. But it was a gift that was meant for the enjoyment of *all* Israelites. So there are clear instructions that it was to be divided up fairly and as widely as possible, across the whole kinship network, with every family receiving a share - an inheritance from God himself. On the other hand, it was still God's land. He was its true owner (Lev. 25:23). And so this divine ownership of the land was the foundation for Israel's economic system. God, as the real landlord, held Israel accountable to himself for everything they did on and with the land. This is what lies behind the detailed laws in the Torah concerning use of the land, preservation of people's share in it, justice and compassion in sharing its produce, protection of those who work on it, special provision for those who become poor and have to sell it, and all the other specific economic mechanisms designed to sustain an equitable distribution and enjoyment of the resources God had given to his people.

From the time of Solomon onwards, this system came under increasing pressure and dissolution. More and more land was accumulated by fewer wealthy families while poorer ones became dispossessed or driven into debt bondage. The courts, far from defending the oppressed, increased the oppression through bribery and corruption. Kings, far from acting with the justice required of them, instead perpetrated the kind of high-handed tactics that the story of Naboth illustrates. As we saw in chapter one, this process aroused the anger of prophet after prophet. In fact, economic issues loom larger in the preaching of the prophets than any other, with the possible exception of idolatry itself. And of course, the two were closely linked. The faith of Yahweh underpinned a system of economic and social justice. Baal was the god of a society of stratified wealth and power. To abandon Yahweh for Baal was no mere spiritual affair, but opened the way to rampant injustice in the socio-economic sphere also – which is very precisely illustrated by the Naboth story, since Jezebel was actively trying to replace the faith of Yahweh with that of Baal. Idolatry and injustice went together. They still do.

Coming back to the New Testament and the Palestine of Jesus's day, we need to recognize that the country was beset by the same economic problems, only made even worse by the imposition of Roman imperial government. Much scholarly study has been given to the social and economic situation in first century-Palestine, and it does not make pleasant reading. There was intensive exploitation of the agrarian peasant farmers, the majority of whom were tenants, since the ownership of land was concentrated in the hands of few wealthy families. Tenant farmers were hard pressed trying to meet a variety of demands on what they could produce – rents, taxes, tithes, debt repayments. And all this before they could think of what they could afford to consume for themselves to stay alive and have something to invest in the next year's sowing. Since many of the landowners lived in Jerusalem, there was antagonism between town and country. Villagers suffered many hardships and discriminations and there was much discontent. There were clashes between Jewish peasantry and Gentile settlers in Galilee and the eastern parts of the land who were perceived as an economic threat. The pressures of debt and dispossession drove some into the extreme revolutionary camp of the Zealots, who attacked both the Roman power and the Jewish aristocratic collaborators. It was a tense and sometimes violent agrarian scene in which Jesus grew up.

Jesus was a carpenter. The trade he pursued was not merely joinery. The word used to describe him, *tekton*, meant somebody skilled in practical small engineering jobs – mostly in wood, but frequently also in stone or other building materials. The carpenter was a versatile person, making or mending agricultural implements, domestic furniture, boats and other large constructions, and also frequently employed for contract work in public building works. They would have a village home base and workshop, but often they would travel around with the tools of their trade, seeking employment from private or public employers – on the farms, with the fishing fleets, in the cities on new building projects, etc.

It is very possible that Jesus, during his twenties, travelled extensively around Palestine pursuing his trade before he eventually laid it aside to embark on his public ministry. Some scholars suggest this on the evidence of the wide range of social contacts that Jesus had both in Galilee and in the Jerusalem region, as well as the breadth of familiarity with so many aspects of everyday life that emerges in his parables. He knew what he was talking about. He had seen life at every level, as itinerant workers certainly do. He was probably a familiar figure, hiring out his skills among the fishing fleets around the shores of the Sea of Galilee, long before he called some of his friends to become his followers in a new venture. It is quite possible that he helped to build the boat he preached from.

So, like the prophets before him, Jesus spoke from a position of close observation of the realities of the situation in which he lived. He would have listened to countless conversations among fellow workers. He would have seen the hard slog of life on the farms and in the vineyards. He would have heard the complaints of the heavily debt-ridden, the murderous mutterings against absentee landlords by aggrieved tenants, the bitterness against tax-collectors. He would have felt the pain of fathers whose sons opted out of the slog and escaped to what they imagined as a good life, or whose daughters ended up in prostitution to pay debts that never seemed to shrink. He would have witnessed violent incidents on the roads, fatal accidents on building projects, crucified criminals ...

So one sabbath, he attended the synagogue round the corner from his own carpenter's shop in Nazareth, read from Isaiah 61 and launched his new ministry on the basis of it. 'Today', he said, this scripture was being fulfilled. In view of the whole social context in which he lived and worked, he could hardly have chosen a more significant text:

> The Spirit of the LORD is upon me, because he has anointed me to preach good news to the poor.
>
> (Luke 4:18)

His mission, he declared, was to be among the poor and for the sake of the poor, and the predominant location of his social intercourse endorsed that policy statement.

The prophecy in Isaiah 61 draws on ideas connected with the jubilee year in ancient Israel. That is almost certainly what is meant by 'the favourable year of the LORD' in v. 2. The original law of the jubilee is in Leviticus 25. It was intended to be a year when Israelites who had been compelled to sell land or dependant members of their family into slavery because of mounting debts would have their debts cancelled and be able to return to full possession of their ancestral family land. It was to occur every fiftieth year. It was thus designed to alleviate the worst effects of continuing indebtedness. One generation's hard times should not condemn all future generations of a family to bondage. A jubilee would occur approximately every other generation and give a fresh start. Its twin pillars were *release* from debt and *restoration* to one's rightful inheritance.

Some scholars have suggested that Jesus came calling for an actual jubilee year to be put into operation, that is, a radical programme of debt cancellation and redistribution of land. In the context of Roman Palestine, that would have been essentially a call for revolution. Most scholars, however, point out that Jesus did not call for a literal operation of the Levitical law, but rather quoted from the prophetic use of jubilary ideas as a way of characterizing his own ministry. In other words, he was deeply concerned about the economic realities that the jubilee had tried to remedy, but his answer was not a straight return to that ancient legislation. Jesus did

not announce a jubilee and hope it would inaugurate the
kingdom of God. Rather, he announced the arrival of the
kingdom of God and then used jubilary imagery to characterize its demands. Jesus's use of jubilary imagery, like the
prophets', takes the themes of release and restoration and
applies them both in the economic sense in which they originally functioned, and also with 'value added' spiritual dimensions. Release from bondages of all sorts, and restoration to
fulness of life and harmony in relation with God and other
human beings were part of the prophetic vision of the age to
come and part of Jesus's vision of the inbreaking Kingdom of
God.

Jesus was not a revolutionary, in the usual sense of that
word. There is no evidence that he sided with those who
advocated violent seizure of land from absentee landowners
and redistribution of it to tenant farmers. He was very much
aware of the problem, though, and the feelings it generated.
The parable of the so-called 'wicked husbandmen' (Mark
12:1–9) shows his familiarity with the murderous bitterness
of tenant farmers and their desire for ownership of vineyards
for themselves. But he shows no sympathy with their actions
or intentions, and rather uses the story (which may well have
had a basis in incidents he himself witnessed) as a means of
condemning the spiritual and political leaders of his people
(it is important to notice whom he was talking to, in 11:27,
cf. Matt. 21:45; the parable should not be construed as a
rejection of the whole Jewish people).

On another occasion, Jesus refused to get involved in a
dispute over land, using the occasion instead as an opportunity to hammer home the dangers of greed that possession
of land can engender (Luke 12:13–21). In a more famous
incident, he would not be trapped into siding with the Zealot
call to refuse the payment of imperial taxes to Rome, choosing
rather to relativize the issue under the higher demand of
what belongs to God (Matt. 22:15–22).

On the issue of indebtedness, however, Jesus had plenty to say. As in the days of the great prophets (cf. Amos 2:6, 5:11–12, Neh. 5), debt was one of the major social evils, source of exploitation and oppression, the prime mechanism by which the rich got richer and the poor got poorer. The jubilary hope of *release* from the chains of indebtedness was as deep as it seemed forlorn. Now the interesting thing is that the word for 'release' in both Greek and the underlying Aramaic and Hebrew that Jesus spoke was used of both literal financial remission of debts (as in Deut. 15:1–2), and also the moral or spiritual forgiveness of sins. About which, of course, Jesus was passionately concerned. So we find that a number of the parables of Jesus use stories about the release of debt to illustrate the meaning of forgiveness – and its personal, relational implications.

A king's merciful release of a debtor from an enormous debt is contrasted with the man's subsequent behaviour as a minor creditor (Matt. 18:12–35). A similar but shorter story illustrates forgiveness in Luke 7:41–3. The story of the so-called 'unjust steward' in Luke 16:1–8 portrays the role of the middle man in the polarized structure of creditor and debtor. His action was not so much to cheat his master by reducing the debt, but rather to remove from the debt the illegal element of interest which had been concealed in the document. It is known that interest, which was technically illegal, was charged at frequently very high rates, by simply stating that the debtor had borrowed an amount which was actually the loan plus interest. The interest did not appear on the document, but the amount said to be owed included it. The steward deleted the hidden interest, and the master could not condemn him without exposing himself. The 'unjust' steward was actually restoring some justice in the sphere he could manoeuvre in, and by his generous action opened up the possibility of new relationships with those who would otherwise have rejected him. Zacchaeus, likewise, after a meal with

Jesus which transformed his life priorities, returned to legality with his fourfold restoration of plundered goods, and went on to a generosity far beyond legal requirements in giving half of his goods to the poor (Luke 19:1–9).

> Release for us our debts, as we also have released our debtors.

> (Matt. 6:12)

The well-known petition in the Lord's Prayer is of course traditionally understood as a request for forgiveness of sins, and indeed is expressed that way in Luke's version (Luke 11:4) and in Matthew's record of Jesus's own further comments. But most scholars believe that Matthew has preserved a form of the petition which shows that Jesus had real debts in mind also. Since his parables linked debt and forgiveness, it is very likely that Jesus had both concrete and spiritual dimensions in mind. There is no reason why we should have to make an exclusive choice, in interpreting the prayer, between literal debt and spiritual sins, any more than we have to spiritualize 'Give us this day our daily bread' or deny that elsewhere Jesus did use literal bread to symbolize spiritual nourishment.

Jesus taught a prayer which, like the beatitudes, engaged with earthly as well as spiritual realities. To pray that God's reign should come, that his will should be done, *on earth* as in heaven, would most appropriately include the desire that God should act to change the social conditions that crushed the life out of people by indebtedness. Especially since it was indebtedness that most seriously threatened the availability of daily bread. The two petitions are closely linked. The radical challenge of the prayer, however, was not just in the plea that God would intervene to relieve the burden of debt, but that those who sought such benefit of the reign of God must respond by themselves acting in generosity and forgiveness. It was authentically prophetic to insist that the vertical blessing must have horizontal effects, in the economic as well as in the spiritual sphere.

Another way in which Jesus strongly reflected the prophetic ethos on economic matters was his critique of wealth. Now Jesus was no ascetic. On the contrary, he was willing to be served (in life and in death) by the relatively wealthy, and his enjoyment of food and drink and company gained him a reputation as a friend of sinners (which was meant as an insult, but taken as a compliment, no doubt Luke 7:34). But in word and act he portrayed the dangers of wealth in terms that even Amos would have envied. He saw the insidious idolatry that wealth generates and warned against its utter incompatibility with serving God (Matt. 6:24, Luke 16:13). It was not so much wealth in and of itself, as its tendency to produce an attitude of complacent self-sufficiency that he so condemned (Luke 12:15–21), because self-sufficiency is the diametric opposite of the prime quality needed for entrance to the kingdom of God – humble dependence on God in faith (Matt. 6:19–34).

And so, to the utter amazement of his disciples, he was prepared to let a rich man, who had enquired about eternal life, turn and walk away because he was unwilling to meet Jesus's demands in relation to his wealth. Jesus loved the man. But he saw his heart. In his case, while he held on to his wealth he was not free to do what the righteousness of the reign of God required. Costly discipleship was not for him.

However, while Jesus stood among the prophets in his critique of wealth, he went much further than them in advocating an alternative strategy. On the one hand, a carefree (though not careless) attitude to material things born of confidence in God's provision (as we saw earlier in this chapter), and on the other hand, a radical generosity that cut right across expected norms of behaviour. These were his twin policies.

Generosity can be upsetting. Jesus himself, for example,

caused great offence by his own generosity in offering his presence and ministering the forgiving grace of God among those whom society regarded as ill-deserving of any such thing. But he reinforced his action by parables which portrayed God the Father as incomprehensibly generous. The story of the landowner who hired workers for his vineyard and then paid those who had worked only a few hours a whole day's wage (Matt. 20:1–16) must have been as irritating to the real hearers as to the fictional workers. For it not only spoke by analogy of the generosity of God that transcended human norms of fair play, but challenged them about real life economic relationships. Anyone who acted like that would be in trouble with neighbouring landowners, and probably also with the best of the labour force as well. Generosity was perceived as injustice. Justice preserved the status quo. Generosity undermined it.

Other stories have a similar double-edge – i.e. both pointing to the nature of the rule of God himself, and also offering models for human imitation. The story of the rich man who is snubbed by his own associates but then goes on to give a feast for all the outcasts of society (Luke 14:16–24), was told not just in answer to a comment about the heavenly banquet of the kingdom of God, but to follow up a specific recommendation by Jesus that people should actually demonstrate that kind of unrepayable generosity in their social lives (Luke 14:12–14). Such action is an investment in the reality of the new order of God's kingdom (Luke 12:32–4). Whether it was two whole days' wages (as the Good Samaritan gave to care for his 'enemy' to whom he acted as neighbour) or two small coins (as the widow gave to God, out of her poverty), Jesus observed and commended. But to give up or to give away for the sake of following Christ and living under the reign of God was no loss – in this age or the age to come (Mark 10:23–31). In the end, as Jesus said, though it is not recorded in the Gospels, it is more blessed to give than to receive (Acts 20:35).

POLITICAL CONFLICT

Some of the people compared Jesus to Jeremiah. Why Jeremiah? Some scholars draw attention particularly to the fact that both Jeremiah and Jesus suffered abuse and rejection. It is also true that Jesus, like Jeremiah, expressed great compassion and sorrow for his people, both in their immediate 'lostness' and in their impending future disaster. The 'weeping prophet' modelled the tears of the Messiah.

But there is another, sharper, reason for the comparison which lies in the *reason* why Jeremiah suffered such rejection. And that was that he brought an uncompromising warning of judgement to come upon his nation (e.g. Jer. 4:5–9). He voiced and acted out prophetic threats against the very heart of the nation – the temple itself (Jer. 7:15, 19:1–15). And as the external threat against Judah grew in intensity from the world power of Babylon, Jeremiah urged his national leaders to accept and submit to Babylon and not embark on futile plots of rebellion (Jer. 27).

In other words, Jeremiah stood out against the whole political direction of Judah's government during its last two decades up to the destruction of Jerusalem by Nebuchadnezzar. For his words and actions he was branded a traitor (Jer. 37:11–15), imprisoned more than once, physically assaulted (Jer. 20:1–2), and very nearly lynched on one occasion (Jer. 26). Jeremiah was not just laughed at as a crank. He was hated as a serious critic and threat. His words and actions were politically intolerable. Two kings and various religious officials tried to silence him, permanently.

So if the crowds saw Jeremiah in Jesus, it presumably wasn't a 'gentle Jesus meek and mild' that caught their attention or provoked their historical memory. The crowds were witnesses to the gathering storm of conflict between Jesus and the authorities. The Gospels show us that on occasion after occasion, the same word or action of Jesus which led the crowds to marvel at his authority, provoked opposition, censure or plotting from the religio-political leaders. Almost everything he said and did collided with the official line. And a major reason for that was that Jesus, like Jeremiah, declared that Israel itself was on a collision course with the judgement of God, and the collision was urgently, horrifyingly, inescapably close. His stance on this was authentically prophetic.

Three features of his words and actions illustrate the seriousness of this aspect of Jesus's prophetic significance: his attitude to the Romans, his rejection of the Pharisaic agenda, and his words and actions in the temple.

i) The Romans

First of all, there was his attitude to the Romans. It is sometimes said that since Jesus did not preach revolution against Rome he must have been apolitical. We have already said that this is very short-sighted because it suggests that revolutionary violence is the only *political* option even in a situation of oppression. But we can go much further. For Jesus himself did. Not merely did he not preach violent revolution, he actually advocated positive acts of love towards the occupying forces. This was swimming against the whole tide of Jewish political sentiment at the time. In that sense it was radical and even more truly revolutionary.

> If someone wants to sue you and take your tunic, let him have your cloak as well. If someone forces you to go one mile, go with him two miles. ... You have heard that it was said, 'Love your neighbour and hate your enemy.' But I tell you: Love your enemies and pray for those who persecute you, that you may be sons of your Father in heaven.
>
> (Matt. 5:40–45)

The command to love your enemies was radical enough, but Jesus was not content to leave it general like that – even though it would be unmistakeable who he was referring to in the context of his day. The confiscation of clothing and conscription of labour for baggage carrying were common features of the Roman occupation. Jesus urged that people, *in love*, should go beyond the limits of what could be legally demanded by those whose laws they only perforce obeyed.

Such teaching would not have endeared him to the Zealot movement, the armed resistance fighters. Yet it must be realized that by commanding love towards the Roman enemy, Jesus was not adopting a pro-Roman political stance, as though to condone the oppression itself, any more than God's sending rain on the unjust condones their injustice. He was even less endearing to the Sadducees, the party of relative collaboration with the Roman administration. For Jesus, the reign of God was supreme over all human authority, as he reminded Pontius Pilate at his trial. He could not be bought by either side in the major political conflict of his day. His radical agenda undermined both.

ii) The Pharisees
Secondly, there was Jesus's conflict with the Pharisees over their definition and practice of holiness. We have already seen something of this above, and pointed out that it was much more than just a matter of sincerity versus hypocrisy. The Pharisees' programme needs to be seen as a wholistic socio-political theology and ethic. They, like the vast majority of Israel, longed for the overthrow of the oppressor and the establishment of Israel as God's people, in freedom in their own land. And they believed that the way to achieve it was neither ascetic withdrawal and waiting (the way of the Essene sect) nor revolutionary armed violence (the way of the Zealots). Rather they sought to achieve a society totally shaped by the Torah, by fastidious observance of every detail, by sharp clarification of who and what was holy, by hallowing the sabbath as the clearest badge of Israel's covenant identity.

And Jesus threatened their whole ideology and programme

from the roots. We have seen how he operated with a different understanding of the key values of the law, and effectively devalued some of the things they set most store by. But more seriously, like the prophets before him, he engaged in activities which were symbolic, or rather, which were signs of the message he brought. Among those prophetic sign-actions which most infuriated the Pharisees, because they undermined and radically criticized their whole system, were his table-fellowship and his actions on the sabbath.

Jesus ate with tax-collectors and sinners. In so doing he broke through one of the major social and religious barriers of his society. The matter of who ate with whom was of great significance, and part of the Pharisees' collective agenda included carefully controlled table-fellowships which excluded those who would not or could not fit in with their pursuit of holiness. Even when Jesus was invited to and attended meals with Pharisees, he created embarrassment by what he said and did (Luke 7:36–50, 14:1–24). But what was worse was that he deliberately cultivated close social relationships with precisely those groups of people whom the Pharisaic programme excluded: 'sinners', tax-collectors, prostitutes.

Jesus also went out of his way to behave in extraordinary ways towards those whom society marginalized for other reasons, the sick (especially leprosy sufferers), women (including the ritually unclean) and children. We must not underestimate the disturbing force of Jesus's actions in this area. He was deliberately flouting the religious and social status conventions which undergirded his society's perception of itself and which were felt to be fundamental distinctions in the quest for the kind of society which would please God and persuade him to cast off the Roman yoke. Jesus showed his rejection of that whole philosophy by his habitual social intercourse. It was not an occasional gesture towards the poor and the outcast. It was not a matter of a few token acquaintances. Jesus got a *reputation* as the 'friend of sinners'. His disciples

were asked critically about his table manners. It was a persist-
ent, intentional policy and it cut right across the dominant
theology and ethos of the spiritual leaders of Israel.

And Jesus healed on the sabbath. Deliberately. In fact, if
you look at the healings of Jesus, it is interesting that whereas
most of them happened at the request of sick persons who
approached Jesus, in the case of the healings on sabbaths, it
was Jesus who took the initiative, unasked. He was *asked* for
healing at almost any time *except* the sabbath (as the synagogue superintendent said was proper, Luke 13:14). He *chose*
to heal *on* the sabbath, precisely when people would have
been reluctant to ask. Again, there is something of a prophetic
symbolic action about this. It was public, noticeable, deliberate, controversial and pointed. And it aroused his opponents
to enmity because he appeared to be trampling on something
they considered a prime mark of a faithful, distinctive people.
Once again, Jesus's understanding of what constituted the
people of God and what was pleasing to God differed radically
from theirs.

iii) The temple
Thirdly, there were his words and actions in and about the
temple. The fact that Jesus threatened the destruction of the
temple, in word and in symbolic action, was one of the most
remembered things about him. Which is not surprising, since
it was just about the most scandalous and provocative of all
his actions. It featured prominently in his trial. Scholars who
sift the Gospel narratives for what they are prepared to consider authentic and historical are all agreed that the so-called
'cleansing of the temple' is firmly grounded in fact, and indeed
some regard it as a major clue to understanding the aims and
intentions of Jesus (Matt. 21:12–13, Mark 11:15–17, Luke
19:45–46).

However, 'cleansing' is no longer regarded as an adequate
term for what Jesus did and meant. It suggests that all Jesus

objected to was the commercial trading in the temple courts. But the exchange and purchase of animals and currency was an integral part of the whole sacrificial system for the many pilgrims from near and far. It was not regarded as 'unspiritual'. There may well have been an element of profiteering involved, but Jesus's action does not seem to have been directed against merely that, but rather at the whole temple machinery.

Some scholars see in Jesus's temple action a prophetic sign, signifying nothing less than the coming destruction of the temple and its whole sacrificial system. They then fit this in with current Jewish apocalyptic expectations that when the messiah would come, there would be an end to the old temple and the arrival of a new temple, fit for the new age of God's reign over Israel and the nations. Jesus believed himself to be initiating this new age, so his prophetic act in the temple (like his riding into Jerusalem on a donkey the previous day pointing to Zechariah 9:9), was a dramatic way of announcing its imminence. This would fit also with the prophecy of Malachi 3:1–3.

Others draw more attention to the role of the temple as the very heart of Israel and the heartbeat of Israel's nationalism. It was the nerve centre where Israel could most truly be itself – holy, distinct, separate, undefiled, exclusive. It was the navel of Jerusalem the navel of the earth. It was the pinnacle of Mount Zion the city of God. Not for nothing, therefore, did the Romans keep a garrison of soldiers right next door, since the temple was the scene of occasional unrest and the hatching of anti-Roman riots. So it has been suggested that Jesus was denouncing the role of the temple as the 'pillar of chauvinism'. It had become the symbol of an Israel at odds with the world, rather than an Israel for the nations. It had become a perversion of the very mission of Israel itself.

This interpretation fits well with the words that accompanied Jesus's prophetic action.

Is it not written, 'My house shall be called a house of
prayer for all the nations'? But you have made it a den
of robbers.

(Mark 11:17)

The direct quotation is from Isaiah 56:7, in a chapter saturated with God's universal desire for outsiders to come and
enjoy the blessings of his salvation. Foreigners and eunuchs
are promised inclusion and acceptance and joy in the house
of God. This echoes but surpasses the prayer of Solomon at
the dedication of the original temple, in 1 Kings 8:41–3.
Instead of being a fortress to keep Israel safe and the nations
out, the temple should have been the beacon of Israel as
God's light to the nations. And for those who had ears to hear
and scriptural memories, the donkey ride on the day before
would have recalled Zechariah's prophecy that when the messiah came he would take away the hardware of warfare and
'he will proclaim peace *to the nations*' (Zech. 9:10).

And the last phrase of Jesus's scathing words brings us back
to Jeremiah. For it is exactly what Jeremiah said to the people
of Jerusalem in the temple itself at a previous time of great
national peril, when the enemy was Babylon (Jer. 7). At that
time also, the temple was the heart of Israel's nationalism and
resistance. Then too the people believed that while the
temple stood, they were safe, protected by the God who
could never destroy his own temple. Safe, said Jeremiah, like
robbers in a den; but not at all safe from the coming judgement of God which would destroy Jerusalem and temple
together.

Jesus gave the words an extra twist, because the word
'robber', *lestes*, did not just mean a thief, but was the current
word for the anti-Roman resistance fighters. Such was the
perversion of the whole ethos of the temple. But it could not
last. Jesus saw in the near future, not an act of judgement by
God on the Gentiles which would finally exclude them

entirely from the temple, Jerusalem and the land, but rather an act of God's judgement on the temple itself as the centre of such exclusiveness, and the beginning of a new extension of blessing and salvation to the nations. This was a thorough and politically intolerable reversal of the temple ideology of his day. That is why it was a major factor in his trial as far as the Jews were concerned.

So, like Jeremiah, Jesus uttered prophetic words of judgement on the temple, and along with it the city and nation. There is no doubt that in this respect Jesus adopted fully the stance of the great prophets of divine judgement on Israel – even though, again like Jeremiah, he did so with intense grief and compassion. There are at least eight clear predictions of the destruction of the temple or Jerusalem in the Gospels and Acts (Matt. 23:37–9, Mark 13:2, 14:58, 15:29, Luke 13:34–5, 19:42–4, 21:20–24, John 2:19, Acts 6:14). And this is only part of a very strong strand of judgement language in the wider teaching of Jesus. One scholar has counted some sixty-seven passages where Jesus issues a warning or threat, coupled with some explanation or call to repentance or other action.

Clearly, Jesus drank deeply from the profound seriousness of the great prophets of the Hebrew scriptures. Like them, he allowed no special immunity from the wrath of God to a people who were denying or perverting the reason for their existence. Like them, he knew that judgement begins at the house of God. Like them, he knew he would suffer for his message. Unlike them, however, as the Messiah he would in a deeper sense take that judgement upon himself.

Jesus, the Psalms and the reign of God

Jesus came to a people who knew how to pray, and to sing. The rich heritage of worship in Israel was part of the very fabric and furniture of the mind of Jesus. So it is not at all surprising to find him often quoting from the Psalms, even with his dying breath. Nor is it surprising to find that the values and concerns which have occupied our attention in this chapter already are deeply embedded in the Psalms, because the Psalms themselves reflect like a myriad mirrors the great themes of the law and the prophets.

We could trace the pervasive contrast between the character, actions and fate of the good, the wise and the godly, on the one hand, and the wicked, the foolish and the ungodly, on the other. It sets the whole tone for the Psalter from the very first Psalm, and surfaces in the sharp edges of the parables of Jesus. We could list the repeated ethical concerns of the Psalms and see them shared by Jesus – like the importance of truth and the damage of falsehood; the high premium placed on humility and walking in personal communion with God; the warmth of generosity and kindness that marks the righteous person in imitation of the ways of God himself; the anger at injustice, hypocrisy and perverted behaviour; the celebration of the abundance of God's good gifts in nature and providence and the matching exhortations to trustfulness and freedom from anxiety; the gratitude that overflows into a commitment to obedience to God's law.

But we shall focus on one major theme in the Psalms which provides an important background for the central pillar of the preaching of Jesus – the kingship of God. Nothing is better known about Jesus than that he came proclaiming that 'the kingdom of God is at hand', and spent a great deal of time explaining what it meant.

It might be somewhat surprising that we have only come to look at the subject of the kingdom of God as we approach the end of this book. Should it not have featured in a prime position of honour near the start? It could have, but my strategy was deliberate. Our whole purpose has been to see how much Jesus was shaped in his identity, mission and teaching by his Hebrew scriptures. And this was as true of this central theme in his agenda as of everything else. The Kingdom of God meant the reign of *this* God – the God revealed in the history, law, prophecy and worship of the Bible he knew and loved. The spiritual and moral *content* of the expression was already contoured by the great teaching and challenges of the Torah and the prophets and the Psalms. And so it has been important for us to work our way through that material *before* we ask what Jesus meant by the kingdom of God.

It is a common misunderstanding that the idea of the kingdom of God was something introduced by Jesus. Certainly there was a freshness and an urgency about his announcement of its arrival (or its imminence, depending on how one interprets 'the kingdom of God *is at hand*'). He was clearly proclaiming that something new was bursting on the scene in his ministry which demanded attention and urgent action. But he was not putting a totally new concept before a bewildered audience. His Jewish listeners knew very well that God was king. Their scriptures stated it often enough, and they sang words to that effect regularly from the Psalms in their synagogue worship. In other words, and in our terms, the kingship of God is an Old Testament concept.

In chapter one we looked at a group of Psalms which celebrate the kingship of Yahweh, with an eye especially on the remarkable way in which they envisage all the nations praising the God of Israel for his saving acts. We now turn back to that same group of Psalms to take note of some other themes that run through them, which would have been part of Jewish understanding of the expression 'kingdom of God' as Jesus used it.

Another pause for Bible reading would be in order! Read through Psalms 24, 29, 47, 93, 95, 96, 97, 98, 99, 145, 146. All of these include references to Yahweh as king, or expressions such as 'The LORD reigns', or 'sits enthroned' or 'rules over the nations'. Apart from that, there is considerable variety in the moods and themes of these Psalms. We shall pick out just three major aspects, which between them are a fairly good summary of how the idea of the reign of God was understood in the Old Testament.

THE UNIVERSAL DIMENSION

The widest aspect of the reign of Yahweh expressed in these Psalms is the affirmation that he rules over the whole earth. He is king of nations and nature. This universal reign of Yahweh was first expressed in a song of praise which is not in the book of Psalms, but in the book of Exodus. It is the song of Moses in Exodus 15, which in the context of the story was sung on the far shore of the Sea of Reeds after the Israelites had safely crossed and the Egyptian pursuing army was washed away. The song ends with the climactic words, 'Yahweh is king, for ever and ever' (Ex. 15:18). One can almost hear, under the breath, the implication, 'and not Pharaoh.' For the whole sequence of events which had just come to their climax at the sea had been to prove exactly who was the real king, who had the real sovereign power. Moses kept pointing it out to Pharaoh, but he never learnt the lesson. Yahweh's conflict with Pharaoh demonstrated not only that it was Yahweh, not Pharaoh, who was sovereign in Egypt, but also that his rule extended over the whole earth (see Ex. 8:22, 9:14, 16, 29). Daniel conveyed the same message, at the opposite end of Old Testament history, to Nebuchadnezzar in words that echo the Psalms (Dan. 4:3, 17, 25, 32, 34–5, cf. Ps. 145:11–13).

The widest and most basic sense of the kingship of God in the Old Testament, then, is this universal sovereignty.

THE REDEMPTIVE, THEOCRATIC DIMENSION

The Psalms celebrate the kingship of Yahweh over all the earth as an act of faith. It was certainly not something evident to the naked eye. Clearly God's kingship is not in fact acknowledged by all the nations. However, Israel, through the covenant relationship, had accepted the rule of God over themselves. God was the acknowledged king in Israel – so much so that for several centuries this belief prevented them from having a human king over them. And when at length the pressure for a monarchy became irresistible, the narrative presents it very ambiguously – as a definite step away from real theocracy, and yet as a vehicle which God could use to express and locate his own kingship.

So, as well as the universal dimension of God's kingship, the Old Testament has this very particular dimension. God's covenant relationship with Israel was in a sense the relation of a king to his subjects. Indeed, the idea of a 'covenant' made use of the political model of the treaties of that era, between imperial kingdoms and their vassal states. That is what lies behind the description of Yahweh as 'the Great King'.

In the ancient world, it was the king's job to protect his people from their enemies and to give them laws and good government (the same basic priorities that we expect from our own governments). The two other texts in the Torah (apart from the one in Exodus 15:18) in which Yahweh is portrayed as king interestingly pick up each of these. In Numbers 23:21–3, Yahweh as king is the protector of his people. In Deuteronomy 33:3–5, his kingship is linked to the giving of the law.

So the kingship of God in Israel had very practical, earthy effects. It was not just a theological item of belief. It was the authority of God as king which lay behind the specific details of Israel's law – with all its characteristics that we surveyed above. There was, therefore, a powerfully ethical thrust to the acknowledgement of Yahweh's kingship. His reign was one of righteousness and justice, earthed in the real world of social, economic and political relationships. And this is what we find in some of the Psalms which celebrate it.

If the King of glory dwells on his holy hill, then Psalm 24 asks who can stand there, i.e. who can worship God acceptably. The answer is clear and ethical.

> He who has clean hands and a pure heart.

A fuller version of what these phrases mean, spelled out in social reality, is found in Psalm 15. Later kingship Psalms emphasize the justice of God's reign.

> Righteousness and justice are the foundation of his
> throne.   (97:2)

> The King is mighty, he loves justice – You have estab-
> lished equity,
>> in Jacob you have done what is just and right.
>>>   (99:4).

Again, this is spelled out in social detail in other Psalms, in terms of practical compassion on all the needy of the earth – man and beast.

> The LORD is gracious and compassionate,
>> slow to anger and rich in love.
> The LORD is good to all;
>> he has compassion on all he has made.
>>>   (145: 8–9, cf. 14–20)

> He upholds the cause of the oppressed
>> and gives food to the hungry.
> the LORD sets prisoners free,
>> the LORD gives sight to the blind,
> the LORD lifts up those who are bowed down,
>> the LORD loves the righteous.
> The LORD watches over the alien

and sustains the fatherless and the widow,
but he frustrates the ways of the wicked.

The LORD reigns forever,
your God, O Zion, for all generations.
Praise the LORD.

(146:7–10)

The Kingdom of God, then, meant the reign of *Yahweh*, and
we have seen enough of the way Yahweh is characterized in
the Old Testament to realize that where he is king, justice
and compassion must reign too. For we saw in some depth
above that one of the very core features of the law was the
imitation of Yahweh. If *he* chooses to behave in the ways
described in Psalm 146, then his people must demonstrate the
same qualities in their own social structures and relationships.
That is precisely the duty laid on the king in particular, as
the embodiment of God's kingship, in Psalm 72.

So when Jesus came proclaiming the kingdom of God, he
was not talking about a place or an idea or an attitude. It was
not just pie in the sky nor joy in the heart. The reality of
God's rule cannot be spiritualized into heaven (now or later)
or privatized into individuals. Now of course it does have
spiritual and personal dimensions which are fundamental also.
But the term itself speaks of the aligning of human life on
earth with the will of the divine government of God.

'Heaven rules', said Daniel – on earth. And the rule of the
God of heaven demands a repentance that puts things right
in the social realm as much as in personal humility (Dan.
4:26–7). Jesus cannot have meant any less. Especially since
his declared agenda, taken as we saw in its precise wording
from Isaiah 61, could as easily have been taken from the
Psalm quoted above – a Psalm celebrating Yahweh's kingship
in specific terms related to human needs and social evils.

To enter the Kingdom of God means to submit oneself to
the rule of God and that means a fundamental reorientation

of one's ethical commitments and values into line with the priorities and character of the God revealed in the scriptures. The point of being Israel and living as the people of Yahweh was to make the universal reign of God local and visible in their whole structure of religious, social, economic and political life. They were to manifest in practical reality what it meant to live as well as sing, 'the LORD reigns'.

THE ESCHATOLOGICAL DIMENSION

So we see in the Old Testament that the kingship of God was in one sense a universal sovereignty over all nations, nature and history. And that in another sense it meant the specific rule of Yahweh over Israel within the covenant relationship where his kingship was acknowledged. But God's kingship, thirdly, came to be thought of in a future perspective also because neither of the first two senses was being realized in full. On the one hand it was obvious that the nations did not acknowledge Yahweh as king, and on the other hand it became increasingly and painfully obvious that even Israel, who acknowledged him as king, did not demonstrate it. He was king in name and title, but not obeyed in reality in the actual life of the nation. This credibility gap between the professions of worship and the practicalities of life was the spot where the sparks of prophetic anger flew thick and fast. The sparks were directed especially at the human kings of Israel who not only failed to reflect God's kingship in its social and ethical demands, but rather perverted and denied it.

So there developed the hope and expectation that at some time in the future God himself would intervene to establish his reign in its fulness over his people and over the world. God would come as king and put things right. This hope is found in the prophets. Jeremiah, after a chapter which surveys the failures of several human kings (22) anounces that God himself will 'shepherd' his people through a true descendant of David (Jer. 23:1–6). Ezekiel, using similar language but in greater depth and detail, combines God's own future kingship with a coming true son of David (Ezek. 34 – a chapter worth reading in full, imagining its impact on Jesus). Shepherds and shepherding were common metaphors for political leadership, and particularly kingship, in the Old Testament. (Which incidentally shows that when Jesus referred to himself as 'The good, or model, shepherd', it was a claim to be the rightful leader of Israel, the embodiment of God's kingship over his people; not just a metaphor for the cuddly compassion of popular portraits of Jesus.)

Isaiah 52:7–10 is the basis for the familiar modern hymn, 'Our God reigns'. In its context it was a word of rejoicing for Israel herself at the time of the restoration from exile (v. 7 – 'say to Zion'), but it also envisages 'all the ends of the earth' joining in the song of praise to God's royal salvation. It is a magnificent eschatological and missionary song.

The same message of future hope and blessing in Isaiah 33:20–24 is linked to the point that God as king will also be lawgiver and judge.

> The LORD is our judge, the LORD is our lawgiver
> the LORD is our king, it is he who will save us.

Similarly, Isaiah 2:2–5 envisages all nations accepting the law and the rule of Yahweh, in such a way that there will be an end to war between nations. The same prophecy in Micah 4:2–5 is followed by an even more explicit reference to Yahweh as king (Mic. 4:6ff.), and by the familiar word that it would be from Bethlehem that the ruler of God's people would arise (Mic. 5:1–5).

Returning to the Psalms, the note of rejoicing on which some of them end is a celebration of the hope of God's coming. The God who reigns now in the affirmations of faith and worship will one day come to put things right for his whole creation. 'Putting things right' is probably the best way to catch what the Hebrew means by 'he comes to judge'. It does not just mean 'to condemn' – though it will certainly mean the destruction of wickedness. But since the coming of God is made the subject of universal rejoicing, it must also include the idea of God re-establishing his original desire and design for his world, in which the liberation of the peoples will spell joy for nature also (cf. Rom. 8:19–25).

> Shout for joy before the LORD, the King.
> Let the sea resound and everything in it,
>   the world and all who live in it.
> Let the rivers clap their hands,
>   let the mountains sing together for joy;
> let them sing before the LORD,
>   *for he comes* to judge the earth.
> He will judge the world in righteousness
>   and the peoples with equity.
>
> (Ps. 98:6–9)

So when Jesus came announcing 'The time is fulfilled, the reign of God is at hand', he was making the sensational claim that what the people were longing for as something future was now present. What they knew as a matter of hope in worship was now among them as a matter of reality in person. The eschatological was breaking into history. God had come to reign. The teaching of Jesus about the Kingdom of God does show that there was still a future dimension even from the perspective of his earthly ministry. That is, it was not yet fully manifest in what he came and did. He likened it to a process that would be at work, even in hidden ways (like seed growing or yeast rising or a net fishing).

But the point was, it had definitely arrived. It was inaugurated. The reign of God was present and operative in the very midst of the people, said Jesus. It gave them an opportunity they must not miss. And it made demands they could not evade. Demands which they already knew about from the riches of their scriptures and all the moral depths of Old Testament faith.

For Jesus did not come to teach people new ideas about some new moral philosophy which he called the Kingdom of God. Of course he sharpened and provoked their thinking with his questions and parables, transforming their perspectives, helping them recapture a God's-eye view of how things were meant to be under his rule. Of course he drove his points right home to the inner recesses of the heart, searching our motives as well as our actions. Of course he brought a new urgency, a new power, a new motivation for the obedience of personal discipleship. But in its major features the Kingdom of God already had its *moral* content from the Hebrew scriptures, with all the range of ethical values, priorities and demands that we have surveyed in the law and the prophets.

There was no ambiguity at all about what was required of the people of God under his kingship. No ambiguity about what it would mean for the world when God would establish his rule. The dynamic power of the message of Jesus lay not so much in *what* the kingdom of God meant as in *the fact that* it had arrived. The Gospel was good news of a present reality. Good news, at least, for those who were prepared to receive it in repentant hearts and a radical new agenda for living.

Good news is the message of Christmas, to return to our starting point at the beginning of the book. Christmas carol services may never feel the same again! Many of the great Christmas hymns are full of allusions to the Hebrew scriptures. It was partly because so many of the biblical phrases and images of those hymns are becoming less and less meaningful to modern Christians that I have written this book. For without the Old Testament, Jesus quickly loses reality and either becomes a stained-glass window figure – colourful but static and undemanding, or a tailor's dummy that can be twisted and dressed to suit the current fashion.

We have seen that the Old Testament tells the story which
Jesus completed. It declares the promise which he fulfilled.
It provides the pictures and models which shaped his identity.
It programmes a mission which he accepted and passed on.
It teaches a moral orientation to God and the world which he
endorsed, sharpened and laid as the foundation for obedient
discipleship.

Perhaps Isaac Watts did not have quite all of this in mind
when he wrote his splendid hymn, so often sung at Christmas.
But he certainly based it on the Psalms that celebrate God's
kingship, echoing their ecstasy, their inclusion of all humanity
and all of nature, their eager anticipation of the fulness of
God's saving justice and love. And in these respects he recognized that the widest significance of Jesus, as Lord, Saviour
and King, is to be found by worshipping him in the light of
his own scriptures.

> Joy to the world! the Lord has come;
>   Let earth receive her king!
> Let every heart prepare him room,
>   And heaven and nature sing.
>
> Joy to the world! the Saviour reigns;
>   Let men their songs employ;
> While fields and flocks, rocks, hills and plains
>   Repeat the sounding joy.
>
> No more let sins and sorrows grow,
>   Nor thorns infest the ground;
> He comes to make his blessings flow
>   Far as the curse is found.
>
> He rules the world with truth and grace,
>   and makes the nations prove
> The glories of his righteousness
>   And wonders of his love.

Bibliography

This book list makes no claim to being a complete guide to the enormous literature on Jesus research or his relation to the Old Testament, but includes most of the more significant recent works, many of which I found helpful in my own preparation. In the absence of footnotes in the text, this bibliography therefore also stands as an acknowledgement of the debt I owe to the work of others. It is confined to books. To have included articles in journals would have made it almost endless. Many of the works cited here include detailed bibliography of relevant periodical literature.

E. Bammel and C.F.D. Moule (eds.), *Jesus and the Politics of his Day*, Cambridge 1984

H. Boers, *Who Was Jesus? The Historical Jesus and the Synoptic Gospels*, Harper & Row, San Francisco 1989

C.L. Blomberg, *Interpreting the Parables*, Apollos, Leicester 1990

M. Borg, *Conflict, Holiness and Politics in the Teaching of Jesus*, Edwin Mellin, New York 1984

J. Bowker, *Jesus and the Pharisees*, Cambridge University Press 1973

S.G.F. Brandon, *Jesus and the Zealots*, Manchester University Press, 1967

F.F. Bruce, *Paul and Jesus*, Baker, Grand Rapids 1974; SPCK, London 1977

W. Brueggemann, *The Land: Place as Gift, Promise and Challenge in Biblical Faith*, Fortress, Philadelphia 1977

—— *The Prophetic Imagination*, Fortress, Philadelphia 1978

J.H. Charlesworth, *Jesus Within Judaism*, Doubleday, 1988; SPCK, London 1989

B.D. Chilton, *A Galilean Rabbi and His Bible: Jesus' Use of the Interpreted Scripture of His Day*, Michael Glazier, Wilmington 1984

B.D. Chilton and J.I.H. McDonald, *Jesus and the Ethics of the Kingdom*, Eerdmans, Grand Rapids 1987

E.P. Clowney, *The Unfolding Mystery: Discovering Christ in the Old Testament*, IVP, Leicester 1988

J.D.G. Dunn, *Jesus and the Spirit: A Study of the Religious and Charismatic Experience of Jesus and the First Christians as Reflected in the New Testament*, SCM, London 1975

—— *Jesus, Paul and the Law*, SCM, London 1989

C.A. Evans, *Life of Jesus Research: An Annotated Bibliography*, Brill, Leiden 1989

R.T. France, *Divine Government: God's Kingship in the Gospel of Mark*, SPCK, London 1990

—— *The Gospel According to Matthew: An Introduction and Commentary*, IVP, Leicester; Eerdmans, Grand Rapids 1985

—— *Jesus and the Old Testament: His Application of Old Testament Passages to Himself and His Mission*, Tyndale, London 1971

—— *Jesus the Radical*, IVP, Leicester 1975, 1989

—— *Matthew: Evangelist and Teacher*, Paternoster, Exeter 1989

J. Goldingay, *Approaches to Old Testament Interpretation*, Apollos, Leicester, updated edition 1990

A.E. Harvey, *Jesus and the Constraints of History*, Westminster, Philadelphia 1982

—— *Strenuous Commands: The Ethics of Jesus*, SCM, London 1990

M. Hengel, *Christ and Power*, Christian Journals, Belfast and Dublin 1977

—— *Was Jesus a Revolutionist?* Fortress, Philadelphia 1971

M. Hooker, *Continuity and Discontinuity: Early Christianity in its Jewish Setting*, Epworth, London 1986

R.A. Horsley and J.S. Hanson, *Bandits, Prophets and Messiahs: Popular Movements in the Time of Jesus*, Winston, Minneapolis 1985

S. Kim, *The Son of Man as the Son of God*, Eerdmans, Grand Rapids 1985

R. Leivestad, *Jesus in His Own Perspective: An Examination of the Sayings, Actions and Eschatological Titles*, Augsburg, Minneapolis 1987

I.H. Marshall, *I Believe in the Historical Jesus*, London 1977
—— *Jesus the Saviour: Studies in New Testament Theology*, SPCK, London 1990
—— *The Origins of New Testament Christology*, Apollos, Leicester, updated edition 1990

B.F. Meyer, *The Aims of Jesus*, SCM, London 1979

S.C. Mott, *Jesus and Social Ethics*, Grove Booklet on Ethics No. 55, Grove, Nottingham 1984

C.F.D. Moule, *The Birth of the New Testament*, A. & C. Black, London, 3rd ed. 1981
—— *The Origin of Christology*, Cambridge 1977

D.E. Oakman, *Jesus and the Economic Questions of His Day*, Studies in the Bible and Early Christianity Vol. 8, Edwin Mellin, New York 1986

A. Richardson, *The Political Christ*, SCM, London 1973

R. Riches, *Jesus and the Transformation of Judaism*, Seabury, New York 1982

S.H. Ringe, *Jesus, Liberation and the Biblical Jubilee*, Fortress, Philadelphia 1985

R.A. Rosenberg, *Who Was Jesus?*, University Press of America, Lanham, New York & London 1986

C. Rowland, *Christian Origins: An Account of the Setting and Character of the Most Important Messianic Sect of Judaism*, SPCK, London 1985

E.P. Sanders, *Jesus and Judaism*, Fortress, Philadelphia 1985

J.R.W. Stott, *Christ the Controversialist*, Tyndale, London 1970

G. Theissen, *The Shadow of the Galilean*, SCM, London 1987

W.M. Thompson, *The Jesus Debate: A Survey and Synthesis*, Paulist Press, New York 1985

G. Vermes, *Jesus the Jew: A Historian's Reading of the Gospels*, Collins, London, 1973 & SCM Press, 1985

D. Wenham, *The Parables of Jesus*, Hodder and Stoughton, London; IVP, Downers Grove 1989

C. Westermann, *The Parables of Jesus in the Light of the Old Testament*, T. & T. Clarke, Edinburgh 1990

B. Witherington III, *The Christology of Jesus*, Fortress, Minneapolis 1990

C.J.H. Wright, *Living as the People of God: The Relevance of Old Testament Ethics*, IVP, Leicester; In the USA, *An Eye for an Eye*, IVP, Downers Grove 1983

J.H. Yoder, *The Politics of Jesus*, Eerdmans, Grand Rapids 1972

B.H. Young, *Jesus and His Jewish Parables*, Paulist Press, New York 1989

I.M. Zeitlin, *Jesus and the Judaism of His Time*, Polity Press, Blackwell, Oxford 1988